MAINTAIN
AND IMPROVE
YOUR POWERBOAT

MAINTAIN
AND IMPROVE
YOUR POWERBOAT

More than 100 Do-It-Yourself Ways
to Make Your Boat Better

PAUL ESTERLE

International Marine / McGraw-Hill

Camden, Maine New York Chicago San Francisco Lisbon London Madrid
Mexico City Milan New Delhi San Juan Seoul Singapore Sydney Toronto

The McGraw·Hill Companies

Library of Congress Cataloging-in-Publication Data

Esterle, Paul.
    Maintain and improve your powerboat : more than 100 do-it-yourself ways to make your boat better / Paul Esterle.
        p.   cm.
    Includes index.
    ISBN 0-07-154934-X
    1. Motorboats—Maintenance and repair—Popular works.   I. Title.

    VM341.E86   2009
    623.82′3120288—dc22   2009001289

1 2 3 4 5 6 7 8 9 10 11 12 13 14 15 16 17 18 19 20 21 22   FGR/FGR   0 9

ISBN 978-0-07-154934-9
MHID   0-07-154934-X

Photographs and illustrations by the author unless otherwise noted. Photo(s) on pages 5 and 6 (left) courtesy Ranger Boats; pages 6 (right) and 7 (left) courtesy Grady-White Boats; pages 11, 12, and 22 courtesy Tempress Products; page 21 courtesy SSI, Inc.; pages 43 (bottom), 129, 200 (bottom), 214, and 263 (bottom) courtesy Moeller Products Company, Inc.; page 84 (top) courtesy Maxwell; page 84 (bottom) courtesy Quick Nautical Equipment; pages 125 and 127 (left) courtesy Taylor Made Products, Inc.; pages 127 (right) and 130 courtesy C. E. Smith, Inc.; pages 182, 184, 185, 186 (top left), 194, 195, and 198 courtesy Blue Sea Systems; page 200 (top) courtesy Poly-Planer; page 202 (left) courtesy Shakespeare Electronics Products Group; page 218 courtesy FloScan Instrument Company.

McGraw-Hill books are available at special quantity discounts to use as premiums and sales promotions, or for use in corporate training programs. To contact a representative please e-mail us at bulksales@mcgraw-hill.com.

This book is printed on acid-free paper.

Contents

Preface

After years in the hospital IT field, I decided to "drop out" and do something fun for a while. My definition of "fun" includes writing about boats, maintaining a mini-fleet of three boats, and working for West Marine. This book was sparked by questions I've heard over and over again from magazine readers and West Marine customers.

A recurring theme of those questions is that boatowners everywhere are interested in doing more of their own work on boats. The ever increasing costs of boats, slips, and fuel, coupled with the difficulty of finding affordable marine services, has resulted in an explosion of DIY boaters.

Even those boatowners who don't do their own work will appreciate this book's insights into the best approaches for and ramifications of a wide range of projects. There isn't room in these pages to explore all possible projects or every possible approach to a given project. Rather, I focus on solutions I have used and know will work for you.

I'm not suggesting that all the projects I've tried on my own boats have turned out superbly or even satisfactorily. Many have, but some haven't. In all cases, however, you can benefit from my experience. We can learn more from mistakes than successes, and working on a boat is certainly no different. And isn't it better when the mistakes you learn from are someone else's?

I hope this book makes your time on the water more enjoyable. Hope to see you out there!

CHAPTER 1

How Boats Are Built

Why do your own boat maintenance, repairs, and upgrades? There are a lot of good reasons, but the most obvious one is financial. Most maintenance tasks are straightforward and can be done by most boatowners. Rather than spending $70 to $90 per hour for a marine mechanic or technician to do a job, do it yourself and save the bucks. Besides, you'll learn more about your boat, be able to recognize small problems before they become big problems, and be able to fix things in an emergency.

Convenience and personal preference are also good reasons to do it yourself. You may have gotten a good deal on a boat that doesn't have exactly the equipment you wanted and now would like to add. Need more storage for cruising gear? Want to make your boat better suited to fishing by installing rod holders or a T-top? Want to brighten up the interior by adding larger portlights? Tired of raising the anchor by hand and want the mechanical assist of an electric windlass? Learning to do the job yourself is an economical way to upgrade your boat to exactly the configuration you want, with the additions exactly where and how you want them.

Even with the advantages of doing it yourself, it's still reasonable to have a professional do some or all of these jobs for you. In that case, this book is here to give you a sound basis for knowing what is involved and to help you decide if the job is being done right in a realistic time for a realistic price.

This book is organized by the functional areas of a boat, starting with the cockpit and moving on to the galley and the cabin, the decks, the "canvas"-covered areas, and the hull. We make no attempt to cover every possible repair or maintenance project for any of these areas. Rather, the intention of this book is to provide lots of good projects to make your boat safer, more comfortable, and more functional, and to keep it that way. Here and there you'll find sidebars giving additional background or explaining procedures that have broad application to many projects. Following our coverage of the structural components of hull, decks, and cabin, we shift our attention to electrical and electronic projects, the engine and drivetrain, and trailers. Then we end with winterization projects to keep your boat in good shape during the off-season and to minimize the work of recommissioning it in the spring.

You will probably jump right to the section you are most interested in and may not read the entire book. For that reason, you'll find frequent cross-references to tips and techniques that are common to projects in various areas of the boat.

Before we begin the projects, let's take a moment in the balance of Chapter 1 to discuss how boats are built. Unless you know a little about the underlying structures and techniques used in making boats, you will be flying blind when it comes to maintaining or modifying them. Since this book is primarily about small fiberglass powerboats, that's where we'll focus our attention.

MATERIALS

Fiberglass boats are built from a composite material known broadly as fiber-reinforced plastic, or FRP. This consists of strands of fibers embedded in a matrix of a hardened plastic resin to form a rigid material that is stronger and has better mechanical properties than either material by itself. Both the fiber strands and the resin can be of several different types.

Fibers

"Glass-reinforced plastic," or GRP, is a slightly more specific term than FRP, and it can be accurately applied to the majority of boats, because fiberglass is by far the most common reinforcing fiber in FRP. Fiberglass is real glass that has been melted and forced under pressure through fine holes in a die. After exiting the die, the glass fibers can be stretched or blasted with steam or air to make them even finer, and the resultant strands are then coated with a sizing and wound onto bobbins.

Fiberglass for boatbuilding comes in a variety of constructions. Tight bundles of fine strands can be woven into *fiberglass cloth*, which formerly (but not so much any longer) found frequent use

as the finished interior surface of a molded hull or component. It is still used in small boats, where its high tensile and flexural strength works well in conjunction with lightweight mat (as discussed later in this chapter).

Larger bundles of coarser strands can be grouped to form a *roving*, which looks like untwisted twine. These rovings can be used in chopper guns (described later in this chapter) or woven into a coarse, heavy cloth called *woven roving*. The fiberglass strands can also be chopped into short lengths and glued into a *mat*, much like felt. There are other configurations as well, some of which we discuss as they become relevant in later chapters.

Each configuration has different properties and is used in different parts of a boat and in different ways. Most fiberglass boat hulls these days are laid up using alternating layers of mat and woven roving, often beginning with two layers of mat under the exterior gelcoat to prevent the weave of the roving from "printing through" the gelcoat to be visible on the exterior.

In the early decades of composite boatbuilding, glass fiber reinforcements were the only choice. Through the miracles of modern chemistry, however, we now have several additional materials, each with different properties.

Carbon fiber is used in high-performance composite parts. Carbon fibers are three times stronger and four times lighter than steel. They add stiffness as well as strength to properly designed and built laminates. These characteristics can be achieved only with a careful orientation of fibers in the resin matrix.

Prepregs are carbon fiber materials suspended in a partially cured resin matrix (usually epoxy). The prepreg material can be handled, cut, and precisely applied to a mold. The resulting lami-

The most common fiberglass reinforcing materials used in boatbuilding are (left to right) mat, woven roving, and cloth, all three of which come in various weights. Because woven roving is coarser and heavier than cloth, boatbuilders use it to build thickness in a hull or deck laminate. But layers of roving must be sandwiched between layers of mat to ensure uniform adhesion and prevent delamination.

nate is then cured under heat and pressure to form a completed part.

Kevlar is a DuPont brand name for aramid polymers. Kevlar is widely used in personal body armor as well as reinforcements in boat hulls. Kevlar is five times as strong as steel for a given weight. It requires careful application, as it tends to float on top of wet resin, and it is difficult to sand and fair.

Generally speaking, the higher tech the reinforcing material, the more precise its application needs to be to achieve its highest potential. Naval architects and boatbuilders spend a great deal of time optimizing the exact composition and configuration of hull laminations and reinforcements.

Resins

Reinforcements are only half the picture. The other half is the resin, which, in boatbuilding, is either polyester, vinylester, or epoxy. These are applied as a thick liquid that has been catalyzed or mixed with a hardener, either of which turns the resin hard so that it encapsulates the reinforcing materials in a rigid matrix. Generally speaking, the reinforcements contribute tensile strength while the resins contribute stiffness. Together these components are more than the sum of their parts, and they are the basis of modern fiberglass boatbuilding.

Heat affects the cure time of any resin system. The higher the temperature, the faster the cure. These resins are exothermic, meaning that they generate heat while they cure. This becomes a problem if you have a large amount of resin in a container. I have seen epoxy and polyester get dangerously hot and even boil over when too much was mixed and not applied soon enough. By the way, the amount of time the resin remains workable in a pot after mixing is referred to as *pot life*.

Polyester resin was one of the first resins to be widely used with fiberglass. A small amount of catalyst (typically 1 to 2 percent by volume) is added to trigger polymerization and cause the resin to harden. The resin-to-catalyst ratio is highly dependant on temperature and humidity and should be adjusted accordingly for best results.

The use of polyester resin began with attempts to develop alternatives for aluminum during World War II. After the resin was perfected in the late 1950s, fiberglass boatbuilding exploded. Early fiberglass boats were touted as being impervious to water and maintenance-free. We know better now, but perfecting this resin fueled the conversion of recreational boatbuilding from wood to plastic.

As time has proven, boats built from polyester do sometimes absorb water and develop osmotic blisters. Early resins were less susceptible to the problem, but resin reformulations in the late 1970s and 1980s produced hulls that were more likely to blister. Blistering problems were worsened by less-than-adequate quality control in some of the lamination processes.

Polyester resins usually come with a styrene monomer added to make the resin less viscous and easier to handle, and to aid in hardening. This styrene was the cause of the familiar "polyester" smell in most mold shops in the past. The fumes are now regulated as volatile organic compounds (VOCs), which has forced boatbuilders to add safety and antipollution equipment and develop new molding methods that greatly reduce the pungent odor.

Polyester resin, by itself, is air-inhibited: it won't cure in the presence of air, and the surface will stay tacky. That is a useful characteristic when you are laying up a hull with successive applications of resin and fiberglass reinforcements, because each layer will chemically bond to the next. Such resins are identified as *laminating resins.*

A wax compound can be added to the resin to create a *finishing resin.* While curing, the wax migrates to the surface of the resin and seals it from contact with air, allowing the surface to cure hard. (This can also be accomplished by spraying on a mold release compound such as polyvinyl alcohol, or PVA.) Finishing resin is used for the final laminations.

Whether building a new boat or making repairs, it's important to select the right resin.

When building up successive laminations, you don't want to use a finishing resin, because the wax will prevent additional layers from adhering and must be sanded off before the next layer can be applied. On the other hand, for a final layer, you do want to use a finishing resin to ensure a complete cure.

The vinylester molecule is chemically similar to polyester but has fewer ester groups. Since ester groups are the resin component most subject to water degradation and osmotic blistering, *vinylester resins* are more resistant to blistering.

Many boatbuilders now use vinylesters, at least in the outer layers of hull laminations. Boats built with these resins often offer extended hull warranties against blistering. The downside is that vinylester resins cost more than polyester.

Epoxy differs from ester-based resins in that it requires a *hardener* as opposed to a catalyst. The hardener is added to the epoxy resin in a critical, defined ratio, typically ranging from 5:1 (resin to hardener) to 1:1, depending upon the manufacturer. (In contrast, just a few drops of catalyst suffice to make a pot of polyester resin "kick." Although adding extra catalyst will accelerate the cure of polyester, adding extra hardener to epoxy will not accelerate the cure but will simply weaken the resin structure.)

When mixed and applied correctly, epoxy is much stronger and more water resistant than either of the ester type of resins. Epoxy's water resistance is so good, in fact, that epoxy can be used as a barrier coat over polyester, and this is often done as a repair in cases of extreme blistering. Epoxy is far more costly than the ester resins, however, so it is not often used as the primary resin in composite boats, with the exception of very high-end racing sailboats where light weight is critical and cost is less of an issue.

Since both components in epoxy—resin and hardener—completely react, there are very few VOCs to worry about. Unfortunately, some people become sensitized to epoxy resin and break out in hives or experience other difficulties in the presence of uncured resin. For that reason, gloves, masks, and other protective gear are recommended when using epoxies.

Resin bonds between two composite parts are referred to as *primary* bonds when there is a chemical reaction between the parts and the resin, so that the two parts become essentially one. A *secondary* bond exists if the resin simply serves as an adhesive that mechanically connects the two parts. During construction, primary bonds are generally preferable, since they are stronger; but to accomplish this, the construction schedule must be carefully planned so that subsequent parts or laminations go together before the previous ones are fully cured. Bonds between parts in repairs are necessarily secondary bonds, and epoxy should be used whether the substrate is epoxy or polyester, because epoxy forms a much stronger secondary bond with either material.

Epoxy has poor resistance to ultraviolet (UV) rays, and sunlight causes it to break down fairly quickly. All epoxy-coated surfaces that are exposed to sunlight must be protected with paint or with a varnish that contains UV-blocking compounds.

THE MOLDING PROCESS

Fiberglass molds are themselves usually made from fiberglass. A prototype of the part to be molded, called a plug, is built. It can be made from foam, wood, or other temporary materials or can even be an actual hull. In any case, it is the exact shape of the finished part. It is sanded, painted, and polished. The finish of the plug will be the resulting finish of the mold, so great care is taken to get it perfect. It is then waxed and a coat of tooling gelcoat is applied. Tooling gelcoat is usually black or red and is harder, and thus more durable, than regular gelcoat.

Layers of fiberglass are then built up on top of the tooling gelcoat to form the structural basis of the mold. Reinforcements and handling aids are then bonded to the shell of the mold. These handling aids allow the mold to be rocked on its side and moved around the mold shop.

Once the mold is removed from the plug, its interior surface—which will be the exterior surface of the hull or other part to be molded—is polished to a fine finish. This finish will be replicated in the molded part, so it must be perfect in every way. After polishing, wax is applied to the mold and buffed several times. This forms

Multiple coats of wax are applied to the hull mold and buffed out. The wax provides a shiny surface and acts as a mold release for the hull. (Courtesy Ranger Boats)

the *mold release*, a finish the fiberglass will not bond to.

Gelcoat is then sprayed into the mold. Gelcoat is a specialized form of polyester resin that forms the shiny exterior surface of the hull or other part being molded and protects the laminations beneath from UV rays. Gelcoat is applied by itself, and needs to be of a uniform thickness, usually 10 to 20 mils. (A mil is one thousandth of an inch—0.001 inch—so 10 mils is 0.010 inch.) Many boats are gelcoated in a single color, but some boatbuilders mask off designs in the mold and spray different colors to create features like bootstripes and covestripes. Great care must be taken to apply the gelcoat in a uniform thickness, especially in corners. A thick web of gelcoat in a corner is likely to chip or crack.

The gelcoat is air-inhibited and remains tacky to the touch. This allows it to bond to the next layer being applied. This layer is composed of short fiberglass fibers and resin. It can be applied either in the form of a mat or with a chopper gun. The mat is composed of short fiberglass strands compressed together with a binder, much like felt. The styrene in the polyester resin dissolves the binder and allows the fiberglass to conform to the curves of the mold.

A chopper gun looks like a spray gun with an attitude. Resin and the catalyst are sprayed from a nozzle. The resin and catalyst mix on their way to the mold. This eliminates any problems with catalyzed resin curing in the gun itself. On top of the gun is an air-driven cutter or chopper. Fiberglass roving—strands of untwisted fiberglass strands—are fed into the chopper. The resultant short strands are also blown into the mold and coated with the now catalyzed resin. Often a red strand is embedded in the roving to give a visual indication of the thickness of the layer being applied.

The mat or the chopper gun layer is then rolled out using grooved rollers. The rollers break up any air bubbles in the mat, compress the

When the female mold is polished and waxed, the lamination of the part (in this case a hull) begins. Here gelcoat is sprayed into the mold to form the shiny exterior finish of the hull. (Courtesy Ranger Boats)

Layers of fiberglass are then built up over the gelcoat in the mold, coated with resin, and carefully rolled out to eliminate air bubbles and consolidate the layers. Each layer is applied before the previous one is fully cured, so that the layers are chemically cross-linked and adhered. (Courtesy Grady-White Boats)

strands, and ensure that they are uniformly coated with resin.

After one or two layers of mat are applied, more layers of fiberglass follow. These additional layers are either woven glass cloth or woven roving, often alternating with layers of mat. The outer layer(s) of mat cushions the next layer and prevents "print-through," in which the weave of the cloth or roving is visible in the final finish. When layers of mat alternate with layers of woven roving, the mat fills in the roving's coarse weave and creates a better bond for successive layers of roving.

Most production boats have a defined lamination schedule, spelling out the size and placement of the reinforcing material. Often these are precut and arrive at the mold ready to place. This schedule is designed to make sure the proper amounts of reinforcements are placed in the right locations in the mold.

Following the initial fabric layers, sections of core are applied (as described later in this chapter). Again, most of the core is precut and is applied in precise locations in the mold. The final, interior skin of fiberglass is then built up on top of the core. This forms the inside, or rough side, of the molded part.

Cored Construction

Early in the fiberglass boatbuilding evolution, it was realized that stronger and lighter structures could be made by utilizing a "sandwich" or "cored" technique. A lightweight center core is placed between two layers of fiberglass. The resulting structure is lighter than the equivalent solid fiberglass structure but thicker and much, much stiffer.

Early cored construction utilized plywood. The usual process was to cut ⅜-inch or ½-inch

Grooved rollers are used to roll out the "wet" fiberglass. Here we see a layer of fiberglass cloth being applied in what looks like the cockpit portion of a deck mold, where cloth's ability to conform to abrupt directional changes makes it preferable to roving. (Courtesy Grady-White Boats)

Most fiberglass boats have a cored deck. This cross section through a 35-footer's deck shows a core of plywood squares sandwiched between upper and lower skins of fiberglass. It's readily apparent how much stiffness is contributed to the deck by the core.

plywood into 6-inch squares and place these between the inner and outer layers of the fiberglass laminate. Cutting the plywood into small squares allowed the core to follow a gentle curve. For areas with more curves, a balsa-based core material was developed. Balsa wood was cut across the grain to create small blocks, about 2 inches square and ⅜ inch or ½ inch thick. The end grain of the balsa wood provided high compressive strength with little weight. The squares were bonded to a mesh-like scrim cloth that could be draped around a curve such as the edge of a rounded cabintop. Once another layer of fiberglass was applied to the surface, a complete sandwich structure resulted.

Cored construction is most often used in decks, cabin soles, and cabintops, although hulls have also been built using cored construction, resulting in a lighter boat.

Both plywood and balsa are subject to delamination or even rot if water is allowed to saturate them. The resulting structure loses much of its stiffness and strength. The condition is usually called *core rot*. In response, plastic foams were developed for use as core materials. These are fairly dense foams with good compressive strength and are compatible with the various resin systems.

Another response to this problem is to avoid the use of cores wherever hardware will penetrate the outer surface of the laminate, especially in areas such as ports, through-hull fittings, and deck hardware. This allows there to be solid fiberglass in an area that might be susceptible to water intrusion. The substitution of solid fiberglass for cored laminate beneath hardware is a sign of a good builder.

Many of the projects in this book involve drilling or cutting into the outer surface of a laminate. Where this exposes core material, we recommend steps to replace a small amount of core with resin to avoid future core saturation.

Advanced Molding Processes

Modern boatbuilders have implemented a range of new processes for molding fiberglass boats. You often see techniques like vacuum bagging, resin infusion, or closed-mold resin transfer molding (RTM) mentioned in sales literature. These techniques produce better and sometimes cheaper hulls and are more environmentally friendly than traditional open molding. They don't affect the way we maintain or upgrade our boats, however, so we need not address them here.

INTERIOR STRUCTURES

Early fiberglass hulls were built with largely wood interiors. Plywood bulkheads and wooden stringers were added to the hull and bonded in place using fiberglass mat and resin. Interior cabinetry was then built in place. Because the locations of the stringers and bulkheads were not precise, much of this work required custom fitting by experienced woodworkers.

This process worked fairly well for small production runs, but it was ill-suited to mass production due to the amount of handwork required. A further problem was that, although the hull was durable, the woodwork was susceptible to rot and delamination.

Structural grids and liner pans were developed as a means of simplifying and speeding production. Structural grids are molded from fiberglass and somewhat replicate the wooden stringer and floor designs used in earlier boats. They also may incorporate the engine beds as well as grooves or notches for locating bulkheads or cabinetry. The grid is molded separately, then trimmed and bonded into the hull.

A logical extension of the structural grid was the development of the hull liner or pan. This is a single part that incorporates the cabin sole, bulkheads, cabinet shells, and other interior features. It too is molded, trimmed, and bonded in place, and then cutouts are made for cabinet doors, sinks, and other equipment. In many cases an overhead pan or liner is also made and bonded to the underside of the deck.

These developments required more extensive and expensive tooling, in the form of molds and trim fixtures. However, the ability to produce and install these components using relatively low-cost labor increases productivity and lowers costs.

ASSEMBLY

Once the fiberglass parts are finished, they move on to the assembly stage. Some components, such as structural grids and liners, are bonded in place while the hull is still in the mold. This eliminates any chance of hull distortion while the boat is being assembled.

Hulls and decks are usually worked on as separate units. If a small boat has a cabin, the cabin and deck are typically molded as a single piece, separate from the hull. There will be a crew installing equipment such as engines and plumbing and electrical systems in the hull while another crew bolts ports, stanchions, bow rails, and other such parts to the deck or deckhouse molding.

Once those two units are complete, the deck is lowered onto the hull and fastened in place. Several different techniques can be used to join the hull to the deck, some being more reliable and leakproof than others. See Chapter 4 for details. Which technique is chosen has great ramifications for the repair process. Pieces and parts that were easily installed while the deck and hull are separate can become inaccessible when the two are joined. It's not uncommon to have to cut a water heater or fuel tank into pieces in order to get it out of the boat. Getting replacements back in is a whole other issue. Wiring and plumbing lines are also commonly run behind or under liners or pans. It may well be necessary to cut away portions of a liner to get at some such components for repair.

Some boatbuilders—Boston Whaler, for example—inject foam between the hull and deck molding to provide positive flotation. This is a wonderful thing as long as you don't have to run another wire or hose. In those cases, radical surgery may be required.

Assembly-Related Maintenance Problems

Most production boats are built to a price. To meet that price, boatbuilders simplify their work as much as possible. For the first five or ten years of the boat's life, that's fine. After that, however, some of those practices come back to bite the owner.

Particular areas that cause problems are any penetrations through a cored section of a hull or deck. The holes are usually quickly cut with a drill or router, some sealant is slapped on, and the part is bolted in place. A few years down the road, the sealant starts leaking. Where does it leak? Why, into the core, of course. That, in turn, leads to core rot and a flimsy deck or hull.

Another recurring problem is lack of access to fastener hardware belowdecks. It may have been easy for the builder to through-bolt a stanchion in place while the deck was off the hull. But after the hull and deck are assembled, it may be impossible to reach the nut on the bottom of the bolt. This can cause real difficulties should there be a need to remove or replace the stanchion, or replace or tighten its fastenings.

REGULATORY STANDARDS

In the United States, boats are required to conform to one or more sets of standards. The United States Coast Guard has issued minimal standards influencing the design of fuel and ignition systems and requiring that boats up to 20 feet long be able to float level even when totally swamped. In addition, all boats made in the United States must have a hull identification number permanently affixed to the boat. Boatbuilders self-certify that their boats meet these requirements and must install capacity and data plates reflecting the certification.

The American Boat & Yacht Council (ABYC) is another agency issuing standards for boatbuilders. These standards, which are more complex and far-reaching than the Coast Guard's, are voluntary but have been adopted by the vast majority of production boatbuilders in the United States. Surveyors inspecting a boat for sale or for insurance purposes will check for compliance to ABYC standards. It is important, therefore, that boat repairs follow ABYC standards in order to avoid depreciating the value of the boat.

The European Community (CE: Conformité Européene) also has its own standards. More and more of the components made in the United States are receiving CE certification, indicated by the CE marking on the part.

When adding or changing components aboard a boat, be sure that the replacement parts are certified for marine use. In the United States, they should carry the Underwriters Laboratory (Marine UL) label. In Canada, Canadian Standards Authority (CSA) does the certification, and a CE mark indicates that a part is certified by the European Union. This is especially important in the case of electrical components. It is tempting to replace a $300 marine starter motor with a $57 unit from an auto parts store. After all, many boat engines are marinized automobile engines, right? That's true, and the starter will start the engine.

However, a starter from an auto parts store is not certified to be ignition-protected. Using that starter in a bilge potentially filled with gasoline fumes could result in a large boom, and going up with that boom will be any protection from your boat insurance. If the insurance company can prove you used noncertified parts, you will end up having your insurance cancelled and will potentially be at risk for a lawsuit, especially if someone is injured.

The moral of this story is to pay the extra money for genuine marine parts. If you plan on extensive modifications and upgrades to your boat, become familiar with the standards, especially the ones formulated by the ABYC. See Appendix B for sources of that information.

CHAPTER 2

The Cockpit

Most of us spend more time in the cockpit of our boats than anywhere else on board. Anything we can do to enhance the utility, comfort, safety, or convenience of the cockpit will provide the biggest bang for our project bucks. Everything described here is well within the ability, time constraints, and resources of the average weekend warrior, so pick your project and get started.

ADDING ACCESS HATCHES

I've never heard of a boat with too much storage space, but I know of many that have too little. In Chapter 1 we discussed how hull liners and pans are designed for efficient manufacturing. Their downside, however, is that they often block access to areas of the boat that may have considerable volume. Adding access hatches can turn these dead spaces into useful storage or permit access to components you couldn't otherwise reach. For example, I've added access hatches that allow me to tighten otherwise unreachable engine mounting bolts.

Access hatch installation involves a number of fundamental procedures that are required for a great many boat repairs and upgrades. We describe them here in detail, and you will find this section referred to in other projects throughout the book.

A wide range of access hatches is available from such marine equipment suppliers as Bomar, Beckson, Tempress, and T-H Marine. Rectangular access hatches come as an assembly that includes a frame, hinges, latches, and the lid, and they range in size from 13 inches by 15 inches to ones that are 30 or more inches long. They are typically made from molded plastic. If you plan to install one where it will be walked on, make sure it is rated for that.

Deck plates are also available for use as access hatches. These are round units that consist of a frame and a plate. The plate can be a screw-in or

A typical rectangular access hatch. (Courtesy Tempress Products)

A threaded deck plate and its mounting ring.
(Courtesy Tempress Products)

pry-out type, and some of these, too, are fitted with an O-ring seal to waterproof the unit. I use these less often for storage than to provide access to components or fastenings in otherwise inaccessible areas.

The three fundamental hatch measurements are (working from smallest to largest) the hatch opening size, the frame cutout size, and the outside dimensions of the frame. (The hatch/deck cross section on page 16 makes clear why the opening you cut for the frame has to be bigger than the hatch opening itself.) Hatches are designed to be installed on a *flat* surface. If the camber from one side of the hatch to the other is ⅛ inch or less, installation is still possible with appropriate care. But if the surface crowns more than ⅛ inch, installation might cause the frame to twist so much that the lid won't seal or even latch. A good way to start your installation is to make a plywood cutout of the hatch's outside dimensions and place it where you think it might fit. If the plywood rocks back and forth, the surface may have too much curvature for proper operation after installation.

One of the most difficult things about installing one of these hatches is determining what is behind the hole you are contemplating cutting. Cutting through plumbing or fuel lines or electrical cables can cause embarrassing and expensive problems.

Your first tool is the Internet. Get on it and find other boaters with the same make and model of boat. There are often owner groups with websites and forums. Go there and check out the discussions and photos. Maybe someone has already done what you are thinking of doing. Maybe they already cut that hole and found the space behind it empty—a perfect place to install new storage. Or maybe they cut the hole only to find the space behind it filled with equipment, in which case they learned a hard lesson you can benefit from.

A handy tool to have, and one you should already have aboard, is an auto mechanic's mirror. These mirrors have extendable handles and swivels to allow the mirror to be aimed at any angle. Use it to look behind trim or removable panels. I found a host of potential trouble spots aboard one of my boats using a mirror like this.

Sometimes the only way to discover what's behind a fiberglass surface is to drill an exploratory hole. Before you start, plan what to do if the area turns out to be unusable. You can cover the hole with a piece of decorative trim or an accessory such as a drink holder, or you can install a small inspection plate and cover. The result will always look better if the hole is centered in the area you are investigating.

Assuming the location is fine, it's time to cut the hole for the hatch. One glance at the hatch frame will show you that there isn't a tremendous amount of room between the mounting holes and the edge of the frame cutout. If you make your opening too large, the fasteners may miss the fiberglass mounting surface and hit the empty space of the opening instead—not good.

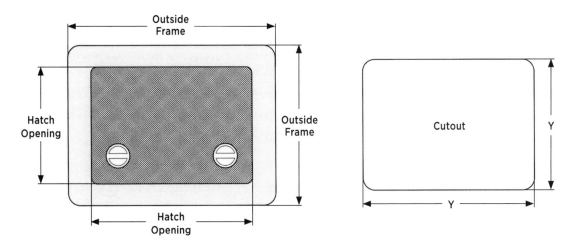

These are the critical measurements for an access hatch. The cutout you make in your deck must be large enough to accommodate the hatch opening and the hatch frame—but no larger. If there was ever a time for the admonition to "measure twice, cut once," this is it. Or better yet, make a template as described in the accompanying text.

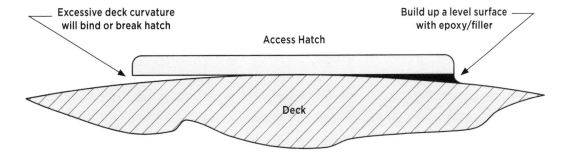

Don't try to mount an access hatch on a deck with pronounced crown. You can accommodate an edge-to-edge crown of ⅛ inch or so by placing neoprene washers on the hatch-frame fasteners as described in the text. Anything more than that, however, will require you to build up a flat base for the hatch frame using thickened epoxy.

To avoid this, make a template. I use artist's foam board, available at most craft stores. It is about ³⁄₁₆ inch thick and consists of a layer of foam sandwiched between layers of cardboard. It is easy to cut with a hobby knife and stiff enough to hold its shape. Place the hatch on the foam board and trace around the opening with a pencil. (That is, trace around the outside of the portion of the hatch frame that will be inserted into the opening when installed.) You can then cut the foam board as a "positive" or "negative" template—in other words, you can use either the piece you cut out of the foam board or the hole that piece leaves behind as your template to transfer the dimensions of the opening to the mounting surface. Either way, check it against the actual hatch to make sure you've got it right.

To avoid scratching the gelcoat of the mounting surface once you start sawing, mask the planned opening with painter's blue masking tape. Cover the fiberglass surface from about 2 inches inside the proposed opening to 3 to 4 inches beyond the outside dimensions of the hatch flange or frame. Then trace around the template onto the tape, marking the location and size of the opening to be cut.

Cut away tape from beneath
where the hatch flange will sit

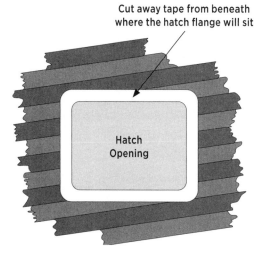

To protect the deck while you cut it, tape all around the hatch opening to a distance of 3 to 4 inches outside the anticipated perimeter of the hatch frame. Blue masking tape works best. Once you've cut the opening, you'll trial-fit the hatch and drill pilot holes for the screws. Then you'll trace the hatch-frame perimeter onto the tape, remove the hatch frame, and cut away the tape inside the perimeter you just traced. Leave the tape in place outside that perimeter, however, to protect the deck from squeeze-out of the adhesive/sealant you use when you install the frame.

You will cut the fiberglass with a metal-cutting blade in a variable-speed jigsaw. (If you will be installing several hatches of the same size, you might want to make a plywood template and do the cutting with a router.) Start the cut by drilling an access hole for the blade inside the hatch opening. Fiberglass is extremely hard on saw blades, and you might have to replace the blade when cutting a large opening. Cut inside the line—it is preferable to cut too small and sand the opening larger than to cut it too large. Keep the cutting speed slow to avoid chipping the gelcoat surrounding the opening, and if your saw allows a variable orbit, set it to minimum.

Trial-fit the hatch and grind or sand the hole larger if necessary. If you cut through a cored section, you will expose the wood or foam core. This needs to be sealed against water intrusion by cutting back the core between the inner and outer layers of fiberglass to a depth of about $3/8$ to $1/2$ inch (in other words, deep enough to surround the fasteners that will hold the hatch frame in place) and filling the space with a paste made from epoxy resin and a thickening agent. Don't skip this step! Failure to properly seal the core from water intrusion will eventually result in core rot, delamination, or both, which will reduce the value of your boat and could be dangerous. After the epoxy plug has cured, test-fit the hatch again, and sand and grind some more if necessary.

If you are unfamiliar with the use of epoxy, see the accompanying sidebar Using Epoxy.

When the hatch fits properly, drill pilot holes for the hatch fasteners, using the hatch frame as a drilling template. In most cases, stainless steel self-tapping screws do a good job of holding the hatch in place. The pilot holes should be tight enough to develop a proper thread, but not so tight that the gelcoat chips when the screw is

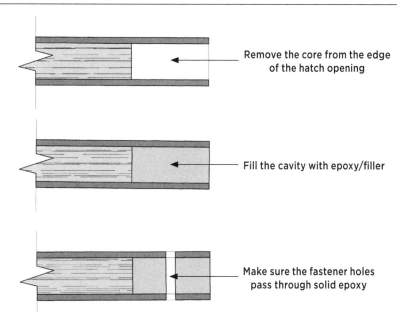

Remove the core from the edge
of the hatch opening

Fill the cavity with epoxy/filler

Make sure the fastener holes
pass through solid epoxy

Cut back the exposed core edges around the hatch opening and fill the resultant cavity with epoxy/filler.

driven. Check against the thickness of the fiberglass laminate *and* the length of the screws for the proper depth of the pilot holes. Don't install the screws yet. Trace around the hatch frame onto the blue tape, then remove the hatch and cut away the tape under where the hatch flange will rest, leaving the tape on the fiberglass outside the flange.

The next step is to choose the right sealant. Many common sealants, such as 3M 5200, will soften the plastic used in the hatches. Read the installation instructions that came with the hatch for the proper sealant. If none is specified, use a marine-grade silicone sealant. While you're at it, go to your favorite hardware store and pick up some neoprene washers. Most hardware stores carry them in their specialty hardware drawers. These should be about ⅜ inch in diameter with a ⅛-inch or 3/16-inch center hole, and about 1/16 to ⅛ inch thick. You'll need one for each fastener in the hatch frame.

Back at the boat, place the fasteners in the hatch frame, then cover the frame edges with blue tape. Turn the frame over, place a neoprene washer on each fastener, and apply a healthy bead of sealant around the frame's mounting surface. Apply more sealant to the opening on the boat, then gently place the hatch in position and start screwing it down. The goal is to snug the fasteners up against the neoprene washers, which are there to keep you from squeezing out all the sealant. Torquing down fasteners in this kind of installation without the washers squeezes out all but a thin film of sealant. That thin film will quickly fail, whereas a thicker layer will better handle the expansion and contraction of the hatch and hull.

Use a disposable putty knife to clean up the excess sealant that has squeezed out onto the blue tape, then you can pull up the tape without any mess. Don't be tempted to go back and

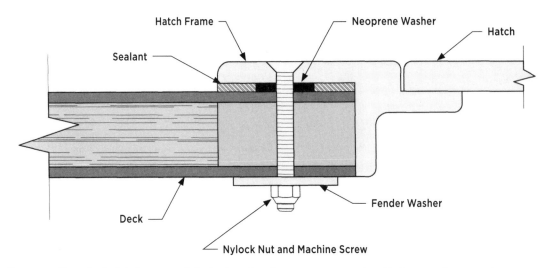

Cross section of a hatch frame and deck, showing the neoprene washer that prevents excessive squeeze-out of the adhesive/sealant.

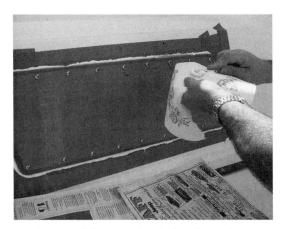

This is a portlight, not a hatch, but the techniques are the same. Note that both the frame itself and the surrounding fiberglass are protected by masking tape. Plenty of rags and a square-tipped tongue depressor will prove useful for cleaning up the sealant squeezed out from under the hatch.

retighten the fasteners after the sealant has begun to cure. This will break the sealant bond around the fasteners and could result in leaks. If you insist on tightening the fastener, make sure someone holds the screw or bolt from turning while the nut is tightened from below. If you allow the fastener itself to turn, you will break the sealant bond around the fastener and provide a path for leaks,

I mentioned earlier that a *slight* camber or crown in the fiberglass mounting surface—no more than ⅛ inch—can be accommodated. To do this, mount additional neoprene washers on the fasteners under the curvature, and temporarily tighten down the frame without sealant. Take note of how tightly you torque the fasteners, and make sure the lid latches and seals properly. You can then go ahead and install the hatch as described above, using enough sealant to fill the gaps. Be sure not to overtighten the fasteners when you install them for good.

If you're replacing an existing hatch or portlight, see "Replacing Ports and Hatches" in Chapter 3. The procedure is largely the same.

Using Epoxy

I use WEST System epoxy from Gougeon Brothers, Inc. There are other excellent brands available, but I know WEST System best, and some of the following discussion is based on my experience with that product. Feel free to use another brand, but recognize that some of the application details that follow may differ.

Epoxy is a two-part material consisting of a resin and a hardener. When mixed together, they polymerize to form a hard plastic material. Modified with the proper additives and paired with appropriate fiberglass materials, epoxy has a myriad of uses aboard a boat. The epoxy/hardener mixture has a consistency prior to setting anywhere from firm, thick, and clay-like to thin and syrupy. Many epoxies on the market today have a mix ratio of 5 parts resin to 1 part hardener, although 4:1, 3:1, 2:1, and 1:1 epoxies are also available.

Most suppliers offer calibrated pumps that fit the cans of resin and hardener. One press of each pump will deliver the appropriate ratio of resin and hardener. You can also use mixing cups with measurements printed on them, but the pumps are a darn sight easier to use.

Epoxy heats up as the resin and hardener chemicals react, and the more heat this exothermic reaction produces, the faster the reaction occurs. As soon as the mixture begins to gel, it is no longer workable, and any unused epoxy in your mixing tub must be discarded.

In contrast with polyester resins, you can adjust the "pot life" (the time the mixture stays liquid or workable) by using a different hardener. Most epoxy brands have several different hardeners available. For example, there are four WEST System hardeners:

205 Fast Hardener—This is a medium-viscosity hardener for use in colder temperatures. It uses a 5:1 mixing ratio and has a pot life of about 9 to 12 minutes at 72°F. This hardener is not suitable for clear coating.

206 Slow Hardener—This is a low-viscosity hardener for use when extra working time is needed or for use in higher temperatures. It uses a 5:1 mixing ratio and has a pot life of 20 to 25 minutes at 72°F. It is not suitable for clear coating.

207 Special Hardener—This hardener is specially formulated for clear-coating wood. It contains UV protection but will still need additional protection from a varnish with UV inhibitors to prevent breakdown. It has good self-leveling properties and will cure clear with a slight amber tint. This hardener uses a 3:1 mixing ratio and has a pot life of 22 to 27 minutes at 72°F.

209 Extra Slow Hardener—This hardener was developed for use in hot or humid conditions. It has about twice the pot life of the 206 Slow Hardener. It uses a 3:1 mixing ratio and has a pot life of 40 to 50 minutes at 72°F and 15 to 20 minutes at 95°F. It is not suitable for clear-coating.

To further extend the working time of an epoxy mixture, cool it in a refrigerator or spread it out in a shallow tray to allow heat to dissipate more readily.

Additives and Materials

Epoxy resin and hardener mixed straight from their cans can be used as is, without further additives, for laminating fiberglass cloth or coating wood or other materials. I epoxy-coat all surfaces of any wood I install in a boat. This helps prevent water absorption and subsequent rot. Epoxy can also be used under varnish to provide a stable base. The varnish will also protect the epoxy from UV rays.

Alternatively, the epoxy mixture can be tailored to a number of specific uses with a wide variety of additives. These additives are usually sold in powder form and are mixed into the resin as soon as the hardener is thoroughly mixed. The most common additives are:

Colloidal (or fumed) silica—This filler is used to thicken epoxy and prevent sagging or slumping on vertical surfaces. Used by itself or in combination with other fillers, it makes a very smooth surface that won't run or sag. It's tough to sand, though, so use it sparingly on a surface you'll need to sand or fair.

Microballoons or microspheres—This lightweight, easily sanded filler material is used to fair surfaces or form fillets. Several types are available for different uses. These fairing fillers should not be used beneath the waterline, as they have a tendency to wick water. Neither should some of these fillers be used under dark colors, as the heat developed in sunlight may affect them. Check with your supplier.

Microfibers—These rayon or glass fibers are used to strengthen epoxy bonds. Epoxy with this filler provides a high-strength bond and is especially good for bonding wood. It provides excellent gap-filling properties.

High-density fillers—These are used to make epoxy noncompressible (for use under bolts, for example). Epoxy with this filler develops maximum-strength bonds, especially when bonding hardware in place.

Graphite powder—This is used to make an extremely black and slippery mix. Epoxy with graphite powder can be used to form bearings around rudder shafts, for example.

Pigments—These usually come in the form of a thick liquid or paste and are used to color the epoxy. This is not the equivalent of a painted coating, however, and it won't protect the epoxy from UV rays. If the surface will be exposed to sunlight, it must still be painted or protected with a UV-inhibitor varnish.

Barrier additives—These are used to form a more water-resistant coating below the waterline, especially for curing hull blisters.

Copper powder—This is used to make antifouling epoxy paint for under the waterline. The jury is still out on the effectiveness of this approach, however.

Several reinforcement materials are used in conjunction with epoxy. Fiberglass reinforcements are available in the form of cloth, cloth tape, and various combinations of stitched cloth, mat, and roving. (Not all fiberglass reinforcements are compatible with epoxy resins. Read labels before you buy.) Besides fiberglass, other fabrics made from aramid fibers (Kevlar) and graphite or carbon fibers are also in common use.

Tools

You will need several mixing and application tools, including tubs of some sort in which to mix the epoxy. I use white polypropylene bowls supplied by the epoxy manufacturer. They are flexible and allow you to crack out the cured resin so you can use the bowls again. I get ten to fifteen uses out of a bowl before it breaks.

Wooden tongue depressors work well as stirring sticks. For economy, buy these at a crafts store, not a medical supply house. Recently, WEST introduced a polypropylene mixing stick. You just flex it to pop off the cured epoxy, making it reusable.

Foam brushes are fine for coating a surface with epoxy. Experiment with brands of brushes, as some tend to dissolve in the epoxy. When applying fiberglass cloth or tape, I use disposable "chip" brushes so I can "stipple" or force the epoxy into the cloth. These brushes usually have unpainted handles and white or buff-colored bristles. I buy my brushes in bulk from marine suppliers like Jamestown Distributors.

Plastic squeegees are also useful. I buy cheap ones from an auto parts store. The epoxy suppliers sell neat notched squeegees, but hardened epoxy doesn't break off these very well, whereas it will pop right off the cheaper flexible ones. If I need notches, I can always cut them with a knife.

Plastic glue syringes are handy for forcing epoxy into holes or tight areas. Plastic frosting bags can be used to dispense thicker epoxy mixtures. Zip-style baggies can also be used: just snip off the corner and squeeze out the epoxy.

Grooved aluminum or plastic rollers are ideal for rolling down fiberglass cloth. They are pricey but work well for wetting out the cloth with epoxy and eliminating voids and air bubbles. Be sure to get the kind you can disassemble for cleaning.

Safety

Another important consideration is safety equipment. Epoxy gives off far less odor than polyester resin, but it has one significant safety hazard. Prolonged exposure can lead to sensitization. Once that happens, any future exposure will cause a reaction similar to an allergic reaction, and you will have to stop using epoxy forever—end of story!

For that reason, always use adequate protection. Many people use disposable latex gloves to keep epoxy at bay. I use heavy-duty rubber gloves because they hold up better, are more resistant to tears, and extend higher up my arms. Work outdoors with excellent ventilation, or wear an appropriate respirator. A mere dust mask doesn't qualify—you need an organic vapor respirator. Safety glasses are also advisable.

You will soon adopt a set of clothes as your epoxy uniform. It will get stiffer and stiffer with repeated use until the hardened epoxy finally forces you to throw the outfit out. If I'm going to be really slopping the epoxy around, I also wear a Tyvek "bunny" suit. If working overhead, I wear a disposable paint hood that slips over my head and hair like a ski mask.

Applications and Techniques

Using epoxy is a lot like cooking: you use a number of basic ingredients in different ways to accomplish the result you are looking for. Epoxy is fairly forgiving as long as you get the resin/hardener ratio right.

From now on, when I talk about epoxy I mean the mixed product with hardener added. This is the starting point for all subsequent uses. Again, the metered pumps supply the proper ratio of resin and hardener to the mixing pot, and the two components must then be thoroughly mixed. This means scraping off all the material clinging to the sides and bottom of the container and stirring it back in. Stir for at least a full minute—two is better.

Unfilled (that is, unthickened) epoxy, with no additives, has several applications, as mentioned previously. It can be used as a coating to waterproof the edges and surfaces of wood and plywood. It can be used as a base for varnish. It is used to laminate fiberglass cloth and other reinforcements. And it is applied to bare wood surfaces prior to gluing them together with thickened epoxy. Pretreatment with unfilled epoxy saturates the wood and prevents it from sucking the resin out of the later adhesive mix. It's an important prerequisite for a strong bond.

When using epoxy with fiberglass, begin by "painting" the epoxy onto the surface you are laminating, then lay the fiberglass carefully onto the surface, avoiding wrinkles from the outset. Apply more resin and work it into the fiberglass with an up-and-down "stippling" motion of the paintbrush. An ideal composition is 50 percent resin and 50 percent reinforcement, so don't apply too much resin. It doesn't increase the strength and wastes epoxy. We discuss the laminating process in more detail later, in other projects.

Various terms are used to describe the consistency of an epoxy/additive mix. *Thick cream* means a mix that can be poured. *Ketchup* consistency is slightly thicker but will still run. *Mayonnaise* consistency is thicker yet and won't run. *Peanut butter* is even stiffer and needs to be troweled in place with a putty knife.

Additives can be mixed into the base epoxy in various combinations to tailor the result for specific applications. For example, high-density filler plus a small amount of colloidal silica will produce an excellent adhesive with gap-filling properties. This is a very useful quality, as it permits the pieces being joined to have less-than-perfect mating surfaces. In fact, filled epoxy joints do not need to be tightly clamped, and tightly clamping two perfectly flat pieces together will squeeze too much epoxy out of the joint and result in a weaker bond.

High-density filler plus a little colloidal silica mixed into epoxy to a thick cream consistency is ideal for sealing core material in fiberglass decks against water intrusion. We cover this in detail in several projects, but briefly, the area around a fastener is cut back, and the cavity is filled with the epoxy mixture. After this epoxy plug cures, a fastener hole is drilled through. The plug keeps water away from the core and serves as a compression strut to keep the tightened fastener from compressing the laminate. The same approach is often used to seal the edges of hatch and port openings.

Microspheres or microballoons, also called low-density or microlight fillers, are added to epoxy to form a fairing compound that is easy to sand. Fairing is the process of filling and sanding a surface to form a smooth, consistent surface without bumps or hollows. The consistency should be thick enough to coat a vertical surface without sagging. If you have a large area or deep section to fair, use a notched spreader to form ridges in the area to be faired. Sand those ridges down until they are at the level required. Then come back with another application of fairing compound to fill the valleys between ridges. This saves both epoxy and sanding.

Cleaning Up

Using epoxy is a messy business. The challenge is to keep it as contained and "cleanable" as possible. Cheap plastic painting tarps are ideal because epoxy doesn't stick to them. I throw one over my bench when I'm coating wood pieces or laminating anything. I have also used adult diapers for protecting surfaces from drips and spills. I spread one out on the cabin sole and place the epoxy tray on it when I'm mixing aboard a boat.

Be sure to clean up the items you are epoxying as you go. Drips and drops are easy to wipe up when the epoxy hasn't cured, but can add hours of miserable sanding time to your project if you wait until they cure. Don't just wipe once and walk away. Epoxy has a habit of oozing out as soon as you turn your back.

There are several choices for cleaning up after epoxy. Acetone is probably the most common but needs to be used outside (don't breathe the fumes!), is a problem to dispose of properly, and releases volatile organic compounds (VOCs) into the air—not good for the environment. One manufacturer offers a cleanup emulsifier you can mix with water. Many people swear by white vinegar for cleaning up. These are all for uncured resin, by the way. The best cleanup tool for cured resin is a chisel or sander.

STORAGE COMPARTMENTS AND TACKLE BOX DRAWERS

Few boats come equipped with what most of us would consider adequate storage. Consequently, some of the most often added features are storage compartments or tackle boxes. These look a lot like access hatches from the outside but open to a variety of interior configurations. They range from a simple box-shaped storage area or liner attached to a hatch frame to a unit subdivided by various numbers and configurations of storage drawers. These compartments promote safety by getting items off the deck and out from underfoot. They are especially useful in areas that would be too deep or hard to reach with a mere hatch access. For example, the area opened up by the access hatch might reach down into the bilge under the cockpit floor, and any item stored there would fall out of reach. The liner limits the area to a useful volume.

The main suppliers of these units are Cabela's, Sailing Specialties Inc. (SSI), and Tempress Prod-

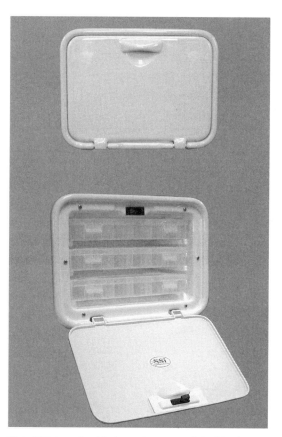

This SSI, Inc., tackle box storage unit holds three individual tackle box storage drawers. (Courtesy SSI, Inc.)

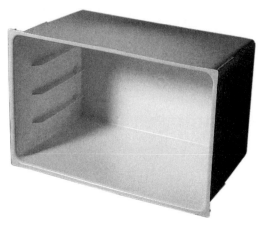

If you don't need tackle box trays, the liner and hatch from the previous photo can be used without the drawers. (Courtesy Tempress Products)

A molded liner can be used in conjunction with an access hatch like the one shown on page 11. (Courtesy Tempress Products)

ucts. The Tempress and SSI units are molded plastic, while the Cabela's units are made from StarBoard plastic "lumber." These units fit into a hole cut in the structure of the boat and are either screwed in place or through-bolted. Through-bolting requires access to the back side of the unit.

Configurations include two-, three-, and four-drawer units. Not all manufacturers make all sizes. The boxes are either custom made for the unit or are standard tackle drawers from suppliers like Plano. Another option is a simple box liner that attaches to the access hatch frame.

As when installing an access hatch, the first order of business is finding a mounting location for the box that is convenient and flat. The only difference between installing an access hatch and installing a storage box is that there must be sufficient depth behind the opening to accommodate

the box. Make sure there are no critical plumbing, wiring, or structural components in the way. Otherwise, follow the same procedures as described in Adding Access Hatches earlier in this chapter.

HANDHOLDS

Additional handholds are cheap insurance against falls on board or even falling over the side. A visit to your local marine store or a marine products website will give you an idea of the variety of handholds available today. They range from traditional teak handholds to stainless steel or even polymer "lumber" units. They come in a variety of sizes and numbers of loops or openings. You also have the possibility of engineering a custom design utilizing standard fittings and handrail tubing.

A teak handhold installed on a cabinet below deck.

Teak handholds have a traditional look that goes well on boats with other wood trim. If you have access to wood and the right woodworking tools, you can always make your own handholds. I have seen them made from cherry, mahogany, and white oak. The advantage of making your own is that the design is limited only by your imagination. Use stock thicker than the common 1-by boards (which are nominally 1 inch but actually only ¾ inch thick) to provide a base wide enough for secure mounting.

You can stain teak to match other colors of wood, and it's possible to mix stains of various colors to achieve a custom look or to match an existing stain. For an interior wood handhold, apply at least eight coats of a good gloss varnish. For exterior handholds, use eight or more coats of satin varnish with UV blockers. There are several

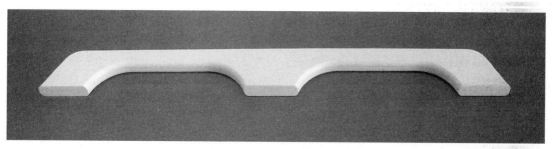

A polymer imitation-wood handhold like this StarBoard product does not need to be finished and is weatherproof.

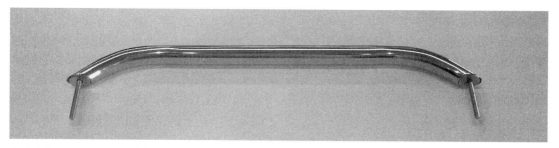

A stainless steel handhold with mounting studs on each end.

other finishes to choose from, including Cetol, Bristol Finish, and Interlux Perfection Two-Part Polyurethane Varnish..

White polymer plastic handholds are also available. The advantage of using polymer lumber, such as StarBoard, is that no finishing is needed. The product also will not absorb water or delaminate. There are a few stock plastic handrail designs available in either white or black. The selection isn't large, but the ones that are available have a modern Euro look. My only complaint about off-the-shelf polymer handholds is that they are typically made from ¾-inch stock, which I feel is not thick enough to give sufficient side-to-side support on something that may be as highly stressed as a handhold, even if it is through-bolted.

Stock sheets of the material are available for custom handholds, and I used this material to replace four-loop teak handrails on one of my boats.

Stainless steel handholds are also an option. They come in several lengths with two different mounting styles. One has a bolt hole in each end

This custom-designed StarBoard handrail replaced a well-worn teak handrail on the cabintop of one of my project boats.

to facilitate through-bolting, while the other has a threaded stud welded on each end. The stud works well as long as it is long enough to go through the mounting surface and the backing plate. There should be enough thread length to allow at least three threads to extend past the nut. The stud can be trimmed with a cutoff disc in a Dremel tool if necessary.

All handholds require two things: proper location and proper installation. I like to temporarily mount hardware with double-backed sticky tape. This allows me to evaluate a potential location, as long as I don't apply any appreciable force to it. Leave it in place to see how it works. This technique has saved me from installing hardware that would have interfered with the opening of doors and ports.

Once a location is chosen, the mounting is the next consideration. A handhold can have a lot of force applied to it by a falling crewmember, and it must be properly backed to be safe. This is achieved by using a backing plate underneath the deck or cabintop (or behind the deckhouse or cabin side). The backing plate spreads the forces applied to the handhold fasteners over a wider area and prevents the fasteners from pulling through the deck or other structure they are attached to.

Installing a backing plate requires under-deck access to the handhold fasteners. Don't be tempted simply to screw the handhold in from topside using long self-tapping screws. These would more than likely pull out of the fiberglass deck or cabin side at the worst possible moment. Handholds should be through-bolted for strength and safety.

The backing plate can be made from ½-inch or ¾-inch-thick plywood, ¼-inch-thick aluminum or stainless steel plate, or a laminated synthetic product called G10. G10 is manufactured

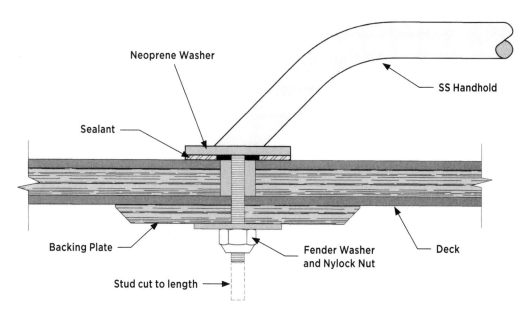

Neoprene Washer

SS Handhold

Sealant

Backing Plate

Fender Washer
and Nylock Nut

Deck

Stud cut to length

Cross section of a properly installed stainless steel (SS) handhold. Note the use of a neoprene washer to prevent excessive squeeze-out of the adhesive/sealant. You want enough sealant in place after the fasteners are tightened to prevent ingress of water.

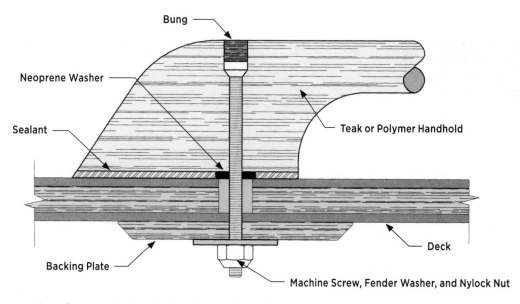

Bung

Neoprene Washer

Teak or Polymer Handhold

Sealant

Backing Plate

Deck

Machine Screw, Fender Washer, and Nylock Nut

Cross section of a properly installed teak or polymer handhold. A plywood backing plate is shown here, but aluminum or stainless steel plate could be used instead.

by several companies and distributed through plastic supply houses, and it can also be found, at great savings, on eBay. I particularly like ¼-inch-thick G10, which is made from multiple layers of fiberglass cloth bonded with epoxy. It makes a strong, corrosion-proof backing plate that can still be cut with a jigsaw.

Once the mounting holes are drilled, inspect the holes for any trace of wood or foam core. If you have drilled through a cored surface, you need to remove the core from around the hole and fill it with epoxy/filler. Once the thickened epoxy has set, redrill the mounting hole through the epoxy plug. The plug will keep water from saturating and rotting a wood core, and it will keep the through-bolt from crushing a balsa or foam core when tightened.

Affix the blue tape around the mounting holes. Remount the handhold temporarily, trace onto the tape around the mounting pads, and cut away the tape beneath the pads. If you are using wooden handholds, tape around the mounting pad bases to prevent sealant from getting into the grain. Place a neoprene washer or an O-ring around the fastener and apply plenty of sealant to the handhold and the mounting area. Bolt the handhold in place, applying only gentle pressure on the nuts for now. Any excess sealant will squeeze out on the tape and can easily be cleaned up.

Allow the sealant to cure fully. For fast-cure products this can take forty-eight hours, but products such as 3M 5200 may require seven days or more. After the sealant has cured, you can snug up the fastener by tightening the nut from below. Have someone else hold the head of the bolt or machine screw absolutely immobile to avoid breaking the watertight bond between the sealant and the fastener.

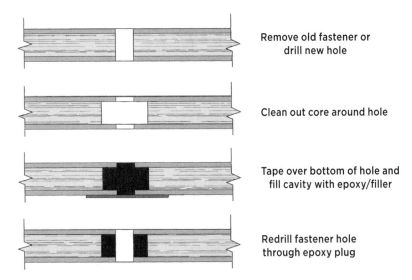

Remove old fastener or drill new hole

Clean out core around hole

Tape over bottom of hole and fill cavity with epoxy/filler

Redrill fastener hole through epoxy plug

When mounting handholds, as when mounting hatch frames, portlights, or anything else through a cored fiberglass laminate, you should replace the core around fastener holes with thickened epoxy plugs to prevent water from leaking into the core. Because this step is critical, this drawing appears in several places throughout the book.

COCKPIT TABLES

A horizontal surface in the cockpit on which to put your lunch and beverage is a luxury. Cockpit tables needn't be permanently mounted; there are several options for mounting and dismounting a table quickly and easily. You can purchase a complete table with mounting accessories or just buy the mounting components and build a custom tabletop.

Before spending money on this upgrade, do some legwork to determine the mounting style, height, and table shape that will work best for you. It's worthwhile to build a mock-up from foam, cardboard, and/or scrap wood, possibly supported at the right height on a piece of cardboard carpet tube. This mock-up won't be strong enough to hold any weight, but it will allow you to slide in

behind it and walk alongside it—or discover that you can't do either. Better to discover a flawed design now, with cardboard and duct tape, than later, with mahogany and epoxy.

There are several common mounting scenarios for cockpit tables. One end can be mounted to a gunwale or cockpit coaming with a piano hinge while the other end is supported by a fold-down leg. Folding the leg up beneath the tabletop allows the table to swing down against the side of the boat, out of the way.

Another option for a gunwale- or coaming-mounted table is to install L-shaped brackets on the underside of the table and a mating receiver on the cockpit side. The L-bracket slides into the receiver socket, and a folding or removable table leg supports the other end of the table. This configuration allows for larger tables than could fold down against the cockpit side on a hinge, and it completely removes the table from the cockpit when not in use, opening up more space for lounging or fishing. On the other hand, it requires

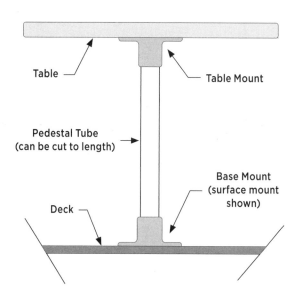

A typical stowable cockpit table mounted on a central pedestal. The surface-mounted socket for the pedestal base is easier to install than a flush mount socket but will become a trip hazard when the table is removed for storage.

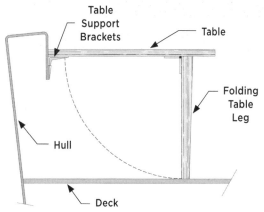

This table is supported at one end by a hinged leg and at the other end by brackets that slide into receivers mounted on the side of the boat. (See the next illustration for detail.)

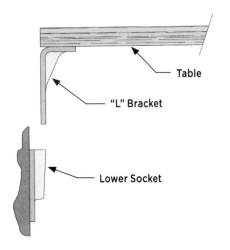

L-shaped table brackets will support one end of a stowable table.

space elsewhere for storage, and the L-brackets can easily ding or damage whatever surface the tabletop is stored against. In some boats a removable tabletop rests on cleats mounted at the front edges of two seats that face each other; when the table is in place it forms a continuous platform that, with the addition of a cushion or cushions, can be used as a single or double berth.

There are also small tables that fit into standard rod holders. These are used more often for bait-preparation or fish-cleaning stations than dining tables. Most are made from StarBoard polymer lumber, which is easily cleaned and never needs refinishing. These tables are generally mounted to extend outward over the side of the boat, taking up no cockpit space, and most have fiddles on three sides to prevent things from sliding overboard.

Most cockpit tables, however, are mounted on a central pedestal. The base of the tubular pedestal fits into a socket installed in the cockpit floor, or sole, while the upper end fits into another socket that is screwed to the underside of the tabletop. The table height can be lowered by trimming one end of the pedestal tube.

Once a location has been determined, the next step when installing a pedestal-type table is to mount the lower socket on the cockpit sole. The socket may be either flush-mounted (also known as recessed) or surface-mounted. A flush-mounted socket includes a center boss, which is inserted through a hole in the deck, and a mount-

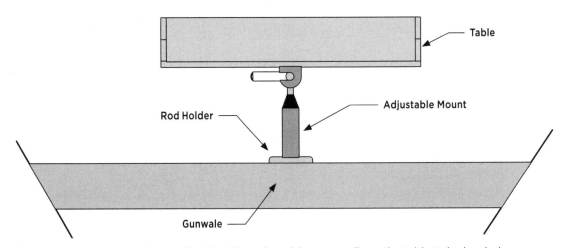

A table mounted on a fishing rod holder. The adjustable mount allows the table to be leveled.

ing flange atop the boss that sits flush with the deck. A surface-mounted socket stands above the deck, creating a possible trip hazard. Both types require drilling holes for fasteners through the deck, while the flush-mounted style also requires a large center hole.

It is imperative that you know what is under the deck before drilling any holes. Many boats have centerline fuel tanks, and you'll find that drilling into one of those can ruin your whole day and then some. Check with your dealer, call the manufacturer, or ask other owners of similar boats. If you don't have access to the underside of the deck—ask!

The method you choose for fastening the pedestal socket will depend on whether or not you have access to the underside of the deck. If you do, things are a little simpler. Cut the center hole, if required, with a holesaw of appropriate diameter to match the boss. Drill holes of proper size for the mounting bolts, which are usually ¼″-20 size (that is, ¼-inch diameter by 20 threads per inch). Notice I said bolts: *Never* use screws to hold down the socket. They will eventually work loose and your table will wobble. It is inevitable that people

will brace themselves against the table at sea, and it must be secure.

Take a look at the sawdust your drilling and cutting have produced. Is there wood dust or plastic foam dust there? Both indicate that the deck is cored, and it is essential to seal it against water intrusion. For the large central hole for a flush-mounted socket, follow the same procedures as described in Adding Access Hatches earlier in this chapter.

The mounting holes are a little more difficult. After drilling the hole for the mounting bolt, cut a slightly larger hole through the top deck surface and through the core using a holesaw. Use a holesaw small enough that the patched hole will be hidden by the socket's mounting flange, and be careful not to touch the lower layer of fiberglass with the holesaw. Pop out the material remaining in the center hole with a screwdriver and clean out any remaining wood. Fill the cavity with epoxy/filler and allow it to cure. Then redrill the fastener hole through the epoxy plug as illustrated earlier in this chapter.

The socket can now be bolted in place with a generous amount of sealant around the bolt holes.

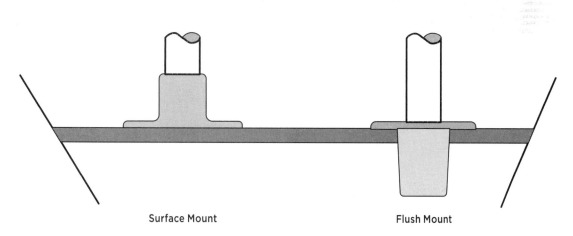

Surface Mount   Flush Mount

Sockets for pedestal bases are available in either surface or flush mounted versions.

These are usually far enough inside the footprint of the mounting flange that I don't tape off the deck or the socket. Don't crank the bolts down tight, because that would squeeze out most of the sealant and cause the remaining sealant to break down more rapidly. The object is to leave a uniformly thick layer of sealant that will flex to accommodate the differing rates of expansion and contraction of the metal socket and fiberglass deck. Placing a neoprene washer on each fastener, between the deck and the socket, will help maintain a proper sealant layer.

Things are a little more complicated if you lack under-deck access. In that case it's necessary to use a toggle bolt. These come in two different styles. For the type with a spring-loaded folding toggle, drill a larger-than-normal hole, sized so the folded toggle nut will pass through. Insert the machine screw through the fastener hole in the socket, then screw the folding toggle a few turns onto the machine screw. Do this with all the mounting holes in the socket. Each toggled bolt nut is then pushed through its designated hole, with the toggle folding as it enters. Once the toggle is through the hole, a spring pops it back out to its extended length. (The screws must be long enough that the upper limb of the toggle can pass all the way through the deck hole and be free to spring open.) Working from above, you then tighten the nut against the top face of the socket.

The second style of toggle has two flexible nylon straps attached to the nut. You pass the nut lengthwise through the hole, and then use the straps to pull it tight against the underside of the

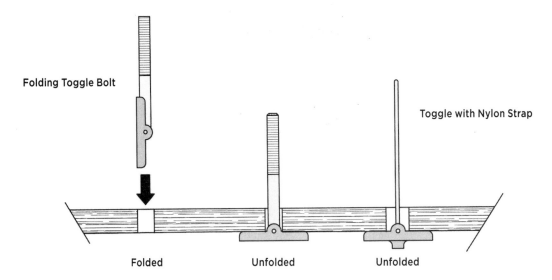

Folding Toggle Bolt

Toggle with Nylon Strap

Folded   Unfolded   Unfolded

Toggle bolts are used where there is no access to the underside of the deck. One type has a spring-loaded folding toggle (left-hand drawing). Insert the bolt through the socket base (not shown) and the oversize hole in the deck or cockpit sole. The toggle then springs open against the deck's underside (center drawing) while you tighten a nut over the exposed, threaded end of the bolt. An alternative variety has the nut attached to two nylon straps. Fish the nut down through the deck hole and wedge it against the deck underside while you thread the machine screw through it (not shown).

deck while threading the machine screw through it. Apply sealant and tighten the fasteners.

Most pedestal table kits come with the upper and lower sockets and a tabletop made of roto-molded plastic. These are lightweight and easy to clean. If the standard top doesn't suit your needs, you can build your own. Solid materials such as ¾-inch plywood or StarBoard are easy to work with but heavy, and aboard small boats, lighter is usually better.

A very light table can be made from insulation foam sandwiched between two pieces of ⅛-inch plywood. Use the blue or pink foam made for home insulation, not white Styrofoam, which would be a very inferior material for this purpose. Place a piece of solid lumber in the middle of the table to hold the fasteners for the top socket, and use epoxy to glue all the pieces of the sandwich together. Then epoxy ¾-inch solid wood strips around the edges for a clean finish, and seal all around with more epoxy.

The upper socket should be fastened to the underside of the table using threaded inserts, not wood screws. Threaded inserts have a helical thread on the outside and a machine thread on the inside, commonly ¼″-20 size (¼-inch diame-ter by 20 threads per inch). Drill a large pilot hole into the solid center, then screw the threaded insert into the hole. The large surface area and coarse thread of the insert provide a strong mounting system that can easily be disassembled if necessary.

Lightweight and rigid, this tabletop can be either utilitarian or lovely, depending upon your choice of materials and how you finish them. Cheap plywood can be sanded, filled, and painted. Good plywood can be stained and varnished. You can apply a plastic countertop laminate like For-

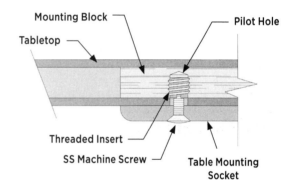

A threaded insert will fasten the table socket securely to the tabletop and tolerates repeated disassembly without loss of holding power.

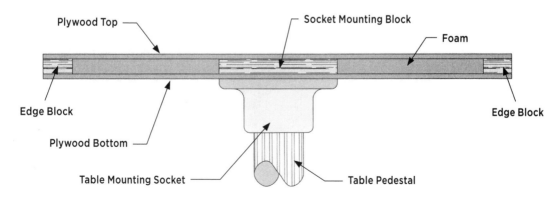

You can make your own lightweight tabletop from plywood and foam.

mica to the top. The use of hardwoods such as mahogany or cherry for the edge pieces can add a touch of class.

INSTALLING A WASHDOWN PUMP

You've had a successful fishing trip. Now you're headed toward the dock and it's time to clean the boat. As you haul bucket after bucket of water aboard, you notice your neighbor standing in his cockpit hosing it down with what looks like a common garden hose. Later, tied up at the dock, you find out that he has installed a washdown pump. Now you want one.

Washdown pumps are becoming more and more popular, especially on fishing boats, where they make cleanup almost a pleasure. And they aren't difficult to install.

The heart of any washdown system is, of course, the pump. Wander down the aisles of any boat store and you will see a wide variety of washdown pumps. Many are simply relabeled freshwater pumps. Washdown pumps are often three- or four-chambered diaphragm pumps driven by a 12-volt DC motor, and are typically rated to deliver 2.8 to 5 gallons per minute (gpm). They come equipped with a pressure switch that turns the pump on when the pressure in the delivery hose falls below about 45 pounds per square inch (psi). Less commonly used are belt-driven diaphragm pumps and flexible impeller pumps.

Be sure to check the duty rating of the pump motor. Freshwater system pumps are designed to turn on, pump water for a short period of time, and then shut off. Your washdown pump, on the other hand, may have to run for a long period of

time while you sluice your decks. If not rated for continuous duty, the pump motor could overheat.

The higher the pump's pressure rating, the more forceful the stream it produces and the better job it can do cleaning your boat. Some pumps specifically designed for washdown systems are rated as high as 70 psi. The West Marine model #7865678 pump, for example, is rated at 3.4 gpm at 70 psi and is equipped with five diaphragm chambers and five valves, resulting in less pulsation in the output supply. It also has a built-in water strainer.

Many manufacturers supply washdown pumps as part of a kit that also includes hose fittings, a spiral hose, and a hose nozzle. Make sure the kit has the components you are interested in, or else buy the components separately.

Other things a washdown system will need are a source of water, power for the pump motor,

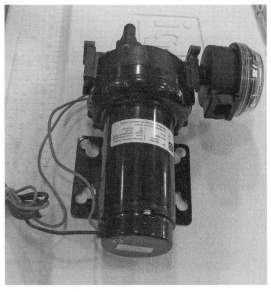

West Marine's model #7865678 washdown pump.

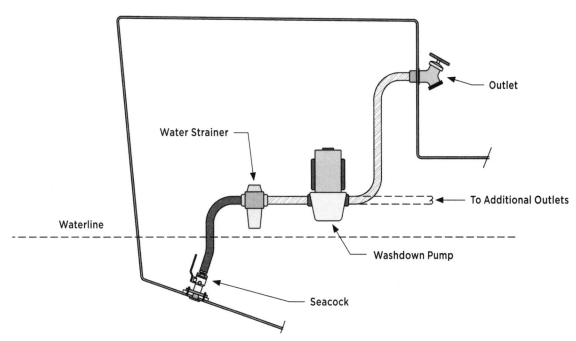

The typical components of a washdown system.

and a means of delivering the water to the right place.

While diaphragm pumps are pretty good about handling small amounts of debris, a water strainer is needed to keep the big chunks out. If your pump isn't fitted with a strainer, you'll need to install one. It should be rigidly mounted to a bulkhead or stringer so it doesn't move around and chafe the hoses. If you mount it above the waterline, you will be able to clean it out without having to close the seacock to which it is connected.

The seacock should be part of a dedicated through-hull fitting below the waterline. (See Chapter 6 for how to install through-hulls and seacocks. If your hull is of cored construction, make sure you clean out the core around the perimeter of the hole and replace it with epoxy/filler.) You may be tempted to tee into another water inlet line, say the water supply for flushing the head or an engine coolant intake line. This usually isn't a good idea, however, as the through-hull flow rate might not be sufficient to supply both systems.

As suggested earlier in this chapter, the pump should be mounted to a bulkhead or other vertical surface above the waterline, and its plumbed end should face down to prevent any water leaks from running down into the motor. Fasten it securely with stainless steel machine screws and nylock nuts, which are locking nuts with a nylon insert to keep them from loosening.

Next comes the wiring. See Chapter 7 for detailed advice, but briefly, the pump needs a source of 12-volt DC power. Wiring must be properly sized for the amperage being drawn and for the distance between the pump and its power source. Refer to wire sizing charts available online and in catalogs like West Marine's. A fuse or circuit breaker must be installed in the power supply line. A circuit breaker provides a convenient means of turning the system off, whereas if you use a fuse instead, you'll have to place an on/off switch in the circuit. To connect the power supply to the pump motor wires, use butt connectors with adhesive-lined heat-shrink tubing for a strong watertight connection. For physical protection, I like to run the wires in a conduit or at least inside spiral wrap, and fasten the wires to something solid on the boat's structure every 18 inches or so with wire clamps.

The pump outlet can be plumbed to as many locations as you want, but remember that the pump will be able to supply adequate pressure to only one outlet at a time. One method is simply to connect a hose from the pump outlet directly to the garden hose and nozzle you will use. Although this works, it does limit the usefulness of the system. A better approach is to plumb two or more different locations—for example, one in the stern for cleaning up fish goo and another in the bow for washing down the anchor rode. Clear reinforced vinyl tubing is fine for this application. You can identify the reinforced version by the white spiraled threads embedded in the vinyl.

Hose fittings may be either the quick-release type or those with standard garden hose threads. The latter can be found with or without shutoff valves, and they look remarkably like the ones on the side of your house. Spigots that protrude from the cockpit wall can be real ankle-biters, so I prefer recessed units. If you choose a garden faucet style of fitting, make sure to locate it where it won't endanger the crew's ankles. Support the supply lines every 18 inches to avoid chafing.

Quick-release fittings for washdown systems can be disconnected while the system is under

A recessed washdown pump spigot.

pressure. These can accept standard garden hose or the spiral coiled washdown hose. I avoid the spiral hose despite—or maybe because of—how well it retracts. Once you let go of this type of hose, it snaps back to where you got it. Call me old-fashioned, but I prefer to drag a regular garden hose around the deck.

The other good thing about a garden hose is that many styles of nozzles are available for it. Stay away from high-volume nozzles if you have a lower-rated pump. Water tends to just dribble out of such nozzles when they're not supplied with sufficient flow or pressure. A nozzle designed for 5 gpm, for example, may not work well with a pump delivering 2.8 gpm.

REPLACING COCKPIT SOLES AND DECKS

This project is confined to plywood decks, which are common on smaller boats. Replacing or repairing a fiberglass deck is an order of magnitude more difficult and isn't covered here.

Tearing up and replacing a plywood sole or deck is a larger task than any we've looked at so far, but it's a viable project for the determined do-it-yourselfer who needs to save both a boat and his or her own money. Sometimes there are no other options if you wish to keep the boat alive. You might have to remove a deck to get at a leaking fuel tank or to replace rotten stringers or other under-deck supports, for example.

Quite often, decks and soles are made from ¾-inch-thick marine plywood laid down on top of the fore-and-aft stringers and side-to-side floors. The plywood panels are screwed and glued to the stringers and may also be bonded to the hull sides with strips of fiberglass mat and resin.

First, clear the decks, taking out seats, tables, and all other hardware that's attached to the plywood. Then remove the screws holding the plywood to the structure beneath. Cut the deck-to-hull tabbing with an abrasive cutoff disc in a right-angle grinder, then attack the deck with pry bars. In some cases it is easier to cut the deck into manageable sections using a portable circular saw set to exactly the thickness of the plywood deck. Don't go any deeper, or you may damage things beneath. In some cases, you might be able to remove the old deck in one or more large sections and use the pieces as patterns for the new deck. Chances are, though, it will come out in small pieces.

After removing the old deck, inspect the underlying structure. Are the stringer and deck supports sound or do they need to be replaced? Is the fuel tank leaking and in need of replacement? (If so, see Replacing a Fuel Tank later in this chapter.) Quite often, hoses and electrical wiring are routed under the deck. Check all these items and, if in doubt, replace them. Nothing could be more

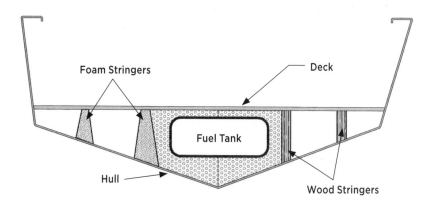

A hypothetical powerboat cross section showing foam-cored stringers to port and plywood stringers to starboard. Both types should be encased and bonded to the hull with fiberglass. Stringers strengthen the hull and support the deck, which is often plywood in small powerboats. The fuel tank is often supported and immobilized by poured-in-place foam.

frustrating than finishing the deck and realizing you need to tear it back out to fix something else.

With the old deck out of the way and any other repairs completed, it's time to consider what to use for the new deck. Marine plywood is a common choice; hopefully it's what the boatbuilder used in the first place (as opposed to an inferior grade). There are several varieties available.

Douglas fir marine plywood is widely available, usually by special order through a "real" lumberyard or boatyard. It is heavier than other marine plywood and has a tendency to check when exposed to the weather. For replacement decks, however, it is a viable option.

Other marine plywoods are made from a variety of tropical hardwoods, including okoume, sapele, and khaya mahogany. These are a little harder to find and will probably have to be special-ordered, unless you go through a specialty supplier. Some of these plywoods, although made with waterproof glue, are not very rot resistant. Okoume, in particular, is susceptible to rot. If you use any of these, they must be properly sealed against moisture intrusion.

Some DIYers lean toward using pressure-treated plywood for a replacement deck. After all, it's supposed to be rot-proof, right? Actually, the preservative is formulated to combat insect damage, not rot. Pressure-treated ply is also, generally speaking, lousy plywood, filled with voids and other defects. It is also usually wet and warped from laying outside in the lumberyard. To top it off, the preservatives are incompatible with many sealants and epoxies. Leave it at the lumberyard.

I use MDO (medium-density overlay) plywood. This type of plywood was designed for outdoor sign use and for concrete forms. Use the sign-grade material, not the concrete-form stuff.

The plywood is of good quality, void-free, and glued with exterior glue. On top of that, it has a phenolic coating bonded to each side. This coating is impressively smooth and hard and readily accepts paint and epoxy or other glues without any surface preparation. The best part is that MDO plywood is cheaper than marine plywood and can be ordered through most good lumberyards (but not the big-box stores).

The plywood you choose will usually come in 4 x 8 sheets. Some suppliers will go as big as 4 x 10 or 4 x 12, but these must usually be special-ordered and cost much more than standard 4 x 8 panels. Larger panels are also extremely difficult to handle.

Now is the time to take stock of the underlying deck support arrangements. The usual course is to subdivide the deck into manageable panels that can easily be handled. I make a scale drawing of the stringer and support structure in order to plan where the joints between panels should fall. The idea is to have the edges of any panel supported by an underlying stringer, floor, or other support.

If the old deck isn't in good enough shape to act as a template, you'll have to develop a new template. Large appliance boxes can furnish big pieces of cardboard for a template. Be careful around the edges of the deck where it meets the hull. The template will define the lower edge of the deck. If the hull has any flare, the upper edge will bevel slightly outward. Don't get too fussy—a ⅛-inch gap next to the hull is perfectly acceptable and will be hidden by tabbing before you're done. Try to get the joints between deck panels tight, though, and take careful note of the locations of hatches, deck plates, and other hardware that penetrates the deck. Now is a good time to plan for extra storage or enhanced access to under-

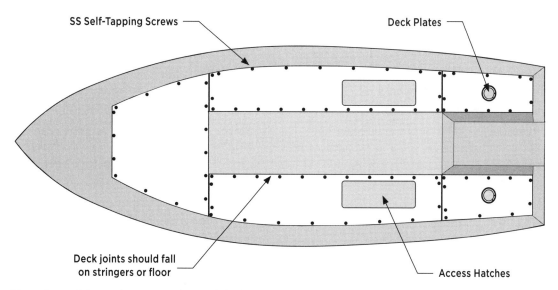

The edges of the replacement plywood deck panels should land on stringers or floors for proper support.

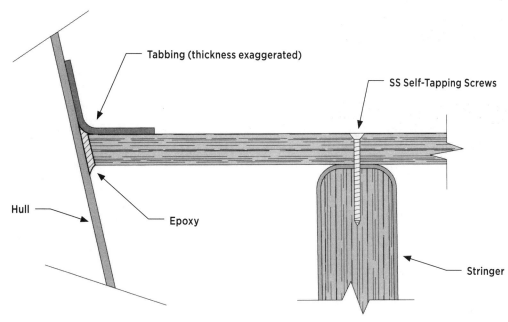

The deck edges are bonded to the hull with tabbing and screwed or glued to the stringers. To seal screw holes from moisture ingress, dip the screws in a polysulfide adhesive/sealant or apply a coat of unthickened epoxy to the entire top surface of the plywood. Better yet, cover with fiberglass cloth and epoxy resin.

deck mechanicals by siting additional hatches or access plates. A powerful circular saw with a good plywood blade is the right tool for making the major cuts. A saber saw may come in handy for some of the details.

Where the outer edges of the panels meet the side of the hull, they may be bonded or "tabbed" in place with fiberglass mat and resin. Clean off this area of the hull with detergent and water, then wipe it down with a dewaxer to remove any old wax, oil, or grease. Finally, wire-brush the surface with a wire wheel in a drill to rough it up for a good bond.

Before installation, the panel edges and bottom surfaces must be sealed against moisture. I apply two or three coats of unfilled epoxy, rolled on thin. This is especially critical along the edges, where end grain is exposed. After the epoxy has cured, apply a bead of adhesive/sealant such as 3M 5200 or filled epoxy (see the sidebar Using Epoxy earlier in this chapter) to the tops of the stringers and deck supports. Fit the panels in place. You can screw them down with self-tapping stainless steel screws run down through the panels and into the stringers and floors. There should be no unsupported panel edges.

Bond the deck to the hull along the edges using epoxy resin and Stitchmat fiberglass cloth. A single layer completely saturated with epoxy should be enough. Cover the top surface of the new deck with unfilled resin. Better yet, apply a layer of fiberglass cloth and resin. Install hatches and deck plates as described earlier in this chapter.

The plywood's epoxy coating provides a good base for the final finish. This could be several coats of a one-part marine polyurethane paint such as Pettit Easypoxy or Interlux Brightside. Apply an antiskid additive, as described in Chapter 4, to give it a safe, nonskid finish. Interlux also makes a nonskid paint called InterDeck with the additives already in the mix, though the available colors are somewhat limited. Interlux Perfection Two-Part Polyurethane paint is tougher than the one-part paints and will also require the nonskid additive. Another brush-on solution is rubberized paint, which has excellent nonskid properties and is available from several manufacturers.

I do not like to use marine carpeting on decks. It retains water and dirt and soon smells. A better but pricier choice is rubber sheet goods with a tread pattern molded in, available from SeaDek and Treadmaster. These materials are durable, have superior nonskid properties, and can be cut to shape with scissors and then glued or epoxied to the deck surface.

Some boats have fine decks made of alternating strips of teak and holly. Woodworking at this level is beyond the scope of this book, but you can get the same look with a lot less work (and at a lower price) by using plywood with tropical hardwood veneers that mimic teak and holly. These

This piece of teak-and-holly plywood has been cut to shape and is in the process of being finished, prior to being installed.

plywood panels are available in thicknesses from ¼ inch to over ¾ inch. I have used the ¼-inch-thick sheets, cut to size and epoxied to an MDO plywood subdeck.

Although this is a lot easier than building a deck with real teak and holly lumber, it can still be a lot of work. The procedures for laying out the panels are similar to those described, however—in other words, not terribly difficult. Take it a step at a time and you'll get through it. Just make sure the boat is worth it before embarking on a project like this. If the boat is old enough to need a new deck, you may not get that money back when you sell.

REPAIRING STRINGERS

In Chapter 1 we talked about stringers being laminated to the hull while the hull was still in the mold. In many older boats, these stringers were made of two or three layers of (hopefully!) marine plywood glued together and cut to fit the curve of the hull. Some boats used solid wood, cut to the hull curve from dimensional lumber (2 x 6 or larger stock).

Newer boats may use prefabricated stringers made from foam and covered with a loosely bonded layer of fiberglass mat. These stringers are also tailored to fit the curve of the hull.

The stringers are then firmly bonded to the hull by covering them with multiple layers of fiberglass roving, mat, or cloth and resin. The fiberglass material is lapped over the hull each side of the stringer by 6 inches or so. These stringers stiffen the hull, and they often become mounting structures for the engines and cockpit floor.

Some boats have a molded grid bonded to the hull rather than stringers. These seldom fail but aren't covered here.

As long as a wooden stringer is well sealed from bilge water, things are fine. Problems occur when hardware is fastened to the stringer without being properly sealed. Water can leak into the wood around engine mounting bolts, for example, or through fasteners used to hold down the deck. This eventually causes wood stringers to rot, delaminate, or both, compromising the engine mounting or the deck structure. While not exactly a fun task, rotted stringers can be repaired. This can be a big job, so be sure the boat is one you are happy with and are willing to spend time and money to save.

Stringer rot is largely confined to wooden stringers. Foam stringer cores aren't really structural. Rather, they are there to provide a convenient form over which to lay up the fiberglass, which then provides the structural strength of the stringer. Thus, wet foam stringers usually aren't a structural problem and can usually be repaired easily.

To repair stringers, you first need to expose them by removing the deck, as described in the previous project Replacing Cockpit Soles and Decks, and in some cases additional internal structures. Take pictures as you disassemble things—it will make reassembly easier. Once the stringer is exposed, you can determine the extent of the water saturation or rot by drilling a hole through the fiberglass on the side of the stringer with a 1-inch holesaw and examining the resulting sawdust and center of the core. Any wet or rotted wood will be evident.

There are no magic bullets for drying out a saturated wood core, and no magic liquids you can inject into a rotted core to stiffen the wood.

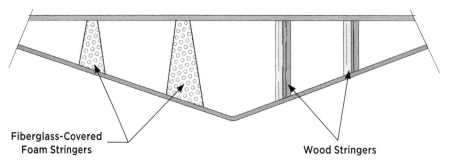

Fiberglass-Covered Foam Stringers

Wood Stringers

Another look at the wood- or foam-cored stringers that are common in production fiberglass boats. The foam is simply a form over which fiberglass is laminated, and the fiberglass provides the stringers' strength. Regardless of materials, stringers are bonded to the hull with fiberglass.

Once it's wet, nothing will bond to it. Besides, it probably took years to saturate the core and would likewise take years to dry out without major surgery.

Given that a foam core contributes little if any strength to a stringer, one method of repairing a delaminated foam stringer is simply to laminate further reinforcing fiberglass over the top. The first step is to clean the surfaces with detergent and water to remove any traces of grease or oil. The surfaces must then be cleaned with a fiberglass dewaxer. As we saw in Chapter 1, wax is added to the final layer of resin to get it to cure tack-free. Failure to remove all the wax will result in a weak bond to the existing fiberglass, just adding another possible failure point. Dewax before you do any further cleaning.

A final step is to wire-brush the surface using a wire wheel in a drill. This will get any loose material off the surface and rough it up for a better bond. While the original boat was probably built using polyester resin, I recommend epoxy to repair the stringer. Epoxy forms a much stronger secondary (nonchemical) bond with the existing structure than polyester resin would. Epoxy is more expensive, but this is a job you don't want to have to repeat.

My choice for a reinforcing material is 24-ounce Double Bias Stitchmat, which, unlike standard fiberglass mat, is compatible with epoxy resin. This material has two layers of unidirectional fibers stitched to a chopped strand mat (CSM). The strands in each layer are oriented at 45 degrees to the material's long axis and at 90 degrees to each other. This allows Stitchmat to drape over a complex surface like a stringer and conform to its shape. It comes in 12-, 38-, and 50-inch widths. Depending on the width needed, a wider piece can be cut into two narrower pieces.

Cut lengths of Stitchmat wide enough to drape over the stringer and extend over the hull 6 inches on either side. Precut all the material you'll need, as epoxy-covered hands do not make for easy scissor work. Mix some epoxy with a small amount of colloidal silica filler, as described in the sidebar Using Epoxy earlier in this chapter. The colloidal silica will keep the epoxy from sagging.

Give the top of the stringer and the hull on either side a coat of the thickened epoxy. Lay the

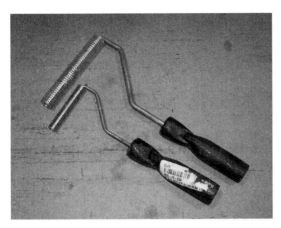

Fiberglass laminate rollers can be plastic or metal. Either construction will last through many projects if you keep it clean.

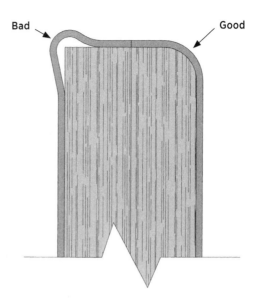

Bad   Good

Stringer corners need a generous radius (at right) to allow fiberglass to conform to the curve. Sharp corners will cause the fabric to pull away from the surfaces and leave voids.

Stitchmat across the top of the stringer and work it down the sides and across the hull. Brush on additional epoxy and roll out the Stitchmat with a grooved roller designed for fiberglass laminating. The roller compacts the rovings, fills the pores with epoxy, and works out any air bubbles.

The fiberglass will turn from an opaque white to a semitransparent color when properly saturated. I like to cover the entire length of a stringer repair with one continuous length of Stitchmat. You can add additional layers if you are concerned about strength.

The downside of this repair is that the stringer ends up being slightly wider and taller than the original. This may complicate the engine mounts, if they are bolted to the stringers. It may also affect the height of the deck or cabin sole and any furniture or cabinetry you may have had to remove prior to the repair.

Another repair method is simply to rip out the existing wood stringers and fiberglass covering. This is best done with a cutoff wheel in an angle grinder. Use the old stringer as a pattern for the new one. Clean the surfaces and epoxy the new stringers in place. Laminate Stitchmat over the stringer to the same thickness of the old stringer covering. The fiberglass will conform much more easily to the top corners of the stringers if you round them.

You can also rip out the old stringers and replace them with preformed urethane foam stringers. These come in various shapes and sizes and have a fiberglass mat loosely bonded to the surface. This mat extends beyond the edges of the foam and is used to bond the stringer to the hull. The foam stringers are cut to length and epoxied in place. Epoxy is applied to the mat covering, and then additional reinforcing is added to form the structural part of the stringer. As I mentioned before, the foam contributes little strength to the equation, serving merely as a form over which the fiberglass can be molded. The downside of this solution is that the new stringers may not even be close to the size or location of the old stringers. This will complicate remounting the engine, deck, and cabin structures.

REPLACING A FUEL TANK

Most permanently mounted fuel tanks don't get any respect. In most cases they are placed below a leaky deck and encased in water-retaining foam. On top of that, they're fed bad gas with water in it and then left to sit all winter. It's no wonder they give up, corrode, and develop pinhole leaks. At least you hope it's a pinhole leak.

In all seriousness, that describes some of the conditions in which many of our fuel tanks live. The main choices for fuel tank material are fiberglass, plastic, or aluminum. Plastic tanks are the best of the lot. Properly supported, a rotomolded polyethylene tank will last a long time.

Fiberglass tanks, on the other hand, are doomed to a short and ugly life in the time of ethanol-laced gasoline. The ethanol in gas will dissolve most fiberglass, and it will send that dissolved gunk down the fuel line into your fuel injectors or carburetor.

Aluminum tanks are a little better but can develop pinhole leaks from internal or external corrosion or can develop cracks if not properly supported. Many permanently installed tanks are, in fact, aluminum.

Unfortunately, most tank leaks are discovered by traces of fuel in the bilge water. It will usually start out as a light sheen on the water. Pay atten-

tion, because this is extremely dangerous, and it's bad for the environment if any gets pumped overboard. It's also illegal, and the Coast Guard will levy a hefty fine against you if you're caught (and the sheen is a dead giveaway).

Before assuming the leak is from the tank, make sure there are no leaks in the fuel lines. Nothing could be more frustrating (not to say expensive) than to replace a tank only to find that the problem was a carburetor leak or a loose fuel fill hose.

Some boats have saddle or wing tanks mounted on both sides. These are usually easy to find and are removable for replacement. They may be behind some sort of paneling, but that isn't normally a big deal. Take the tanks out, find replacements that match the old ones as closely as possible, and reinstall them.

While you're at it, replace all the hoses associated with the tank: the fill hose, the vent hose, and the fuel line. Chances are if the tank is old enough to leak, it's time to replace the hoses. Besides, the stress on old fuel lines during their removal is often enough to crack or damage hoses. Replacing them is cheap insurance.

Under-deck tank installations are more work. The deck covering the tank must be removed. If you don't want to remove and replace the entire deck, you'll need to determine the dimensions of the tank and its location under the deck. Good luck. Unless you can find somebody with a similar boat who has done the job or get the information from the boatbuilder, it's exploratory surgery time.

In most cases, the tank is located between the main stringers and near the fore-and-aft center of the boat. This is to keep the boat in trim as the fuel is used up. The tank will have been placed in a compartment formed by the two stringers on

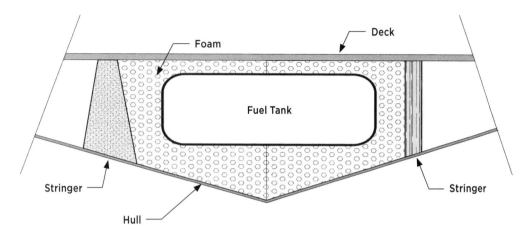

A small powerboat's fuel tank will often be found near amidships beneath the plywood deck. It is likely to be foamed in place between plywood or foam-cored stringers, and will be further secured by floors running from side to side at its forward and after ends.

the sides and floors forward and aft. It probably had foam poured around and under it to keep it firmly in place.

The foam is soft enough to be dug out with hand tools like screwdrivers or putty knives. Once the tank is exposed, you can measure it and search for a replacement. If you are extremely lucky, you will be able to find an aftermarket tank that is an exact match from a company like Moeller or Todd. Tempo was formerly a major supplier but has gone out of business. These tanks will be neutral, dark gray, or black rotomolded polyethylene. Note that red tanks are for above-deck use, not for permanent installation belowdecks. The under-deck tanks come with fuel level sending units installed. Don't worry about compatibility: they work with all electric fuel gauges.

If you can't find an exact replacement tank, find one that's close and, before you buy it, replicate it in a simple cardboard mock-up. Place this in the space occupied by the old tank to confirm the fit and to ensure that the tank fill, vent, and

This rotomolded polyethylene fuel tank is similar to ones typically foamed in place below many decks. (Courtesy Moeller Products Company, Inc.)

drain fitting locations work with the hose locations in your boat.

If your tank is aluminum, you will have far fewer choices. If the manufacturer of your boat is still in business, you might be able to purchase a direct replacement tank from them. Don't look for it to be cheap, however. If your boatbuilder is out of business, there is a slim chance that a marine consignment store may have purchased their old inventory. It's worth checking, perhaps online.

Failing that, it's back to the Internet or your favorite boating magazine to find a custom fuel tank builder. There are many of them, and shipping can be expensive, so try to find one near you. Look for a tank maker that builds to ABYC (American Boat & Yacht Council) standards and make sure they pressure-test it. Then go to the bank and take out a loan.

You'll have to take detailed, accurate measurements, and digital photos may help. You can't ship the old tank to the fabricator to use as a template; UPS and other couriers won't accept it for shipping. If the shape is complex, you might consider building a replica out of artist's foam board, tape, and glue, and shipping that to the tank maker.

If your fuel is diesel, check your old tank. Diesel engines sometimes have a fuel return line back to the tank. If so, make sure the tank you get has a fitting for that return line.

While you're waiting for the new tank to arrive, clean out the area where the old tank resided. Clear out all traces of the foam to ready the space for the tank installation. It's a good time to check the stringers and floors for any structural issues such as rotted or waterlogged wood.

If the old tank was foamed in place in a center compartment, there should have been a pipe or conduit installed beneath it to allow easy movement of bilge water between the compartments forward and aft of the tank. If the pipe or conduit needs to be replaced, PVC pipe works well. You can cut a piece of PVC pipe in half and glue it in place, concave side down. Be careful to seal all the edges and ends so the new foam won't sneak in and seal off the channel, and so that bilge water won't come in contact with the foam.

Be careful to maintain the original mounting height of the fuel tank. Clearance is often limited under the deck area, and you will need that clearance for running the fuel hoses. Tanks are often secured to the stringers or placed on temporary wood supports. This is just to properly locate the tank, not to fully support it and its load of fuel.

The foam around the tank is used to support the tank and keep it firmly in place. Foam with a 4-pound density is recommended for use around fuel tanks. The foam comes as two separate liq-

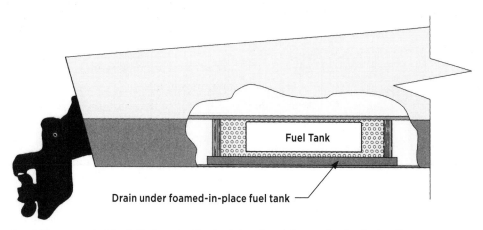

Drain under foamed-in-place fuel tank

Fuel Tank

There should be a conduit installed under the tank to allow bilge water to drain aft.

uids, Part A and Part B. Mixing the two together starts a chemical reaction that produces the foam. This reaction happens quickly! You have a limited time to mix the foam and pour it into place. Be sure to follow the foam supplier's recommendation for the proper temperature range for application. Colder temperatures mean slower foaming and longer hardening times.

Mix the foam in small batches using a wire mixer in a drill to ensure that both components are thoroughly mixed. Use disposable containers. I usually measure out several sets of small containers so I can mix batches without having to go back and pour out more chemicals.

Start by pouring the liquid foam under the tank. The idea is to fill all the voids under the tank. Pour a batch and then wait fifteen to twenty minutes for the foam to fully expand and harden. If you pour too much foam at once, it could push the tank out of position or even cave the tank in

or damage the boat's structure. Once the area under the tank is filled and the foam has hardened, you can pour along the sides and ends of the tank. Try to replicate the same distribution and amount of foam as it was installed around the original tank.

Be careful to keep access to the fuel sender and the tank inlet and outlets clear of foam. If the foam rises above the level of the stringers or deck mounts, let it harden and then trim it level with a handsaw, being careful to avoid cutting your new tank.

Once the foam has finished hardening, you can install the new fuel lines. Do not use just any hose you find at a building supply store. Fuel line hoses must be rated for use with fuel and must be installed with two hose clamps at every connection. Replace the deck and finish it off as described in Replacing Cockpit Soles and Decks earlier in this chapter, and you are good to go.

CHAPTER 3

Cabin and Galley

The cabins on our small boats range from non-existent through cuddy cabins with basic amenities to accommodations that include a combined galley/saloon and a minimalist but separate stateroom or two. Unlike our marina neighbor's 50-foot power cruiser with its onyx-countertop galley that puts our home kitchens to shame, our smaller boats can inevitably benefit from easy-to-implement improvements and additions to the galley and other accommodations.

BUILDING A GALLEY BOX

Many small boats lack adequate storage for the dozens of items a galley requires. Another common problem is the lack of a proper place to use a portable stove, whether it is a single-burner backpacking stove or a big, two-burner propane unit.

After years of carrying my galley gear in a couple of plastic milk crates, I decided to design a galley box to organize it. My objectives were to create a simple way to store and carry spices and all nonfood galley items and to provide a stable platform for a two-burner Coleman propane stove. I wanted the box to be easy to move around so that I could carry the whole galley into the cockpit when I wanted and just as easily pack it up and return it below when I finished a meal.

My galley box design features separate compartments for plates, bowls, and mugs. You can size these compartments for disposable plates, bowls, and cups, but I like unbreakable dinnerware such as Melmac or Corel, which makes mealtime a lot less like camping. Slotted compartment fronts allow access to the dishes while restraining them in place. Slide-out plastic trays hold the silverware and most galley tools. The frying pan fits in the top of the bowl storage area under the stove. A block in the top of the box holds knives, while two other compartments hold the spice kit and a small coffeepot nestled in the small pot. The spice kit is the only "food" carried in the galley box; all perishables are stowed separately, and "iron rations" (canned goods) are likewise stored in other locations. When leaving the boat, I have only to take off the cooler and perishables. The rest of the galley, including the galley box, stays on board 99 percent of the time.

I left the top of my box open to receive the stove. I use a couple of bungee cords to secure it in place and keep it from bouncing out in rough weather or during transport.

Another feature I added is a front panel that folds down to form a work surface. Small chains

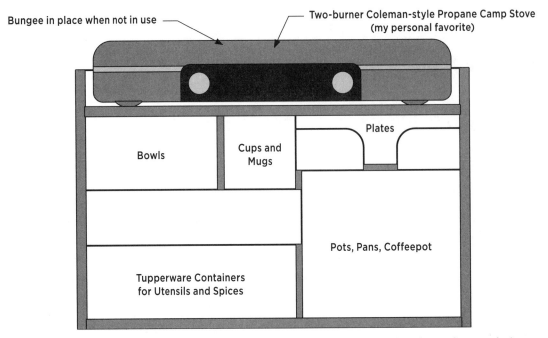

Front view of my galley box. The stove fits in the top recess and is bungeed in place when not being used. Design the internal compartments to meet your needs.

hold the panel level when it's open, so it doesn't need any other supports. Handles fastened to the box make moving it around easy.

The galley box comes in handy for car-camping, too. I can remove it from the boat, put it in the car, and know that I have *nearly* everything I need, already organized. I just need to remember to take a propane canister along. On the boat, propane canisters are stored in a holster attached to the stern rail. (See the next project in this chapter, Propane Cylinder Holsters.)

I'm a great proponent of making mock-ups of major projects before cutting expensive material or discovering that your wonderful improvement doesn't fit the available space. A mock-up will allow you to put the gear in place and then place the galley box where it's intended to live. It sounds like a bit of work, but mock-ups are well worth the

trouble for discovering any potential faults or problems in a design like this.

My favorite material for a mock-up of this size and complexity is artist's foam board. This material consists of a layer of stiff foam with card stock laminated on both sides. The product is easy to cut yet stiff enough to stand a certain amount of use to determine the utility of a design. It is available in 3/16- and 3/8-inch thicknesses. For this project, the 3/8-inch material works well, as it is close to the thickness of the materials you will use for the box.

The first steps in designing a galley box are to decide what will go into the box and where the box will go. It is good to have some prior experience cooking on your boat, as I did, so that you know what gear the box should accommodate. Here is my list to get you started:

Galley Gear

Stove (fuel is carried outside the cabin)

Dishware: plates, mugs, soup bowls

Cookware: Frying pan, pot, teakettle/coffeepot

Silverware

Galley tools: stove lighters, can opener, church key, spatula, large spoons, cooking knives

Spice kit

Toothpicks

Hot pads

The first design iterations can take place on paper. Sketch out alternative ways of packaging all this equipment in the space available. If necessary, you might have to adjust the equipment to make it fit the available space. Consider smaller plates or cookware and fewer tools if necessary.

Once you have a plan that you think will work, make a mock-up from the foam board. An X-Acto knife with a #11 blade and a metal straightedge make cutting the board easy. The parts can be taped together with regular tan masking tape (it

sticks better than the blue masking tape) or glued with white glue.

The box can be made from plywood or Star-Board polymer "lumber." In either material, ⅜-inch thickness for the case and ¼-inch thickness for the partitions would provide a good strength while keeping weight down. I recommend against using standard exterior plywood, as it's too rough and too subject to rot. Instead, use okoume, A/A fir, or MDO plywood, all of which can be found online or at specialty lumberyards. StarBoard in ⅜- and ¼-inch thicknesses is hard to find at retail stores, but it is available.

If you're working with plywood, the sides, back, and bottom of the box should be glued and either screwed or nailed together. (As nothing sticks to StarBoard, the entire box will have to be screwed together with stainless steel self-tapping screws.) All exposed surfaces should then be well sealed to protect against water damage. For additional protection, round over the bottom edges of the box and apply a layer of 3-inch-wide fiberglass tape with epoxy. Fasten a pair of handles on the ends.

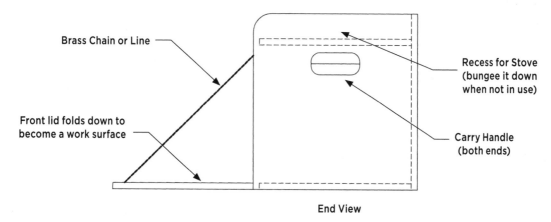

The front panel of my galley box is hinged, and I attached brass chains to hold the front horizontal when open, making a convenient work surface.

Whether you build the box from plywood or StarBoard, I recommend making the front panel from StarBoard. Hinged down and held in place by chains, it can be used as a work surface or a cutting board.

No two galley boxes will be the same, but that's a good thing. You can customize the box for exactly the equipment and the space you have on board.

PROPANE CYLINDER HOLSTERS

Portable propane stoves are a good option for cooking aboard many small boats. They're compact, inexpensive, easy to use, and generally quite safe. The fuel cylinders are also reliable, but they have been known to leak on occasion. Cylinders must not, therefore, be stored inside the boat. Any leaking propane would migrate into the bilges, where a single spark could make it go boom.

You need a way to protect and contain propane cylinders in the cockpit or on deck. Special-purpose fabric bags are available that snap over a pulpit or railing, allowing the fumes to vent overboard. Another approach, which provides even better protection, is a holster made from common 4-inch PVC pipe and pipe end caps. The bottom cap is glued on and a vent hole drilled in it. The top cap slips on and off and is retained by a short lanyard. It is fastened to a stanchion or pulpit so the fumes will also drain overboard.

If you store two cylinders in the holster, make sure the bottom one is fitted with the little plastic cap that came with it, to protect the threads on the end fitting.

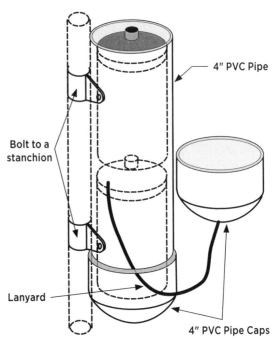

Holds two 1-pound cylinders

You can fabricate a convenient storage device for propane cylinders from standard PVC plumbing components.

A PVC propane canister holster mounted to a stern pulpit stanchion, with a propane canister next to it.

IMPROVING AN ICEBOX

Many older boats have installed iceboxes with too little insulation. It isn't uncommon to see a scant 2 inches of insulating foam on the box sides, and lids with even less insulation or none at all. You can significantly improve the performance of your icebox by adding insulation.

Adding insulation to the inside of a box reduces its storage volume and requires that the surface of the foam be covered with epoxy and fiberglass and finished off so that it is durable and can be kept clean. It is far preferable to add insulation to the outside of the box. This can be done with foamed-in-place material from a spray can or with rigid sheets of blue or pink construction foam, available at building centers. It may be possible to leave the box in place while fitting the foam around it, but in most cases you will want to remove the icebox from the boat.

Sections of rigid foam can be held in place with lots of duct tape or glued in place with vari-ous adhesives. Test the adhesive on a scrap of foam to make sure the materials are compatible. You can also mold a fiberglass shell around the insulation, using procedures identical to those described in Molding a Storage Bin later in this chapter. Make sure you have clearance before proceeding. Adding insulation to the lid, or rebuilding it with fiberglass and rigid foam, will also improve the efficiency of the box and extend the life of the ice.

As ice melts, the water should be drained away for best cooling efficiency. If your box doesn't have a drain, it's an easy matter to install one, as shown in the accompanying illustration. Most iceboxes drain into the bilge, so that anything spilled in the icebox ends up there, adding to that unmistakable bilge smell. The drain hose also lets the cooler, heavier air drain out of the box—just what you don't want. One solution to this problem is to put a water trap in the drain line and direct the water to a collection box that can then be drained and cleaned.

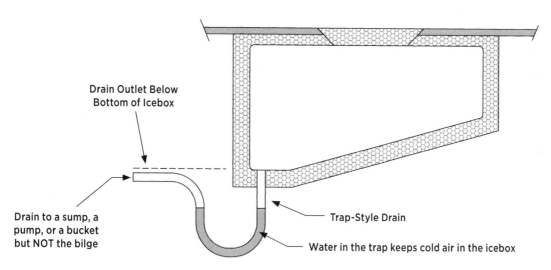

Drain Outlet Below Bottom of Icebox

Drain to a sump, a pump, or a bucket but NOT the bilge

Trap-Style Drain

Water in the trap keeps cold air in the icebox

A trap-type icebox drain allows water to be drained from the icebox without allowing cold air to escape.

KEEPING WATER POTABLE

The best way to keep drinking water fresh in a storage tank during the boating season is to use it. Leaving it sitting unused will almost surely result in bad tasting water. Once that happens, you have to empty the tank as much as possible. That can take some work if you have only a manual pump.

The next step is to "shock" the entire water system, meaning the tanks, lines, and pumps. You do this by adding bleach and water at the rate of 8 ounces of bleach to every 10 gallons of water. This concentration of bleach is for sanitizing, not drinking! Pump this solution from the tank through the entire system. Leave the solution in the system for at least eight hours but no longer than twenty-four hours.

At the end of this time, flush the system with fresh water. Do this to each outlet until all the bleach taste and smell go away. Most people think the water tank is the usual source of the bad tasting water, but the rest of the system, especially the water lines, can also be at fault. I once bought a boat in which all of the clear vinyl water lines were black on the inside from algae growth. The only solution was to replace all of them. I also removed the tank and had it steam cleaned.

A SIMPLE FOOD-PREP STATION

Galley counter space is always in short supply aboard a boat, and space for a cutting board usually doesn't exist. An easy solution to your food-prep needs is a combination wastebasket and cutting board.

Since we're assuming that storage space is in short supply, we'll use your boat's current garbage receptacle as the base. On top of that will go a cutting board as large as you wish, as long as it doesn't make the assembly top-heavy. You can use a store-bought wooden or plastic cutting

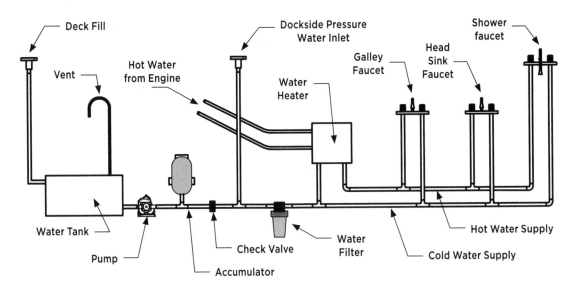

Schematic of a representative pressurized water system.

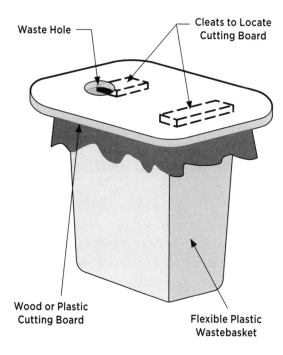

Waste Hole

Cleats to Locate
Cutting Board

Wood or Plastic
Cutting Board

Flexible Plastic
Wastebasket

This wastebasket cutting board makes a handy food-prep station in a small boat.

board or fabricate your own from StarBoard cut to any size.

Measure the inside dimensions of the garbage can's opening. Cut and screw cleats to the bottom of the cutting board so that they fit snugly into the rim of the garbage can, then use a large hole-saw to cut an opening inside the cleats.

To use the cutting board, double-bag the garbage can, then place the tray on top. You can relax in the cockpit with the setup between your knees while you prepare food on the cutting board and scrape the trimmings right through the hole into the can. Cleanup is easy. If you are underway, you can tie a loop of line through the hole in the cutting board and hang it over the side of the boat to clean it.

Finding Storage Space

One of the most often-felt needs on a boat is additional storage space and storage options. I call it "searching for spaces in all the right places." Most boatbuilders do a fairly good job of providing cabin storage, but there is always room for improvement. As discussed in Chapter 2, many boats with interior liners or pans have dead space that can be turned into valuable storage. Refer to that chapter for general tips on finding these spaces.

Areas that may hold exploitable space for cabin storage include:

- areas behind or beneath steps from the cockpit
- bilge areas below the cabin sole
- areas under berths, especially V-berths
- enclosed seats or settee bases
- dead space behind existing cabinets (between the cabinet back and the hull)

Once you locate a hidden area that can be converted into a usable storage space, plan the best method for accessing the space and what changes, if any, need to be made behind the opening. You may be able to utilize an off-the-shelf storage compartment, as discussed previously in Chapter 2.

A nice option for very small spaces is a round access plate with a fabric pocket built in. You'll likely find lots of places in the cabin where these will fit. But if off-the-shelf solutions don't work, you might have to fabricate some kind of shelf, container, or receptacle to make effective use of the available space.

A round access plate (see Chapter 2) with a built-in fabric pocket offers convenient storage in hard-to-fit spaces.

BUILDING A STORAGE COMPARTMENT FROM PLYWOOD AND FORMICA

On one of my boats I found an area behind the steps going down into the cabin that turned out to be a prime storage area. It was bounded on the sides and top by raw, unfinished fiberglass, and was open on the bottom down to the bilge. The space was deep, and any manufactured storage solution would have wasted a great deal of the available depth, so I decided to go the custom route.

First I cut an opening into the flat section of the vertical fiberglass panel, sizing it to match the biggest louvered door I could find at a marine store that fit the available space. I screwed two wooden cleats to the sides of the compartment to support a plywood bottom. I cut thinner plywood panels to fit the sides and ends, and applied several coats of epoxy to all the plywood pieces to seal them from moisture. For a smooth and easy-to-clean finish, I covered the exposed surfaces

with white Formica laminate left over from another project. I mounted the louvered door with stainless steel hinges and a toggle latch. The storage area is 12 inches wide, 10 inches high, and over 26 inches deep—an ideal space to store canned drinks.

MOLDING A STORAGE BIN

Rather than building a storage bin out of plywood, consider making it out of fiberglass. You can choose either polyester resin for economy or epoxy because it's less nasty to work with. For a mold, you can use a plastic container, such as a Tupperware or Rubbermaid bin, a wastebasket, or any other object of appropriate shape and size. If the shape and other dimensions of the container suit, you can cut down the height to adjust the depth.

Place the container upside down on a flat piece of plywood and fasten it in place with hot-melt glue. Thoroughly wax both the container and the plywood with good-quality carnauba wax, applying it with a cloth and buffing it to a shine. Don't use a silicone-based wax.

Fiberglass mat provides adequate strength for this project and builds thickness quickly. To help it conform to the mold at the corners without bulges or wrinkles, cut the mat into strips, and don't try to apply it in a single piece. Brush on a coat of resin, and begin building up layers of mat and resin. Work the resin into the mat until the mat turns translucent, indicating that it is saturated. Build up overlapping layers of mat until it is about ⅛ inch thick. Be sure to extend the fiberglass on each side of the container onto the plywood by a few inches to form a mounting lip. Roll out the layers with a fiberglass roller to eliminate air bubbles. You can also use biaxial Stitchmat to build up the thickness faster. Build up the appropriate thickness, say ⅛ to ³⁄₁₆ inch thick, and let it cure.

It is easier to trim the mounting flange while the molded box is still on the mold. Once the flange is trimmed to shape, you can pry your new bin off the plywood base and remove the plastic container from inside it. Remove the wax from the inside of the box with a dewaxing solvent such as Interlux 202 Fiberglass Solvent Wash, then sand, prime, and paint.

Affix blue tape onto several inches around the opening, then dry-fit the molding into the open-ing. Drill the pilot holes for mounting it, and trace around the flange. Remove the molded part and cut away the tape that would otherwise be under the flange. Place the fasteners in the molded bin's mounting holes, and tape over the top of the flange. Place a neoprene washer on each fastener, then apply a heavy bead of sealant to the flange. Screw it in place, snugging up the fasteners against the neoprene washers, then clean up the excess sealant, remove the tape, and you are done. You could epoxy the storage bin in place, but I find it easier to use screws and sealant. The epoxy solution requires that the bin be held in place until the epoxy cures, usually necessitating a screw or two anyway.

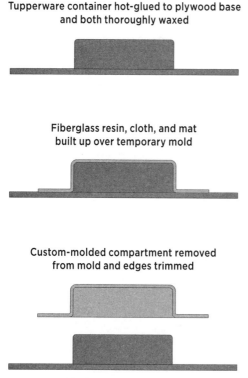

A custom-molded compartment liner is a fairly simple project.

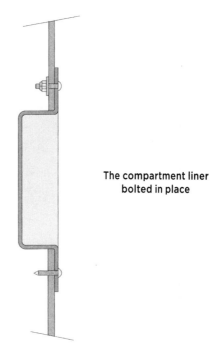

The compartment liner bolted in place

The compartment can be fastened in place with machine screws and nylock nuts or with stainless steel self-tapping screws. Use plenty of sealant under the flange to seal it in place.

V-BERTH STORAGE

Very useful storage options may lurk under the V-berth. This is a common area for boatbuilders to install storage, but on one of my boats a holding tank had been mounted under the V-berth in a secure compartment. That, it seemed, was that— until I had to replace the plywood panels that formed the V-berth bunk flat (that is, the top surface on which the cushions rest). Once I opened it up, I found that the central portion of this area was walled off by the vertical plywood partitions that formed the compartment for the holding tank. Forward and outboard of these partitions, however, were three triangular compartments that were empty and therefore available for storage. With the holding tank isolated behind the vertical partitions, these compartments were perfectly attractive and usable.

I made a new bunk flat using ½-inch MDO plywood, and into it I cut additional access openings over the unused areas. I added a "ring" underneath each opening to support the lid. Each ring had an outside diameter about two inches larger than the opening in the bunk flat and an inside diameter an inch smaller than the opening. This provided an inch-wide lip around the opening to support the access lid. A 1¼-inch hole in the lid provided a finger hole for lifting it. I coated the undersides of the bunk flat panels with epoxy

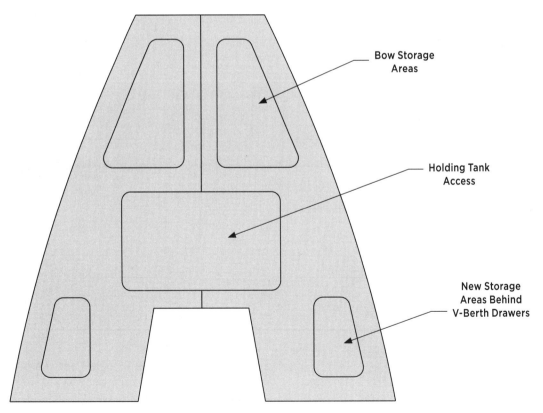

V-berth openings have been added for additional storage.

to seal them from water leaks, and I painted the bottom of the compartments with Interlux Bilgekote paint, a heavy-duty paint designed to hold up in bilges and storage areas.

I covered the top surfaces of the bunk-flat panels with a pale yellow Formica laminate to provide a waterproof and easy-to-clean surface. I use an old-fashioned contact cement for jobs like this, the stuff that really smells of solvent. I find that it is more durable and waterproof than the new, low-VOC type. For this job I thinned the contact cement with MEK, another unfriendly solvent, and applied three thin coats to each surface.

After the laminate dried almost tack-free, I put it in place and rolled it out with a laminate roller. I did the final trim with a laminate trimmer equipped with a trimmer bit and ball bearing follower. In eight years of use, none of the laminate has separated.

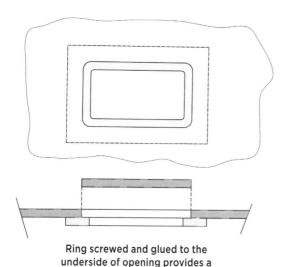

Ring screwed and glued to the underside of opening provides a lip to retain the access plate

The access-hatch configuration I used in the V-berth panels.

SMALL-PARTS STORAGE

Just above the V-berths in many forward cabins, small shelves are mounted along the inside surface of the hull or liner. I find these shelves to be pretty useless, so I turn them into useful storage space for small parts by removing the fiddle (the front lip of the shelf) and building a cabinet extending up from the shelf to the overhead. This cabinet can be large enough for a small cupboard at each end and a central storage area for more than a dozen parts trays.

The compartmentalized trays can be purchased at any hardware store in a variety of appropriate sizes. Build the cabinet from ½-inch MDO plywood and coat it with epoxy. If you wish, you can cover the MDO with Formica laminate, which I prefer to priming, sanding, painting, sanding, and painting some more. The laminate surface is very durable.

To support the parts trays, buy a few lengths of aluminum angles, cut them to length, and drill and screw them to the sides of the cabinet. Then

This project converted the useless shelf above a V-berth into a storage compartment. There is a cupboard on each end, a middle section for parts trays, and a fold-down work surface.

hinge a cabinet door at the bottom so that it swings down to the horizontal, where it is held with chains. The open door provides a useful surface for sorting parts and finding just the right fastener you're looking for, and when closed, the door keeps the parts trays from sliding out. Make sure there's a good, reliable latch to hold it closed when the boat is bouncing around.

REPLACING CUSHION FOAM

A decent set of berth cushions makes life aboard a fiberglass boat much more comfortable. Old cushions diminish in comfort as the foam compresses or crumbles with time, the speed with which this happens depending on the type of foam used. Custom cushions present a wide range of replacement options, but the prices may give you sticker shock.

But you have another, less expensive option if your cushion covers are in decent shape and only the foam needs to be replaced. (We'll assume that your cushions have zippers through which the old foam can be extracted and new foam inserted.)

We often hear it suggested that we use the old foam inserts as patterns for new ones. This is a bad idea, since the old ones are broken down and suffer from years of shape-changing abuse. You are better off making new patterns.

Choosing the proper foam is the first step. We are talking here about open-cell foam for interior uses—not the closed-cell foam used for deck cushions. Open-cell foam is available in various formulas and formats, and most types come in a variety of densities for firmness. The "right" firmness is a purely subjective judgment, one best made by actual contact between your body and

the foam. When choosing foam for one of my project boats, my wife and I went to a cooperative foam supplier and sat and lay down on foam of several different densities before buying. The usual tendency is to pick too low a density—that is, too soft a foam—for long-term use.

Lay a sheet of brown wrapping paper on the bunk flat or other area where the cushion will go. Trace the outline of the base of the cushion and cut the pattern. Quite often the rear or side edges of the cushion will flare outward toward the top. If this is the case—if, for example, the outside edge of a berth cushion flares outward against the hull side—draw a series of lines on the paper pattern perpendicular to the hull, and erect a square at the edge of the pattern so that the base of the square aligns with each of the lines in turn. Measure the distance from the vertical edge of the square to the hull at a height equal to the thickness of the foam, and write this dimension on the pattern.

Place the pattern on top of the foam to be cut, aligning the square edges of the pattern with the foam edges. This surface of the foam will be the top of the cushion, and it helps keep things straight if you mark it as such. Place a ruler on the lines you drew with the square and measure out from the pattern edge the distances noted on the lines. Place a dot at each resulting mark with a Magic Marker. Connect the dots to make a continuous line. This line defines the top edge of the foam.

Now turn the foam over and place the pattern on this side, once again aligning the square edges of the pattern with the foam edges (the *same* foam edges you used for the top surface; better double-check this!). Now trace around the edge of the pattern. This line defines the bottom of the cushion.

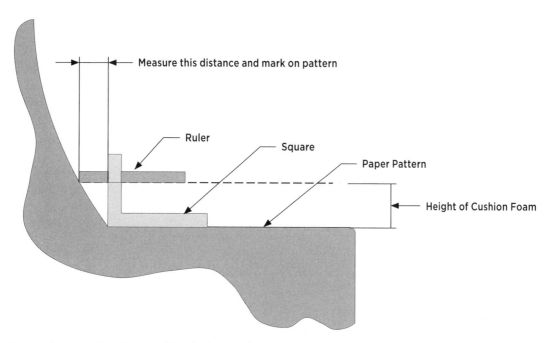

Measure this distance and mark on pattern

Ruler

Square

Paper Pattern

Height of Cushion Foam

Developing a pattern for a cushion is simple when the cushion is square edged and only a little more complicated when the cushion has a beveled edge. See the accompanying text for an explanation. Once you obtain the outboard flare dimension measured by the ruler in this illustration, you will want to note it on the paper pattern.

Turn the foam back over so the top side is up, and cut along the curved line marking the top edge. The foam can easily be cut with an electric knife—so easily, in fact, that it's worth buying one just for this job. Don't worry about minor imperfections in the foam; it is pliable, after all. Cut vertically along the line; you don't cut the bevel with this cut.

Once that edge is cut, turn the foam upside down again, so that the outline you drew for the bottom edge of the cushion is visible. You can now trim the flare (from top edge to bottom edge of cushion) freehand with the electric knife. This sounds like a lot of work, but making two cuts rather than one enables one person to do this job alone. If you have a helper you can combine the two cuts into one, with each of you responsible for keeping the knife on the line on his or her side of the foam.

Taking the old foam out of the cushion will alert you to how hard a process getting the foam back in can be. Simplify it with this trick: Form a bag for the foam using a plastic painter's tarp and tape. Slide the cushion into this bag and seal the end around a hose attached to the suction end of your vacuum cleaner. Turn it on and suck the air out of the bag and the foam. This will greatly reduce the volume of the cushion and make inserting it a snap. The plastic can stay on the foam.

Sewing new cushion covers is a rather specialized skill that few weekend do-it-yourselfers are

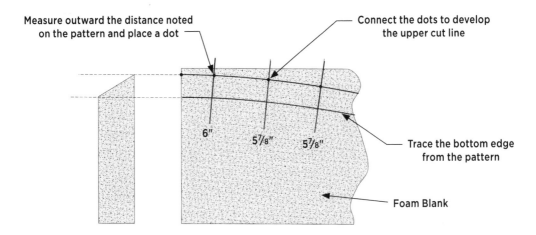

Measure outward the distance noted on the pattern and place a dot

Connect the dots to develop the upper cut line

6"   5⅞"   5⅞"

Trace the bottom edge from the pattern

Foam Blank

This is how to lay out the flared top edge of the cushion on the top surface of the foam blank. Having noted the amount of flare at each baseline where you erected your square in the previous step, you know how far outward from the pattern edge to measure along that baseline before you make a dot. Connecting those dots with a smooth curve gives you the top edge of the cushion. Then turn the blank over and trace the bottom edge of the cushion directly from the pattern.

eager to tackle. If you're one of the few, I recommend visiting Sailrite's website (www.sailrite .com) and purchasing their video on making cushions. Another good resource is *The Big Book of Boat Canvas*, by Karen S. Lipe.

REPLACING PORTS AND HATCHES

Chapter 2, The Cockpit, begins with the procedure for adding an access hatch. The procedure for replacing a hatch or portlight is much the same, and the placement of these projects in Chapters 2 and 3 is somewhat arbitrary. Indeed, either project could have been placed just as logically in Chapter 4, Decks.

There are many reasons for replacing ports and hatches. They may leak; they may be broken

and you can't find parts; the glazing might be cracked, frosted, or discolored; or you just might want to upgrade the look of your boat. Replacing existing ports or hatches with the same parts or similar units of the same dimensions is relatively easy. Changing to ports or hatches of a different size, however, raises the complexity of the project a notch.

If you want to make a direct replacement, the first step is to find out if new units are available. While many boatbuilders install stock hatches from the original equipment manufacturer (OEM), others opt for custom units they produce themselves. Still other boatbuilders subcontract an outside vendor to customize units for their boats.

Inspect your hatches and ports to see if any identifying marks or trade names appear on them. Popular names include ABI, Bomar, Bomon, Hood, Lewmar, Beckson, Taylor Made

Products, and Fuller. Even a part number will help. Use the Internet to search. Owners' groups are other good sources of information about replacements. If your ports or hatches need replacing, chances are other boats of the same model have needed it too, and their owners may have found sources.

There are several possibilities for locating replacement units. If they're still in production, you can buy them through regular retail outlets. Out-of-production units may be located on online auction sites or marine consignment shops. Several shops specialize in selling new old stock (NOS) items from manufacturers' overruns and firms that have gone out of business.

Even if you can't find exact replacements in stock, you may not be out of luck. Several manufacturers, like Bomon, will custom-build hatches or ports for you. These will not be cheap and will take time to produce, but they will simplify installation.

Failing that, it's time to look at other options. There is some level of standardization in port sizes (4 inches by 10 inches, and 5 inches by 12 inches are common sizes, for example). But even if you find a port with the right nominal dimensions, it might not work as a direct replacement, because details like corner radii and the required opening size might be different. Hatch sizes don't follow even this minimal level of standardization. Hatch manufacturers each have their own sizes, cutouts, and mount dimensions. I have found that most new hatches tend to be square, while most older hatches are rectangular.

If you can't find similar-sized replacements, you have a further choice to make: bigger or smaller. If you choose to install a larger port or hatch than you have now, you will have to cut a bigger opening to receive the replacement. This

requires cutting away a portion of the hull, deck, or cabin surrounding the current opening, sealing the perimeter of the opening, and reinstalling the hatch or port. This assumes that the hull, deck, or cabin surface on which the new port will be mounted is flat over a large enough area to accommodate it. Any more than about ⅛-inch camber in the surface makes the project exponentially more difficult and should probably be avoided.

Installing smaller units will require closing up the area around the existing opening. This will require some fiberglass work and repainting to match the exterior. Depending on the size of the unit, this too can be an extensive job. The new area must be built up to the same thickness and strength as the surrounding structure for safety's sake.

Rather than building in from the sides of a hole to reduce its size, it is more time-efficient to fiberglass the entire opening closed, then cut the new port or hatch opening. While wasting some material in the cutout, it makes the job of fairing the newly fiberglassed area into the existing contour of the hull or deck much easier and guarantees smooth contours around the new unit. I recommend this approach for all but the largest hatch openings.

You may choose to remove the old units before purchasing their replacements. This allows you to precisely determine the opening size and whether the new units will fit. On the other hand, you may take your chances and buy the new units before removing the old ones. That will eliminate the possibility of rain or dust getting into the boat while the hatches and ports are out.

Many boatbuilders use silicone sealant when installing ports and hatches. This will make them relatively easy to remove, as silicone sealant isn't a

SEALANT CHOICES

Sealant	Mfg	Type	Above Waterline	Below Waterline	Adhesive Quality	Flexibility	UV Resistance	Cure Time	Okay for Plastics?	Sandable/Paintable
3M Marine Grade Silicone Sealant	3M	Silicone	Y	N	Poor	Excellent	Good	24–48 Hrs.	Y	N/N
3M101	3M	Polysulfide	Y	N	Good	Excellent	Good	14–21 Days	N	Y/Y
3M4000	3M	Polyether	N	N	Fair	Good	Excellent	24 Hrs.	N	Y/N
3M4200	3M	Polyurethane	Y	Y	Excellent	Good	Good	24 Hrs.	N	Y/Y
3M4200 Fast Cure	3M	Polyurethane	Y	Y	Excellent	Good	Good	24 Hrs.	N	Y/N
3M5200	3M	Polyurethane	Y	Y	Excellent	Fair	Good	5–7 Days	N	Y/N
3M5200 Fast Cure	3M	Polyurethane	Y	Y	Excellent	Fair	Good	24 Hrs.	N	Y/N
BoatLIFE Life-Calk	BoatLIFE	Polysulfide	Y	Y	Good	Good	Good	1–3 Days	N	Y/Y
BoatLIFE LifeSeal	BoatLIFE	Polyurethane/ Silicone	Y	Y	Excellent	Excellent	Good	24–36 Hrs.	Y	N/N
GE Silicone I	GE	Silicone	Y	N	Poor	Good	Good	24 Hrs.	Y	N/N
GE Silicone II	GE	Silicone	Y	N	Poor	Good	Good	24 Hrs.	Y	N/N
Sikaflex 291	Sika	Polyurethane	Y	Y	Excellent	Fair	Good	3 Days	N	Y/Y
Sikaflex 292	Sika	Polyurethane	Y	Y	Excellent	Fair	Good	24 Hrs.	N	Y/Y
Sikaflex 295	Sika	Polyurethane	Y	N	Excellent	Good	Excellent	24 Hrs.	Y	Y/Y

very good adhesive. It should be possible to gently pry off the old ports and hatches with a putty knife. A downside of silicone sealant is that it "poisons" the surrounding fiberglass, making it much harder to paint.

Polysulfide and polyurethane adhesive-sealants, though more durable and easier to paint than silicone, may attack a plastic portlight. Furthermore, a polyurethane adhesive-sealant such as 3M 5200 will make it harder to remove old ports and hatches because it grips like welded steel. There are some new solvents that claim to dissolve 5200, but check to make sure they won't damage the surrounding fiberglass. Thin knives or putty knives can be used to cut the sealant and free the unit. Take great care if you are planning to save and reuse delicate items like trim rings.

Another trick that sometimes works is to wrap each end of a thin length of piano wire around a short dowel. Then use the wire as a saw, with the dowels acting as handles, working the wire behind the port or hatch frame and cutting the sealant. Once the hardware is removed, clean off all the old sealant around the opening.

The procedures for enlarging an opening are identical to those used for cutting an opening for an access hatch or storage compartment. (See Chapter 2 for details.) If the fiberglass structure is cored, make sure the core is cut back beyond where the fasteners will go and the area is sealed with filled epoxy.

Reducing the size of an opening is virtually identical to the process of repairing holes in the hull, as described in Chapter 6.

In any case, after the opening has been recut to the proper size, mask around it with 3 to 4 inches of painter's blue tape. Place the port in the opening, trace around the edge of the frame onto the tape, and drill the fastener holes. If your ports have chamfered fastener holes, use a Vix bit to drill the holes. A Vix bit has a spring-loaded outer sleeve that centers the drill in the fastener hole.

If your fastener holes are into solid epoxy, you're home free. If you've hit core material, enlarge the holes through the outer skin and the core. If you will be through-bolting the hardware, don't redrill through the bottom skin; instead, tape over the small hole that you've already drilled on the inside. Next, fill the cavity with filled epoxy. After it has cured, redrill the fastener holes.

Cut away the blue tape under where the port or hatch frame will sit. Place the fasteners in their holes in the port frame, and tape over the top surface of the frame. Place a neoprene washer on each of the fasteners from the underside. Run a generous bead of sealant (see the table Sealant Choices) around the flange of the port and the mounting surface. Place the port in its opening and evenly tighten the fasteners. The fasteners should tighten up against the neoprene washers, keeping you from squeezing out all the sealant. I use wooden tongue depressors with their ends cut square to clean up the excess sealant that squeezes out. Once the sealant has been cleaned up, remove the tape and let the sealant cure. As with similar projects, don't be tempted to go back later and retighten the fasteners. This will break the bond between the sealant and the fastener and provide a potential leak site. If you feel it necessary to further tighten the fastener, wait until the sealant has cured, and then have someone hold the head of the fastener while you tighten the nut from below. If the fastener turns, it will break the sealant bond around the fastener and provide a sure source for leaks.

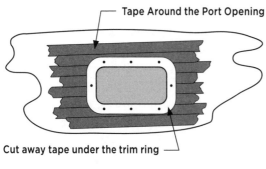

Tape Around the Port Opening

Cut away tape under the trim ring

Tape the trim ring

Installing a replacement portlight. The area has been taped off with blue masking tape. The portlight frame perimeter was traced on the tape, the fastener holes were drilled, and the tape was cut away from the frame seat. Note that the finished surface of the frame has been taped in order to shield it from squeeze-out of the adhesive/sealant when the fasteners are tightened.

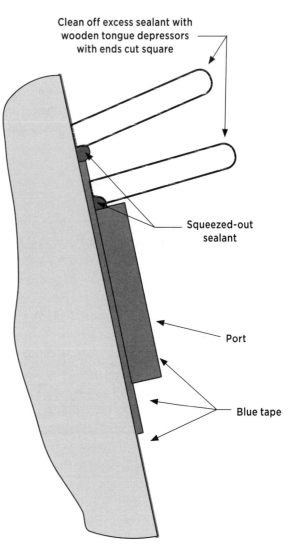

Clean off excess sealant with wooden tongue depressors with ends cut square

Squeezed-out sealant

Port

Blue tape

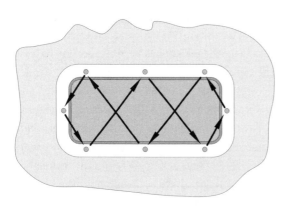

Tighten fasteners evenly by alternating from side to side

Tighten the portlight fasteners by increments.

Once any excess gobs of sealant have been removed, as shown here, you can remove the tape and allow the sealant to cure.

REFINISHING OR REPLACING PLASTIC GLAZING

While there are many valid reasons for replacing ports and hatches, clouded or scratched glazing may not be one of them. Before going to the trouble and expense of replacing an entire unit, consider refinishing or replacing the plastic glazing. In the case of a discontinued or hard-to-find hatch, reglazing may be the best way to proceed, as it will avoid the problems of changing the hatch size or configuration.

Often scratched or clouded glazing can be brought back to life with a thorough polishing. The polishing removes minor scratches and the clouded surface layer. One of the often-used products for this purpose might surprise you. It is the tried-and-true Flitz Liquid Metal Polish. You can apply it to the glazing and buff it out with a power buffer. Be careful not to "burn" the surface by holding the buffer in one location too long. Another product that can be used to polish acrylic (Plexiglas or Lucite) or polycarbonate (Lexan) glazing materials is common, ordinary tooth-

paste, which contains just enough fine abrasive to do the job.

If you can't polish out the cloudiness and scratches, consider replacing just the glazing material itself. Some hatch makers, such as Bomar, supply replacement hatch lenses and the sealant used to bed them. If you can't find replacement lenses, have one made by your plastics supplier, or buy flat stock and cut one yourself. (See the next project, Replacing Plexiglas or Lexan Fixed Windows, for advice on cutting plastic sheet stock.) Follow the plastic manufacturer's recommendations for the appropriate sealant. Some sealants do not have sufficient adhesive qualities for this application, while others may damage plastic hatch frames or finishes.

REPLACING PLEXIGLAS OR LEXAN FIXED WINDOWS

Many boats have fixed windows or portlights that do not have any frames. These are made from

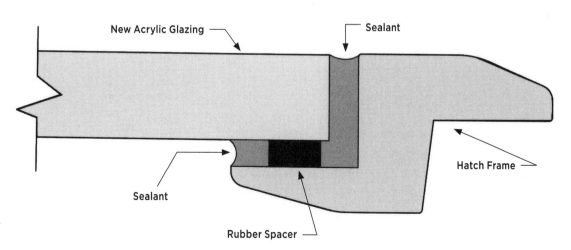

Reglazing a hatch lens can save a costly hatch replacement bill.

Plexiglas (acrylic) or Lexan (polycarbonate) plastic stock and are either screwed or glued in place, or both.

Remove the old windows using any of the methods discussed in the previous project, Refinishing or Replacing Plastic Glazing. Hopefully the old windows will come off in good enough shape to act as templates for new windows. If not, you'll have to make your own patterns from cardboard. Frameless plastic windows should be about 1½ inches bigger all around than the opening. This allows plenty of room for mounting hardware and plenty of width for sealant.

Plexiglas and Lexan are widely available at plastics supply houses. Most cities have one or more of these places; look under plastics suppliers in the phone book. Many glass shops also sell Plexiglas and Lexan. Plexiglas is more scratch resistant and less expensive, while Lexan is stronger. I generally use Plexiglas, but both are good choices.

You can have your supplier cut the new window from your template, or you can buy a sheet of stock and cut it yourself with either a band saw or a good variable-speed jigsaw. In the latter case, use a medium-tooth wood-cutting blade.

The plastic comes with a protective paper cover on each side. Leave this on! Trace your template onto the protective paper, then cut out the window, leaving the line you traced. Run the saw at a slow to medium speed, and don't push it along too quickly. If you run the saw or push it along too fast, you risk overheating the plastic, which will then fuse back together after the blade passes.

Whether you cut them or your supplier cuts them, the window blanks need further finishing before they can be installed. The edges must be as smooth as the surface; any micro-cracks left in the edges tend to propagate further cracking. Block-sand the edges, starting with a medium grit and progressing through finer grits. Each succeeding finer grade of sandpaper removes the scratches from the prior grade and further smoothes the edges. Keep going at least to a 600-grit sandpaper.

After the sanding is complete, buff and polish the edges. I do this by hand with a Tripoli buffing compound and a clean rag. You can use a power buffing wheel if you are careful. The end result should be an edge as polished and shiny as the surface of the plastic.

Fixed windows can be glued in place without the use of fasteners. However, most of the adhesives suitable for this purpose are industrial-strength two-part adhesive/sealants not commonly available to amateurs. Check with your plastics supplier to see if they have the proper material. If not, you may have to screw or bolt the windows in place. In either case the fasteners must go into solid epoxy/filler and not penetrate any wood or foam core.

If you decide to through-bolt the windows, consider your choice of hardware. Simple hex nuts and washers will look industrial and ugly and pose a hazard from the sharp exposed threads. Acorn nuts will provide a more finished look. Barrels nuts are also an option but may require you to cut the fasteners to the correct length. You can also plan to cover the entire area with a wooden or plastic piece of trim molding.

Allow about 2 to 2½ inches between fasteners. Establish a centerline for the fasteners, then subdivide this line into equal segments for the fastener holes. Take extra care here, as uneven fastener spacing will be painfully obvious in the finished job.

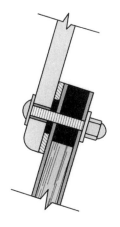

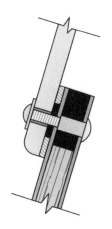

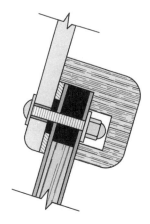

An acorn nut provides a more finished appearance than a plain nut

A barrel nut is another finishing option

The fasteners can also be covered with a wood or plastic trim piece

Inside fastener and trim options for a fixed port. In all cases the laminate core must be cut back and replaced with epoxy/filler where the fasteners penetrate the deck core.

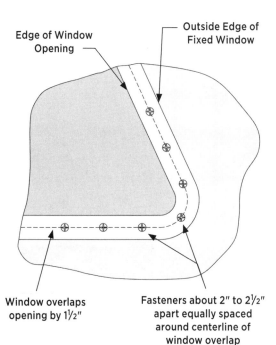

Edge of Window Opening

Outside Edge of Fixed Window

Window overlaps opening by 1½"

Fasteners about 2" to 2½" apart equally spaced around centerline of window overlap

Fastener layout for a fixed port. An even spacing is aesthetically desirable.

Drilling holes in Plexiglas or Lexan requires some precautions. A standard twist drill will "grab" and chip the edges of the hole. You can use a special drill bit designed for drilling plastic, or you can make your own from a conventional bit by grinding the leading edges of the drill to dull them. This allows a slower cutting rate that doesn't chip the plastic. Drill slowly and carefully or you'll ruin an expensive window blank. It pays to practice on some plastic scraps first.

Plexiglas and Lexan expand and contract more than the surfaces they are mounted on. This means that the fastener holes must be drilled oversize to allow for this movement. For ¼-inch fasteners, use a 5⁄16-inch drill bit. The fasteners should be round head, pan head, or truss head. Do not countersink the holes and use flat- or oval-head fasteners, as these would act as wedges and wouldn't allow the plastic to expand or contract, causing it to crack in short order.

After drilling the holes in the plastic, place the window in position and mark the location of the fastener holes on the hull or cabin. Trace the shape of the window opening on the protective paper on the inside of the window.

Drill the fastener holes and check if there is any core material exposed in the holes. If there is, use a bigger bit to enlarge the holes through the outer skin and core. Tape off the holes on the inside if you're through-bolting the windows, then fill the holes with filled epoxy and let it harden. After the epoxy has cured, redrill the fastener holes to the proper size.

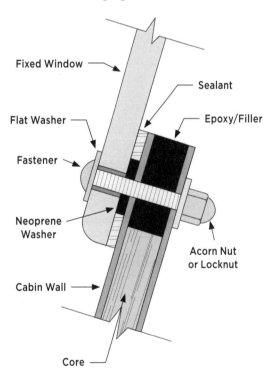

Cross section of a fastener in a fixed port. You want round-, pan-, or truss-head fasteners; countersunk heads would generate cracks in Plexiglas or Lexan. A neoprene washer on the fastener prevents excessive squeeze-out of the sealant.

Using a sharp razor knife, carefully trim and remove the protective paper from the narrow strip traced around the edges on the inside surface of the window blank. This will be where you will apply the sealant before fastening the window in place. Sealant applied to the edges of a fixed window can discolor or turn blotchy over time. To disguise this, sand the exposed plastic with 80-grit sandpaper and then give it two coats of marine paint that match the surface the window will be mounted on. This step isn't essential from a functional point of view, but it results in a more finished and professional appearance.

Affix blue masking tape around the window opening out to 3 to 4 inches. Put the window back in place, trace the window outline on the tape, and cut away the tape beneath the window. Tape the edges of the window to keep excess sealant off the bare plastic.

From here on it's the standard drill: Place fasteners in the holes, place neoprene washers on the fasteners, then apply sealant to both the window

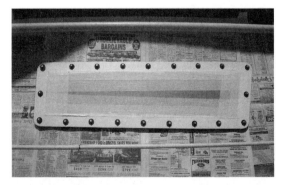

This view of the back side of a fixed window (that is, the side that will mate with the cabin side when installed) shows the sanded and painted perimeter as well as the fasteners in place with neoprene washers installed. The protective paper is still in place over the rest of the window.

and the mounting surface, as described in Chapter 2. Choose the sealant based on the plastic you chose and the manufacturer's suggestions (see the table Sealant Choices earlier in this chapter). Many sealants, such as 3M 5200, will attack and soften some of the plastic glazing materials. Tighten the fasteners gradually, working back and forth around the window. You will be squeezing out sealant, so let it ooze. The fasteners don't have to be torqued down tightly. Simply snug them up against the neoprene washers and let it go at that. Squeezing out all the sealant is a sure invitation to future leaks.

Clean up the excess sealant with wooden tongue depressors with their ends cut off square, then pull off the tape and let the sealant cure.

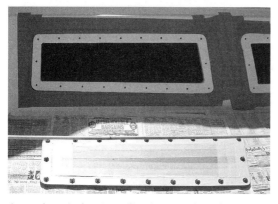

Once the window's outline is traced on the masking tape, cut the tape away from the mounting surface.

Apply a thick bead of sealant around the mounting surface of the window. Cut a narrow strip of masking tape to protect the edge of the window from sealant.

Tighten the window fasteners incrementally, following the pattern shown on page 64. The fasteners are snugged up gently on their neoprene washers.

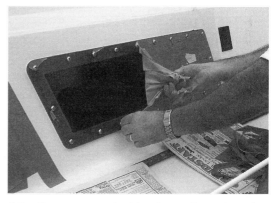

After the excess sealant has been cleaned up, the masking tape and the protective paper on the window can be removed.

REJUVENATING OR REPLACING HEADLINERS

If you have a cuddy or other small cabin, chances are it has a headliner installed to obscure the raw fiberglass and make it look more presentable. That headliner could be part of a molded fiberglass liner or some sort of fabric, similar to an automotive headliner.

Molded fiberglass headliners seldom go structurally bad. They can, however, get dirty, stained, and faded over time. In one of my project boats, the molded headliner was suffering from many years of accessories being screwed in and then removed. Riddled with dozens of screw holes, gouges, and scuffs, it looked so bad I decided to refinish it.

The absolute first step in refinishing any fiberglass surface is to dewax it. I like to use Interlux products, so the dewaxer I use is their Fiberglass Solvent Wash 202. Other paint manufacturers have their own products, and they're all good. I recommend choosing one brand and using that manufacturer's products consistently, from solvents to final paint, in order to ensure maximum compatibility. Mixing and matching brands is a factor in many bad paint jobs.

Apply the dewaxer using a clean rag and wiping in one direction only, switching rags often. After I dewaxed that overhead, I filled in all the old fastener holes with epoxy/ filler. (See Repairing Chips, Dings, and Gouges in Chapter 6 for a detailed discussion.) After the epoxy cured, I sanded the entire overhead with 80-grit, then 120-grit sandpaper. I then rolled on three thin coats of Interlux Brightside one-part polyurethane paint. The result was, in my opinion, every

This molded fiberglass overhead liner looks as good as new after being patched, primed, and painted.

bit as good as any two-part paint application. The project was helped along because I had already removed the ports and hatches for renovation.

Fabric headliners are a different story. Many types of fabric have been used through the years, from short-napped "monkey fur" to foam-backed vinyls. The latter are particularly nasty, as the foam tends to turn into brown powder over time, and the adhesive used to hold the fabric in place is hard to remove.

Other fabric headliners use metal support rods running from one side of the cabin to the other. These rods slide into sleeves sewn into the top surface of the headliner fabric. The fabric eventually becomes hard or even impossible to clean. The stitching on the fabric loops also starts to give way, and the headliner starts to droop. The edges of overheads of this type are usually held in place with staples driven into wood strips mounted around the cabin edges.

The chances of finding an identical replacement fabric are slim, but the good news is that other suitable fabrics of all types are available.

Few marine stores stock fabrics, but most have sample books you can look at and order from. Before you order anything, however, do a little planning. Find out what widths the fabric comes in. If the old headliner is too damaged to serve as a pattern, make a new pattern from cheap cloth to determine the best widths and the amount of cloth you need. It's much better to mess up with a cheap pattern than with more expensive headliner fabric.

If you have a rod-supported headliner, you can either reuse that design or remove the hardware and glue the fabric directly to the overhead with a spray adhesive or contact cement. Gluing anything to an overhead can, however, be an exercise in frustration, so do some trial runs with your choice of adhesive and a scrap piece of fabric. Make sure the solvent in the glue doesn't melt the foam or discolor the vinyl.

Spraying adhesive inside a boat will almost ensure that every surface gets sticky overspray on it, so apply spray adhesive to the fabric outside the boat. The next step is for you and as many helpers as are needed (you did do a trial run, didn't you?) to get the fabric inside the boat and in position to be applied without its glued surface touching anything.

One major problem with fabric headliners is that they cover all the hardware fasteners that may be through-bolted through the deck or cabintop. This makes it difficult to troubleshoot leaks and requires that the headliner be removed to inspect, re-bed, or replace hardware. For that reason a panelized overhead makes a great deal of sense. The rigid panels can be thin plywood, flexible plastic panels similar to those used to line shower enclosures, or similar products. These panels can then be held in place with wood trim strips or even hook-and-loop tape (for example, Velcro).

I used this panelized system on one of my project boats. I first made a scale drawing of the overhead and then divided the area into convenient panels. I adjusted the panel sizes and locations to provide maximum access to the overhead while keeping the panels small enough to be easy to handle.

I then bonded plywood strips to the overhead with thickened epoxy, matching the location of the seams between the panels. Spring-loaded closet rod did a good job of holding these strips in place until the epoxy cured. The strips were wide enough to accommodate a center teak trim batten and a strip of Velcro along each side. I made the panels from ¼-inch lauan kitchen underlayment, which is an exterior-grade plywood. (Lauan is also called meranti or Philippine mahogany.) I covered the panels with white marine-grade vinyl, wrapping it around the edges and stapling it on the back side.

I then fastened industrial-strength Velcro strips to the backs of the panels and matching Velcro strips to the overhead. (The Velcro has a pressure-sensitive adhesive to hold it in place, but I also stapled it to hold it for the long term.) The result was a clean-looking headliner with panels that can be removed for access to the overhead. An additional benefit was that the plywood strips helped create a pocket in the overhead that I filled with Reflectix insulation. Sold in most home improvement stores, this looks like several sheets of bubble wrap bonded together and coated with aluminum foil. It is flexible and can be cut to fit any opening with a pair of scissors. I usually cut it slightly oversize and force it into an opening to hold it in place.

Installing a panelized overhead like this one is a little more complicated. Each of these panels is a piece of ¼-inch marine plywood covered with marine-grade vinyl. The panel layout is designed to give convenient access to the overhead. I glued strips of plywood to the overhead where the panel seams would lie, then fastened industrial-strength Velcro strips to the backs of the panels and to the plywood strips. Teak trim battens bonded to the plywood strips separate the panels. (In the background both port and starboard you can see where lengths of teak batten have yet to be installed.)

Marine Sanitation Systems

A suitable marine sanitation system will make life aboard much more enjoyable for all concerned. Many guys complain that their significant others don't enjoy the boating life. Although a woman may not say it, the proper amenities may go a long way toward encouraging her aboard. In addition, a marine sanitation system is helpful to the environment and also a condition for qualifying your boat as a second home and obtaining the resulting income tax deductions for loan interest.

I once heard a health expert say that if you haven't peed after being out on the water for more than three hours, you are in the beginning stages of dehydration and should immediately begin drinking fluids. That always begs the question of the ultimate result: where to do the deed. Old-timers always championed the "bucket and chuck it" approach, but that is pretty uncouth, especially in mixed company, and it's now illegal in most places anyway. If you want to spend time on the water with your friends, some sort of sanitary system is highly desirable.

In the United States, standards for marine sanitation systems are set by the Environmental Protection Agency (EPA), and these standards are implemented through U.S. Coast Guard (USCG) regulations and enforced by the USCG as well as by state and local marine officers. Marine sanitation devices (MSDs) are classified into three basic types:

- **Type One MSDs** treat the sewage and then discharge it overboard. The treated effluent must meet EPA standards for bacteria count and suspended solids. These MSDs are not legal for use in areas that have been declared no-discharge zones.
- **Type Two MSDs** are more powerful versions of Type One systems, typically found aboard larger vessels (over 65 feet) because of the amount of power required to operate them. These are also illegal to use in no-discharge zones.
- **Type Three MSDs** consist of a toilet connected to a holding tank. The sewage is held for later disposal at a pumpout station or offshore.

Basically it is illegal to dump sewage overboard on inland or coastal waters of the United

States. Sewage can be pumped overboard if you are beyond the 3-mile coastal discharge limit. Some states impose further restrictions. For example, boats that are transiting Lake Champlain are required to have any overboard discharge lines disconnected from their through-hull fitting, or the boatowner will be fined. Simply locking the Y-valve to prevent overboard discharge does not suffice. The potty police check for overboard discharge by placing dye tablets in the toilet and having you flush it. If they see the dye in the water under the boat, you'll pay the fine.

Systems can range from a simple Porta-Potti (considered a Type Three MSD) in a canvas enclosure to a full-blown system with a holding tank and electric head. If your boat didn't come equipped with an MSD, consider adding one yourself.

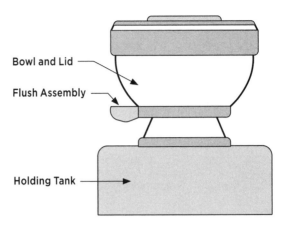

Front View

The Marine Traveler Head from SeaLand Technology is completely self-contained. Hook up a water supply and connect to a pumpout fitting, and it's ready for use.

INSTALLING AN ALL-IN-ONE MSD

An all-in-one Type Three MSD is a compact, practical creature comfort for some small boats. This self-contained unit has the toilet bowl mounted on top of a holding tank and requires only a flush water connection, a vent line, and a 1½-inch discharge line. A typical unit, the Marine Traveler Head by SeaLand, is only 20 inches high, 19 inches wide, and 21¾ inches deep. On the far side of $500, it is expensive, but its compact size and ease of installation make it a better choice for many small boats than a conventional marine head with a separate holding tank. An all-in-one

head does not have an integral pump for overboard discharge—you must empty the holding tank at a pumpout station—but if you do your boating on inshore waters, you shouldn't be pumping overboard in any event. The unit uses only a small amount of flush water, so a 9½-gallon holding tank should give you adequate time between pumpouts.

You will need to build a sturdy foundation capable of supporting the weight of a full waste tank plus a human occupying the seat. Use at least ¾-inch marine or MDO plywood as the base, with lumber supports fiberglassed and epoxied in place underneath.

Some all-in-one toilets offer the option of using the boat's freshwater system for flushing. This eliminates the odor that marine growth might otherwise cause in a saltwater intake line, and the toilet flushes with as little as a pint of water, so the freshwater drawdown is not high.

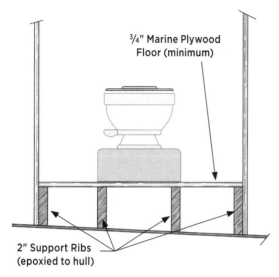

3/4" Marine Plywood
Floor (minimum)

2" Support Ribs
(epoxied to hull)

A self-contained head requires a substantial support platform to hold the weight of the unit, the holding-tank contents, and a person.

For saltwater flushing you'd need to install a through-hull fitting and seacock below the waterline for the flushing water, as described in Chapter 6. (Obviously, the boat must be out of the water for this part of the project.) Install a vented loop in the supply line between the through-hull and the toilet. A vented loop is an upside-down U-shaped device with a valve on the upper end. This valve opens under vacuum and will stop any siphoning in the supply line. The vented loop should be installed so that it remains well above the waterline even when the boat is heeled over.

The holding tank will need a vent line, usually a ⅝-inch-diameter hose. The vent should be placed on the hull as high as possible above the waterline; it allows air to enter or exit the tank as it is emptied or filled. The last requirement is a 1½-inch discharge or pumpout hose. This hose connects the bottom of the holding tank to an access port on deck.

INSTALLING A HOLDING TANK SYSTEM

A typical full-blown marine sanitation system consists of a toilet, either manual or electric, and a separate holding tank. Manual marine toilets have pumps to empty the bowl, and electric heads have a combined pump/macerator powered by an electric motor to grind up the sewage before moving it to the holding tank.

A simple installation passes the sewage from the toilet directly to the holding tank, which also has a discharge line through which the sewage is emptied at a pumpout station. A more complex installation may include a Y-valve to direct discharge from the toilet to the pumpout line or to an overboard discharge. Some overboard discharge lines employ an additional pump, which may be either manual or electric. Note that dumping sewage overboard within 3 miles of shore is illegal in all United States coastal and inland waters.

Installing the head itself, including the water supply, is identical to the procedure for installing an all-in-one system described in the previous project, Installing an All-in-One MSD. But where a separate holding tank is involved, new issues arise.

The first of these is the location and size of the holding tank. There are no hard and fast rules for locating the holding tank. The closer it is to the toilet, the better, as this will minimize the length of the required hoses. Properly plumbed, the tank can be above or below the waterline and above or below the height of the toilet. In most boats, there are only a few spaces available to consider for a holding tank installation. The trick is finding an appropriate location for a reasonably sized tank.

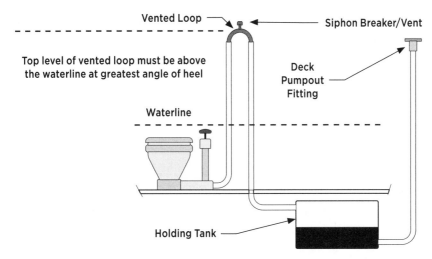

A simple sanitation system includes a separate holding tank connected to the toilet with a vented loop, which prevents back-siphoning of the tank into the toilet even if the tank is installed higher than the toilet. In this case there is no provision for pumping overboard, which is illegal inside the 3-mile limit. Not shown here is the toilet's intake line for flushing water, which should also have a vented loop installed.

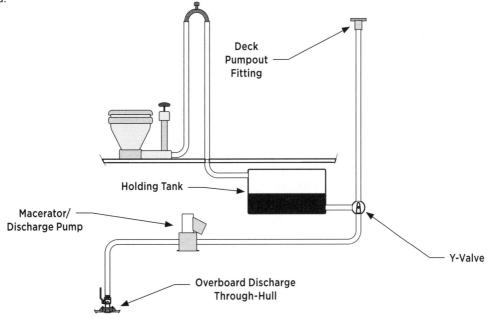

This sanitation setup offers the option of pumping overboard outside the 3-mile limit. Larger cruising boats operating frequently outside the 3-mile limit often install the Y-valve upstream rather than downstream of the holding tank, so that flushed waste need never enter the holding tank, but for small boats it's appropriate for all waste to pass through the holding tank.

Installing a too-small tank will cause frustration, as you'll have to have the tank pumped out too frequently. A further consideration is the effect a full holding tank has on the trim of the boat. Consider that a full 12-gallon holding tank weighs over a hundred pounds, and you can see that all that weight in the very bow or to one side of the boat could affect trim and stability.

Sufficient room for the tank isn't the only consideration. The tank will need to be properly supported, and there needs to be adequate room to run the required plumbing to the toilet and the required outlet and vents.

Water weighs a little over 8 pounds per gallon, so even a small 10-gallon tank will weigh over 80 pounds when full. This usually means a support structure made from ¾-inch plywood, properly supported underneath and securely fiberglassed to the surrounding boat structure. Substantial wood cleats are used to hold the tank in place laterally.

Most small to medium-sized boats use molded polyethylene holding tanks. These are available in a wide range of sizes, and you can probably find one in a marine catalog that fits your available space. If not, you can have a tank custom made (at considerable expense), or you can build one yourself out of plywood and epoxy. Don't laugh: these can be quite successful. Make sure you use lots of epoxy to build up a really good waterproof coating over the plywood.

If you are planning on purchasing a premade tank, consider making a template or sample tank from cardboard to the exact size of the tank. Try to fit it in the place you have chosen, to verify that there is enough room to get the tank in place and then to run the required hoses.

Stock holding tanks have a 1½-inch inlet on the side near the top, a 1½-inch outlet near the bottom, and a small vent fitting. The usual practice is to install threaded hose barbs in the fittings and then run flexible hose to the various connections.

The large inlet and outlet hoses should be rated for sanitation use. There are several grades available, but you should buy the best you can find. Eventually, odors will permeate any sanitation hose, but the better grades postpone that agony longer. A trick proposed by marine sanitation expert Peggy Hall is to wrap the hose with Saran Wrap prior to installing it. She insists that only Saran Wrap is acceptable, not a substitute.

The hose runs should be laid out so that there are no low spots where "stuff" can gather in them; it should all drain down to the tank. But looking at the standard plumbing scheme, you will notice that as the tank is filled, the "stuff" will begin to fill the outlet hose.

One way to avoid the effluent standing in this portion of the hose is to replace it with a standpipe made from standard PVC plumbing components. Solid PVC is highly resistant to odor permeations, as testified by its use in household plumbing applications.

If you are planning an offshore passage, you might want to consider adding a Y-valve to allow overboard discharge. As noted above, discharging sewage overboard is illegal unless you are at least 3 miles offshore. For this reason, your choice of a Y-valve should include a provision for installing a padlock or other device to seal the overboard discharge. Note that some bodies of water (Lake Champlain, for example) require you to actually disconnect the overboard discharge line.

The last bit of plumbing will be the tank vent(s). Most premade tanks have a single ⅝-inch vent line. This should be run to a through-hull fitting placed just below the gunwale or rubrail. This

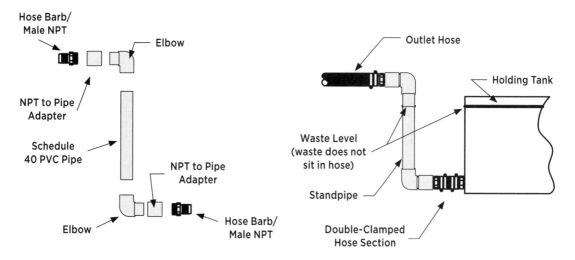

A standpipe of rigid PVC in the holding tank's discharge line will eliminate the odor you might otherwise get from sewage standing in a more permeable flexible hose.

vent line is critical for proper filling and emptying of the tank. Insects have a habit of building nests in these lines, so keep a sharp lookout to make sure the lines are free and venting.

That venting can produce a very disagreeable smell. For this reason, several manufacturers make carbon filters for vent lines. While expensive, they make life at a dock much more bearable for your neighbors. Installation is straightforward. The vent hose is cut at a convenient location and the filter, with a hose barb on each end, is inserted in the line. The filter comes with a mounting band so that it can be fastened to a nearby solid surface.

A final word about vent lines also comes from marine sanitation expert Peggy Hall. Holding-tank odors are produced by anaerobic bacteria, those that thrive in the absence of oxygen. Properly venting a tank encourages aerobic bacteria, which do not produce disagreeable smells. One way of properly venting the tank is to provide at least two 1-inch-diameter vent lines.

Boat Ventilation

Let's be honest: our boats sit idle more than they get used. Who among us hasn't opened up the cabin to the dreaded "boat smell"? The key to curing this problem is proper ventilation. Developing airflow through your boat will help dissipate the smell as well as keep the cabin free from mold, mildew, and condensation.

Ventilation can be passive or active. Passive ventilation depends on proper placement of vents and natural airflow resulting from convection and wind. Active ventilation is a fancy term for an electric fan.

Good ventilation means that it is easy for air to get into and out of every part of the boat. Installing a single vent or a series of vents all pointing the same way doesn't necessarily accomplish this. A single intake vent in the bow and an exit vent in the stern may allow air to flow through, but the airflow may bypass compartments such as the head. Additional vents may be needed to ensure

Air is sucked out
this solar vent

Air is sucked in
through this solar vent

Establishing an adequate amount of ventilation airflow is important in keeping a boat sweet smelling.

that enclosed spaces or areas that the main airflow bypasses are not missed.

Nicro Ventilation has an excellent primer on boat ventilation, *Boater's Guide to Cabin Ventilation*, available at www.marinco.com/docs/guides/n_vent_guide.pdf. Although the book features Nicro products, it is nevertheless a good overall reference. It is also available in hardcover at many marine stores.

INSTALLING SOLAR VENTS

Propping a hatch open a crack or leaving a port slightly open will promote circulation but is an invitation to rainwater or, worse, a thief. A better plan is to install solar vents. These have a small electric fan powered by photoelectric cells during the day and by a rechargeable battery at night, providing steady, twenty-four-hour airflow. Although the motor runs constantly, there is a damper that can be pulled down to shut off the airflow when you're aboard and want to limit circulation.

Another appealing feature of solar vents is that they come with two sets of fan blades with opposite pitches, so a vent can be made to draw air in or push it out. Normally, you draw air in at the bow and expel it at the stern. But if your boat is docked so that the prevailing wind is moving from aft to forward, you can easily reverse the direction of the fans to make the most of it.

The most popular solar vents are made by Marinco/Nicro, and you will find them in almost every marine store. They tend to be expensive, so watch for them to go on sale. I would be leery of off-brand knockoffs, as I have heard several reports of short service lives and defects. The Nicro units are available in white plastic and stainless steel, but the two are actually identical except that the stainless version has a thin metal cover installed over the plastic. The advantage of the more expensive stainless unit is that the covered plastic is less subject to deterioration from UV rays.

I installed two Nicro vents on a 20-footer: one in the bow hatch and one in the companionway hatch. These vents are rated as highly water resistant, which means they will keep out the majority of rain and spray. I'm sure a breaking wave would force water through the vent, but I have never encountered any water below in the several years I have had these vents installed. They keep the interior cool, dry, sweet smelling, and mildew-free during hot summer days and through the winter storage period. (Obviously this won't work if your boat is shrink-wrapped or tarped during the winter.)

The best way of developing effective airflow is to mount one unit in the front of the boat and one near the rear of the cabin or cuddy. The mounting locations can be in a hatch or on the deck or cabintop. In the former case, you'll cut through the clear glazing material; in the latter, you'll have to cut through (probably cored) fiberglass laminate.

The hardest part of the installation is cutting the mounting hole. You can cut the hole with a jigsaw, a rotary tool, or a holesaw. If you are going to install several vents, I recommend the holesaw, which is easy to use and more accurate. The instructions give the required hole size, which is typically 3 inches or 4 inches in diameter. Few home improvement stores stock holesaws this big, but they are easy enough to find online.

After choosing the mounting location, tape off the area around where the hole will go. This protects the surface from scratches and provides a surface on which to lay out the precise hole location. Accuracy is important, especially if you are installing the vent in a hatch, because it will be painfully obvious if the vent is installed off-center.

If you are using a holesaw, first drill a pilot hole to locate the drill bit in the center of the holesaw. If you're using a jigsaw, mark the diameter on the tape with a compass, then drill an access hole for the jigsaw blade. Slow and steady is the trick for either saw.

If you are installing the vent in a cored deck or cabintop, refer to Adding Access Hatches in Chapter 2 for the proper procedures for removing core material and screwing into fiberglass. If you are installing the vent into a hatch cover, you will drill fastener holes through the glazing and use short bolts and nuts to through-bolt the unit.

After all the holes are drilled, you can proceed with the installation. The top cover is held onto the base with several very small screws. Remove them and *don't lose them*! The cover will come off, exposing the base and the three mounting holes. You can trim the blue masking tape close around the base of the vent, or remove it altogether if you are careful with the sealant: the base is wide enough that squeeze-out may not be a problem if you work clean. Either way, run a generous bead of sealant around the base and fasten it down with the three screws. You may want to use through-bolts if you are installing the vent in a hatch. Snug the screws down only medium-firm to make sure that a decent amount of sealant stays in place.

All that's left to do now is to reassemble the top onto the base. Make sure the right fan blades are installed for the direction of airflow you want. The fan will be running but isn't powerful enough to hurt your fingers if you inadvertently touch it. If you want to get fancy, you can cut a wood or plastic trim ring to fit around the inside vent opening.

Step #1 for installing a solar vent in a hatch cover is to mask off the installation area, then drill a pilot hole, as shown here, to guide the holesaw.

Step #2 is to cut the hole, done here with a holesaw. I removed the masking tape for this photo so that the sawdust from the balsa core would be more visible. This tells us that we'll have to dig away the exposed core from the hole's perimeter and replace it with thickened epoxy, as described in Chapter 2.

Step #3 is to drill the fastener holes, apply sealant to the solar vent's base, and fasten the base in place.

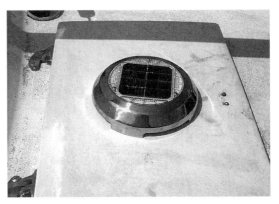

A finished solar vent installation. I actually added two such vents on this boat—one pulling air in and one pushing air out.

The only maintenance item on these fans is the rechargeable battery, and even that is low maintenance. I've had vents in place for years and never had to replace the batteries.

By the way, you can use these same procedures to install passive vents (no fan), but I heartily recommend the powered ones for better ventilation.

RIGGING A HOME AIR CONDITIONER

Marine air-conditioning ranges from simple portable units to complex permanently installed systems, but they all require a large amount of electrical power. That means that you use them only when plugged in at a dock, unless you have a substantial onboard generator.

One of the most popular portable systems is the Dometic Carry-on Portable Air Conditioner. This unit is designed to fit over a deck or cabin hatch and be removed and stored below when under way. The cool air outlet fits into the hatch while the unit itself sits outside. A fabric cover is provided to seal around the unit and keep rainwater out. New units are nominally 7,000 Btu and weigh about 75 pounds. While they are effective at cooling a boat, I can speak from experience

that it takes two people to maneuver one of these below or back on deck.

The price difference between a household air conditioner and a marine unit is eye-opening. Household units are not typically built of corrosion-resistant marine materials, but given the price difference, they can be replaced every couple of years for less than the cost of a marine unit. The other difference is that you will have to rig up a way to mount a household unit so that it can be (tolerably) easy to install and remove. One of the more common and practical mounting locations is the companionway, and our project will address the common tapered companionway opening with dropboards.

Before you begin, however, be aware that it is extremely awkward to get in and out of the cabin by stepping over an air-conditioning unit in this type of installation. Unless you have convenient

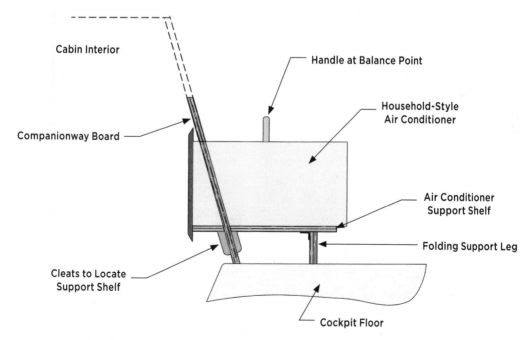

A companionway installation for a portable household-type air conditioner.

egress through a forward hatch, this could present a hazard in case of a fire.

Most dropboards are about ¾ inch thick, so choose an exterior plywood of that thickness for the air conditioner mount. You can get fancy here and use teak- or mahogany-faced plywood, or go with standard fir. Just make sure that it is exterior grade, as it will be exposed to the weather.

The first step involves the air conditioner itself. You will be lifting the unit in and out of the mounting, and most units aren't well equipped for this. Position the unit on a dowel or small piece of wood to find the balance point fore and aft and side to side. Install a handle on top of the unit at this balance point. A standard garage door handle works fine. A handle at the balance point will make the unit easy to pick up without it being heavy on one end or the other. Make sure you know what is underneath the air conditioner case before drilling it to install the handle, as drilling a hole through a cooling line will void your warranty—and it won't do much to improve the unit's efficiency either.

The air conditioner mount will be installed in the lower dropboard. Cut the board to size, with the top and bottom edges sloped to match the angle of the companionway opening. Lay out an opening for the unit, making it about ⅛ inch wider on each side, which will allow the unit to slip easily into place but won't be so wide as to allow lots of cool air to escape. Notice in the accompanying illustration that the top of the lower board has been cut off. Make sure that this board is fairly substantial, as it helps lock the unit in place and prevents it from tipping.

With the top section of the lower board cut away (remember to cut it at the same angle as the top and bottom of the rest of the board), you can cut out the center section. Cut carefully, as this center section becomes the support shelf for the unit.

You now need to find the proper location for the support shelf. It should be far enough inside the cabin so that the top section of the lower board clears the inside flange of the unit, helping to lock it in place. With the proper position determined, you can fasten two locating cleats to the bottom of the support shelf. These should be spaced far enough apart to allow the shelf to slip down over the lower edge of the dropboard and prevent fore-and-aft movement.

A rear leg is needed to hold the weight of the support shelf. If you wish you can hinge this to fold up compactly. When you calculate the height of this leg, remember to allow the air conditioner to slope a few inches to the rear, so that condensate will drip outside the cabin, not in it.

You might want to slip a piece of foam rubber under the unit to reduce vibration and noise. The unit itself can be secured in place with a bungee cord wrapped around the shelf and the unit.

The final step is to apply a finish to the plywood and lumber. I recommend sealing all the voids in the end grain of the plywood with epoxy/filler and giving the plywood several coats of epoxy to seal it well—just don't build up so much thickness that the boards bind in the companionway slots. Finally, apply a couple coats of marine paint if you used fir plywood. If you used a better grade of plywood and are finishing the unit "bright," apply several coats of varnish with UV protection.

CHAPTER 4

Decks

Your boat may or may not have a cabin, but it will certainly have a deck. Projects in this chapter will enhance the safety, utility, comfort, and appearance of that deck. Since our focus in this book is on boats of less than, say, 35 feet, anything we can do to better utilize the limited deck space of a small boat is going to constitute a positive change.

ADDING AN ANCHOR WINDLASS

Recent years have seen great improvements in the quality of electric windlasses, even as their prices have become more affordable. There is no doubt that an electric windlass on the bow of your boat makes life aboard more enjoyable. This is especially true if you are an avid fisherman, frequently lowering and raising your anchor while moving from one fishing spot to another.

When thinking about a windlass installation, first consider your boat. A boat with a substantial foredeck or cuddy cabin is a good bet for an easy installation. The open bow of a walkaround or bowrider configuration presents a more difficult proposition, however.

The first step is to look to the boat's manufacturer, even if you intend to install the windlass yourself. See if a windlass is a prescribed option for your boat. If so, find out how the manufacturer mounts it and which units they use. There's no sense in reinventing the wheel. Failing that, ask owners of boats similar to yours what they have done and how it has worked out.

If you draw blanks, head back to the drawing board for some more research. Windlasses are available in two basic styles, vertical and horizontal. The motor of a vertical windlass mounts belowdecks, while the shaft with the gypsy or rope drum mounted on it extends vertically abovedecks. Horizontal windlasses have their motor on deck, and the motor and gypsy shafts are horizontal.

Vertical windlass motors are more protected from the elements but require substantial space belowdecks. Horizontal windlasses require less space belowdecks but still require belowdeck access for installation of the fastener hardware and wiring. Both types require sufficient space belowdecks for a chain locker to store the anchor rode.

Windlasses can be configured to operate power up/power down (that is, with the motor operating and engaged whether the anchor is

The abovedeck portion of a vertical-axis windlass. The motor is mounted belowdecks, where it is protected from the weather and salt water. This gypsy will handle both chain (in the perimeter chain teeth visible in the photo) and rope (in the gypsy's narrow central groove, as shown). To use a chain-rope gypsy like this, you must splice your rope rode to the chain leader, as shown in the photo. You can easily see that a thimbled eye splice shackled to the chain would not work with this gypsy. (Courtesy Maxwell)

A horizontal windlass has its motor abovedecks, requiring less space below. This Quick Mini Genius is designed for boats up to 23 feet long and achieves a maximum pull of 1,210 pounds. The gypsy will handle both chain and rope. (Courtesy Quick Nautical Equipment)

being hoisted or lowered) or power up/free fall down. Free fall windlasses typically deploy the anchor rode quicker than power up/power down windlasses.

Manufacturers' literature and marine catalogs and websites give general rules about sizing a windlass to your boat. If your boat is on the borderline between two units, always choose the larger of the two. I've never heard anyone complain that their windlass had too much power.

Electric windlasses are DC power hogs, and providing that power is a major consideration. You can run cables from your existing batteries to the bow, but such a long wire run will require very heavy and expensive cables to avoid excessive voltage drop and provide the needed power. Another option is to install a dedicated windlass battery near the bow and run much shorter cables to the windlass motor. You will still need to run smaller wires from the dedicated battery back to the battery charger, however, or else provide alternate battery-charging options. You will also need to provide proper overcurrent protection in the form of fuses or circuit breakers. The proper sizing of the wiring will depend on the size of the unit chosen and will be spelled out in the installation manual for the windlass. See also Chapter 7 for wire-size guidance and wiring installation advice.

Controls for the windlass can take the form of a deck-mounted foot switch or remotely mounted control switches acting through a relay. The relay option allows multiple locations for windlass activation, so you can have a switch at the helm as well as on the foredeck.

Unless specifically designed for a windlass installation, most deck areas are not built strongly enough. This is especially true in the case of cored

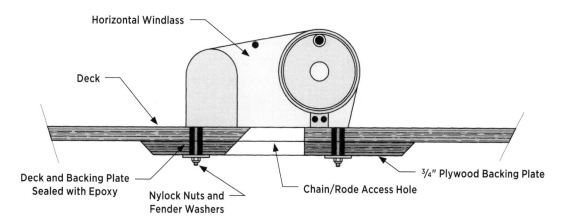

A horizontal-axis windlass mounting.

decks. Simply bolting the windlass to the deck will cause the deck to flex and ultimately fail. A backing plate under the deck is needed to spread the windlass load over a wider area. These are commonly made from aluminum or stainless steel plates or marine plywood.

Windlass installation manuals provide layout templates showing exactly where to cut mounting holes and drill for fasteners. The vast majority of decks are cored, so to prevent water intrusion and the inevitable deck rot that will follow, remove the core for an inch or more beyond the edges of the

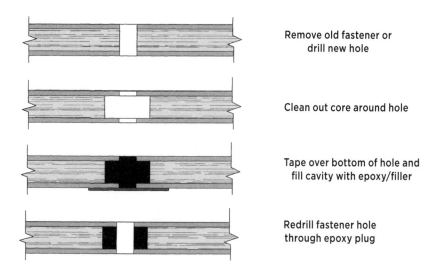

Sealing fastener holes through a cored deck with epoxy/filler. This technique is central when installing hatches, portlights, and deck hardware, and is referenced in several places in this book.

opening and fill the cavity with thickened epoxy, as described in Chapter 2 and also in the sidebar Strategies for Sealing Deck Hardware, later in this chapter.

Bolt the windlass in place using liberal amounts of sealant under the abovedeck portion and between the backing plate and the underside of the deck. Do not use polyurethane sealants such as 3M 5200, as they adhere too powerfully and are nearly impossible to remove. Since you may need to remove the windlass someday for servicing, use a good but removable sealant such as 3M 101.

Once the sealant has cured, you can further tighten the nuts from below as long as someone holds the bolt heads from above with a wrench to prevent them from turning (which would break the seal).

ANCHOR DOOHICKEY

A friend approached me recently with a problem. He had installed a new windlass and a bow roller, mainly in order to be able to deploy his anchor without having to go forward. The problem was that when the anchor was pulled up securely in the bow roller, the shank would drop down slightly past the horizontal, altering the anchor's balance point. The result was that when he attempted to deploy the anchor, he had to go forward and manually raise the shank beyond the horizontal before the anchor would drop overboard. Nothing gained!

We looked at several anchor locks and anchor guides, but nothing really fit the bill. We then started sketching out possible solutions. Our first and best idea was to mount a block of wood of an appropriate height to raise the shank of the anchor enough to self-launch. A half-oval stainless steel rubstrake screwed to the top of the wood block would protect the wood from wear.

As something of a traditionalist, however, I dislike adding wood to a boat's exterior. You either have to varnish and protect it religiously, or you let it go until it becomes unsightly and possibly unsound. My preferred exterior material is StarBoard plastic "lumber," which is tough, doesn't absorb water, doesn't need finish-

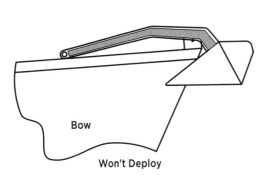

Bow

Won't Deploy

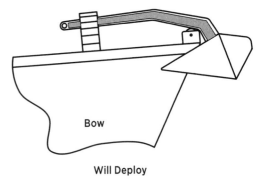

Bow

Will Deploy

The anchor on this boat wouldn't self-deploy from its bow roller (left), forcing the operator to go forward and lift the shank beyond the horizontal. What was needed was a simple foredeck installation (right) to keep the shank above the balance point.

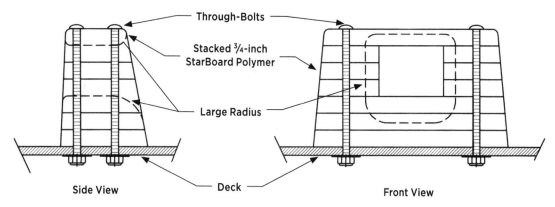

Through-Bolts

Stacked ¾-inch
StarBoard Polymer

Large Radius

Side View   Deck   Front View

The solution was to build an anchor "doohickey" from layers of StarBoard imitation lumber that would raise the anchor shank high enough to self-deploy. While we were at it, we added a central chain passage.

ing, and can be worked with ordinary woodworking tools. Based on the use of StarBoard, I sketched out the design shown in the accompanying illustration.

Several layers of ¾-inch StarBoard gave us a high enough buildup to elevate the anchor stock to the right angle. We then added several more layers of StarBoard to form towers on either side of a central chain passage. If you make the towers high enough to clear the top of the anchor stock, you can also add a bridge across the top of the mount to restrain the anchor in rough weather.

Two bolts through each side will hold everything in place. Don't be tempted to use only one bolt per side, as Starboard is slippery stuff, and the tower pieces will rotate out of place. Also, forget about gluing the layers together: you can't glue StarBoard.

Once the pieces are temporarily bolted together, all the edges can be rounded over. You can get fancy and cut the bottom layers wider than the subsequent layers to give the whole assembly a sleek, tapered look. You can sand it to

final shape with a belt or orbital sander. Start with coarse grit until you get the right taper, then sand with progressively finer grit until smooth. The chain passage edges should be given a generous radius so the chain, swivel, and anchor stock can pass through without snagging.

The unit can then be bolted to the deck, making sure the holes through the deck are properly sealed and that plenty of sealant is used under the anchor mount.

ADDING CLEATS

I admit to being a sailor as well as a powerboater, and of course there is a certain amount of overlap between the two activities, even if the participants themselves don't often mix. Chief among those similarities is that builders of sailboats and builders of powerboats always seem to skimp on deck hardware.

I didn't realize how inadequate the cleats on my 20-foot sailboat were until I got it off the trailer and started keeping it at a dock and anchoring out more. Actually I should say *cleat*, because other than the ones for the jibsheets, there was just one tiny cleat on the foredeck. When I pulled into my assigned slip the first time, I had to use the stern pulpit as a tie-off point, so it was clear that I had to do something.

More cleats, and bigger ones, are usually better, but before we begin adding them willy-nilly, let's look at a typical docking arrangement. If you are tied alongside a dock or pier, you need several mooring lines to be secure. You need a bow line and a stern line, of course, to keep the boat parallel to the dock and prevent it from being blown away. You also need spring lines—one leading forward (the *forward spring*) and one leading aft (the *after spring*) from a midships cleat—to prevent the boat from being blown forward or back relative to the

pier. And if you tie up between pilings in a slip with your bow or stern to the dock, you'll need to repeat the entire array (bow line, stern line, and two springs) on both sides of the boat. Finally, you'll also need adequate tie-off points from which to hang fenders. With all this in mind, you can decide how many cleats you need, and where.

Back to the original problem, my poorly equipped 20-footer. The cleat on the foredeck was so small that it wouldn't even accommodate the bow line, so the first step was to replace the cleat with a decent one.

I chose a large anodized aluminum "four-hole, open-base" cleat, so called because it has four $5/16$-inch mounting holes and an opening between the mounting legs. You can pass the eye of a dockline through this handy opening, then flip it over the horns of the cleat, making a secure

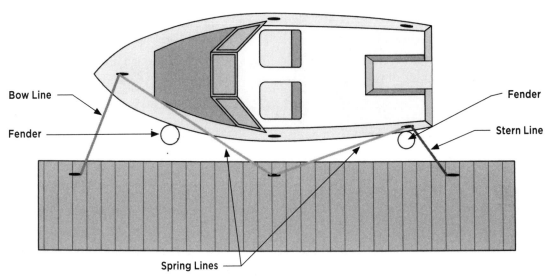

Bow, stern, and spring lines are used to keep a boat properly positioned in a slip or at a dock. Here the springs lead forward and aft from a midships cleat on the dock. Alternatively, if you have a midships cleat on your boat, you can lead the springs forward and aft from there—a convenient and effective arrangement. Some boats, however, simply don't provide a good mounting location for a midships cleat.

This anodized aluminum open-base cleat replaced the too-small cleat on the bow of my 20-footer.

mooring attachment. I made the cleat large enough to hold several docklines.

Luckily, the fasteners of the existing cleat were accessible from underneath in a small forepeak area. The original cleat was simply bolted through the fiberglass deck with no reinforcement. I removed it and filled the mounting holes with epoxy/filler, as the new cleat didn't come close to matching the existing cleat mounting holes.

Considering the force that can be exerted on a mooring cleat, I knew I had to provide additional support for the larger new cleat. An additional complication was the camber, or crown, in the deck where the cleat would go. Reinforcement can take the form of aluminum or plywood backing

plates or additional thicknesses of fiberglass. I chose to use three layers of waterproof ¼-inch birch aircraft plywood, which is available at many hobby shops. I made the first (top) layer the largest, the second layer somewhat smaller, and the last smaller still. By laminating three thin layers of plywood in place, as opposed to using a single layer of ¾-inch plywood, I would be able to make a rigid, strong backing plate that conformed perfectly to the curved underside of the deck.

I laid out and drilled the new mounting holes through the deck and the three pieces of plywood. I buttered up the plywood pieces with epoxy/filler, coated the bolts with grease so the epoxy wouldn't bond to them, and temporarily bolted everything in place. Once the epoxy had cured and the new backing plate was securely in place, I removed the bolts and cleaned up the holes by drilling them slightly oversize. Several coats of epoxy on the birch plywood and inside the holes protected the deck and plywood from water intrusion.

If the deck had been cored, I would have had to drill the holes oversize, then fill them with epoxy/filler as described in previous projects. After the epoxy cured, I then would have redrilled the mounting holes through the solid epoxy. The epoxy seals the core from any water intrusion.

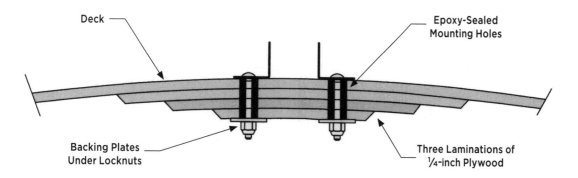

A curved backing plate made from three laminations of thin plywood epoxied together.

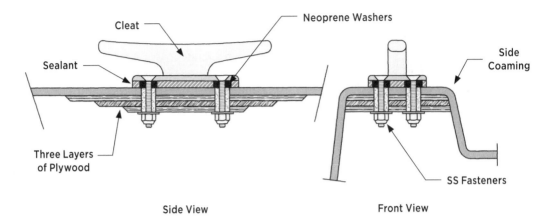

Side and front views of a stern cleat mounted on a molded, uncored fiberglass coaming.

With everything sealed, I reinstalled the cleat using 5/16-inch stainless steel oval-head machine screws, with stainless steel fender washers and locknuts on the underside and a neoprene washer and plenty of sealant between the cleat and the deck. Initially I tightened the nuts just beyond finger tight; then, after the sealant had cured, I retightened the nuts, compressing the sealant to form a better seal. Make sure someone holds the fastener from above while you tighten the nut from below. If you let the fastener turn, it will break the sealant bond around the fastener and provide a convenient path for a leak.

The cockpit was utterly devoid of cleats for docking or anchoring lines, and I was afraid that any storm or even a large boat wake might tear the stern pulpit loose. I decided to add cleats on the port and starboard cockpit coamings. Luckily again, I was able to access these areas from inside the boat. On some boats, you may have to go through stern lockers to get to the underside of a new cleat location.

The installation process was exactly the same as for the new bow cleat. The stern cleats were a little smaller than the bow cleat, since there was less room on the cockpit coaming, but they were still large enough to tie off two docklines on each.

ANCHOR RODE STORAGE

Where do you stow your anchor and rode? Is it thrown in a locker or tangled underfoot? Here's a simple, effective anchor organizer you can build easily and cheaply from items available at your local discount store. It's made from a tough rubber or plastic tub and a plastic wastebasket, and it will keep your anchor line untangled and ready to deploy.

The wastebasket will be mounted upside down in the center of the tub. The anchor line coils around the wastebasket, keeping the line tidy and ready to go.

The first step is to find the appropriate size tub and wastebasket. The channel formed around the outside of the wastebasket and inside the tub needs to be large enough to hold your anchor line and chain (if any). Invert the wastebasket inside

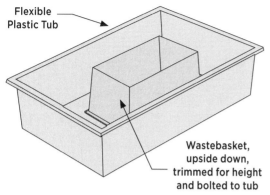

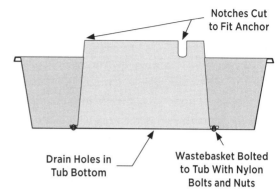

An anchor rode container made from common household items.

Here the basket in an anchor rode container is notched to receive a Danforth-type anchor.

the tub. Drill six to eight holes through the flange of the wastebasket and bottom of the tub.

With the wastebasket in place, trace a line around the basket at the height of the tub rim. Just lay a straightedge across the rim and mark the basket with a grease pencil.

Now it's time for a design decision. You could cut the basket off along this line, so that the sawed-off basket is the same height as the tub that surrounds it. This works well if you have some other place to properly store your anchor. A second option is to cut about an inch or two above this line. You can then cut notches in the new edge to locate your anchor. This works well if you have a Danforth-type anchor.

If you choose the latter option, drill several holes in the rim of the tub so you can hold the anchor in place with a couple of bungee cords.

Final assembly is simple. Bolt the wastebasket in place using nylon nuts and bolts (to keep from scratching your deck or gelcoat). It's also a good idea to drill several holes in the bottom of the tub. This will allow any water that collects to drain out. In fact, I've cleaned my anchor line by just

putting the anchor organizer on the dock, hosing it down, and letting it drain dry.

You might also want to drill a hole in the side of the tub through which to pass the bitter end of your anchor line. That way you can tie it off before you start paying out the line (don't ask why I think that's important). I store my anchor on the bow rail of my 20-footer with brackets (available at any marine store) and the anchor organizer in a locker. Since the center of the organizer (the cut-off wastebasket) is open, I store a lightweight lunch hook and its rode in there.

This anchor rode container has been in use aboard my 20-footer for years and shows no wear.

LINE ORGANIZER

Now that we've solved the problem of organizing our anchor rode, let's move on to organizing other lines. Most of us have a collection of lines aboard—docklines, small stuff, miscellaneous lines, and short lengths that are just too good to throw out. Often they're all simply thrown in a locker or tangled underfoot.

A plastic wastebasket again comes to the rescue. These can be found at just about any discount store, but get the strongest, most flexible ones you can find and make sure you have an appropriate place on board to stow them. It won't do any good if your line organizers are constantly tipping over.

The other materials needed are a length of teak batten stock and some stainless steel machine screws, washers, and acorn nuts. (I recommend teak because it doesn't rot when wet.) Cut lengths of the batten stock long enough to extend 8 to 10 inches above the rim of the basket and about 10 inches below, say 18 to 20 inches long.

Bolt two battens on the wide front face of the basket, two on the back face, and one batten on each of the two narrow sides. All battens are inside the basket. Put the round heads of the machine screws inside so the lines won't snag, and acorn nuts on the outside to avoid sharp bolt ends. Drill several drain holes in the bottom of the basket.

To use, just coil your line and drop it over a batten with the coil inside the basket. Several lines can be stored on each batten, and wet lines can drain and dry. Wedge the basket in place or secure it with a bungee cord. You can also use a five-gallon bucket if it fits your available space better. Make several of these line organizers: they are simple and cheap!

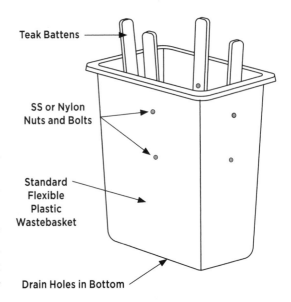

Teak Battens

SS or Nylon
Nuts and Bolts

Standard
Flexible
Plastic
Wastebasket

Drain Holes in Bottom

An effective line organizer can be made from a wastepaper basket and wood battens.

ANCHOR MOUNTS

Small boats frequently have problems with weight distribution. The smaller the boat, the greater will be the effect of shifting a few pounds aft. Closed-bow runabouts especially have this problem; when there's a crowd in the cockpit, the boat often runs bow-high.

You may not be able to put your guests on a diet, but you can try to shift some of the more inert gear forward to even out the load. Ground tackle is a prime candidate for weight redistribution if you store an anchor and chain in a cockpit locker aft.

Several solutions exist. The simplest is to attach a length of PVC pipe to a bow pulpit stanchion with stainless steel hose clamps. Then slide the anchor shank with rode attached into the PVC pipe, with the flukes hanging out of the top

A Danforth anchor mounted on a bow pulpit.

The flat flukes (sometimes called mud palms) of a Danforth and other so-called plate anchors provide maximum holding power with minimum weight, making them the most popular anchor style for small boats. But those sharp fluke points are painful when bumped, and the ideal stowage arrangement will take this into account. On this boat I mounted a stanchion bracket to capture the crown of the Danforth, then I bungeed the shank to the top of the stanchion. The chain leader runs aft to the locker where I stow my rope rode, making it convenient to anchor when I'm singlehanding.

of the pipe. To deploy the anchor, you simply lift it out of the tube and throw it over the side. You did tie the bitter end of the anchor rode to the boat, didn't you?

Alternatively, you can buy a rail-mounted bracket that fits most Danforth-style anchors and holds the anchor by its flukes. This bracket is available in horizontal (for pulpit railing) or vertical (for pulpit stanchion) models. Your choice will depend in part on which provides a more convenient way to secure the anchor shank.

The best solution for one of my small boats was to mount a bracket on a bow-pulpit stanchion and bungee the anchor shank to the top of the stanchion. The chain falls along the toe rail, and when preparing to anchor I lead it from there to the stern, where I usually stow the anchor rode.

There is a small forward compartment in that boat that could loosely be defined as an anchor locker, but there are good reasons not to use it as such. First, there is no opening to the deck above

for the anchor line and chain to pass through, and if there were, chances are it would leak—and there is no provision to drain water from the compartment overboard. Second, the compartment is directly in front of the V-berth, and an anchor rode and chain stowed there wet would soon smell. I don't want odors like that in my V-berth. So I keep the rope portion of the anchor rode stored in a stern locker and attach it to my anchor chain when I intend to anchor out.

ADDING ROD HOLDERS

Every angler knows the benefits of rod holders, and virtually every boat designed and sold as a fishing boat is amply equipped with them. But many owners of family runabouts like to do some occasional fishing, and adding rod holders can be a worthwhile project to improve the "fishability" of a runabout, deck boat, or other general-purpose craft.

Bracket-type rod holders that stick up several inches on top of a gunwale can be problematic: they can snag lines or boarding passengers and get broken easily. Flush-mounted holders are much to be preferred in many cases. These consist of a flange that sits on top of a gunwale or deck with (usually) three mounting holes, and penetrating the flange at roughly a 30-degree angle is the rod holder tube. You can mount the unit so that the tube angles straight aft as it rises—for simple rod storage when under way—or so that it angles somewhat outboard as well as aft, for more effective trolling.

Although everything is stronger when through-bolted, this may not be feasible if the boat has a full molded liner that prevents access to the underside of the deck or gunwale. When this is the case, it's still possible to make a secure installation by screwing the hardware into the fiberglass deck, as long as you pay attention to certain details.

As usual, the first job is to determine where you want to mount the item, and whether there is clearance for the part that will extend below the surface. (See Adding Access Hatches in Chapter 2 for tips on finding out what lurks in hidden spaces.) Remember to account for and allow clearance for the angle of the rod holder tube, since it doesn't extend straight down.

To cut the hole for the main tube, I prefer a holesaw with a center drill to control any tendency to wander and scratch the surrounding fiberglass. *Use the right size holesaw*, one that makes a hole just big enough for the tube to slip through, even if you have to go out and buy one. Too big a hole reduces the strength of the fiberglass around the mounting holes.

A second choice to cut the hole is a jigsaw with a carbide blade. Tape the area around the hole and draw the outline of the hole on the tape. The tape will keep the bottom of the saw from scratching the surrounding fiberglass. Again, cut as small a hole as possible.

You may have to use a half-round file on the inside of one side of the hole to accommodate the slant of the tube. If so, file away just enough to get a good fit.

Examine the edges of the hole you have just cut, and if you find exposed core material, refer to Adding Access Hatches in Chapter 2 for the measures you must take to seal the hole against water intrusion and provide solid epoxy into which you will drive the mounting screws.

Use stainless steel self-tapping screws for this purpose. First you must drill a pilot hole of the proper size. What is the proper size? I wish there was a clearance chart to tell you, but different fiberglass layups react differently, so you have to figure it out. If the pilot hole is too big, the screw may pull out under even a slight load. The pilot hole should be as small as possible without causing the fiberglass to crack when you install the screw. Start with a bit that's about the same diameter as the shaft of the screw (inside the threads), and drill a test hole in the piece you just cut out. Then drive in a screw and see how it goes.

Okay, all the holes are cut and all the pilot holes drilled. What next? Plenty of blue masking

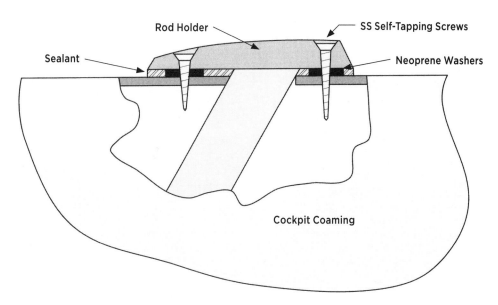

A flush-mounted rod holder installation with recessed tube.

tape. Tape the area around the hole for several inches. It may seem like a waste of tape, but you will appreciate it when cleaning up. Position the hardware and trace around it, then remove it and cut away the tape inside the circle you just traced. Tape the edges of the mounting flange.

Go to your local home improvement store and purchase some neoprene or rubber washers. They should be ⅟₁₆ to ⅛ inch thick and fit over the fasteners you are using. Place the screws through the mounting holes in the rod holder and put the neoprene washers onto the screws. Trim the washers with scissors if they extend beyond the edge of the flange.

Apply a generous amount of sealant to the bottom of the rod holder and fasten it in place—snugly, but not with enough torque to squeeze out too much sealant. (As discussed in Chapter 2 and in previous projects, the purpose of the neoprene washers is to help keep this from happening.) Don't skimp on the sealant—you want this job to

last for years. If you've used enough sealant, some will squeeze out all around.

If you used enough blue tape around the rod holder, cleanup will be simple. Use tongue depressors with the ends cut off square to clean up excess sealant. Then peel the tape away and you are done. Let the sealant cure fully (read the package) before applying any load.

BOARDING LADDERS

While many of us have ladders installed on our boats, I'll bet a goodly number of us haven't actually tried them to determine how well they work.

Boarding a boat from the water, especially after a swim when you're tired, isn't easy. "Soft" ladders made from rope or webbing have a tendency to fold back under the boat, leaving you looking at the sky with no easy way to board.

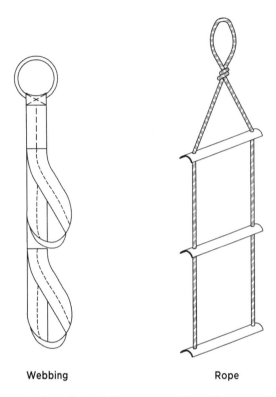

Webbing   Rope

"Soft" ladders can be made from flat webbing or round line. These can be hard to use, however.

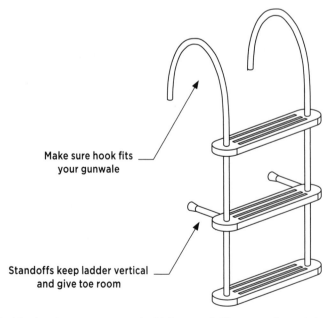

Make sure hook fits
your gunwale

Standoffs keep ladder vertical
and give toe room

A "J" ladder hooks over a gunwale. Make sure it fits properly and doesn't slip off under use.

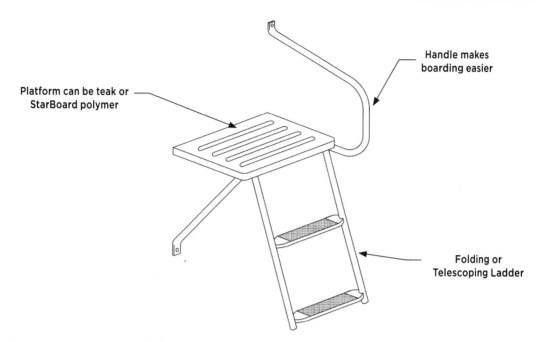

Handle makes
boarding easier

Platform can be teak or
StarBoard polymer

Folding or
Telescoping Ladder

A transom-mounted swim platform combined with a folding or telescoping ladder provides user-friendly boarding. Such units are available in teak or polymer plastic (for example, StarBoard).

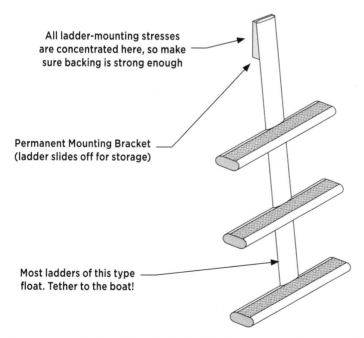

All ladder-mounting stresses
are concentrated here, so make
sure backing is strong enough

Permanent Mounting Bracket
(ladder slides off for storage)

Most ladders of this type
float. Tether to the boat!

Sport ladders are rigid ladders that attach to the transom. They were developed so divers could get their swim fins on the rungs. Make sure your choice will float!

Some lightweight aluminum ladders also fold up under pressure or pop off the gunwale when most needed. I use two main criteria for judging the usefulness of a ladder:

- It must extend far enough below the water to allow you to comfortably get a foot on the lowest rung. Many ladders don't go far enough, making it difficult to leverage yourself up and out of the water.
- It must remain vertical when under load. Being on your back with your feet and the ladder extending under the boat is not a practical way of boarding.

Most permanent ladders bolt onto a transom swim platform. One style, called a sport or diver's ladder, has a large-diameter central tube with steps or rungs welded to each side. These are much easier for divers wearing swim fins to mount. They lock into a bracket bolted to the side or transom of the boat and are rigid and strong. You will need to ensure the mounting area on your boat has adequate strength, as these ladders concentrate a large amount of stress in a small mounting footprint. Instead of folding, they are removed from the bracket for stowage.

Before mounting a ladder to a transom, make sure the structure will support the load. Transoms on outboard boats are usually strong enough, being reinforced with more than an inch of plywood. Other transoms, however, may need reinforcing with plywood, StarBoard, or metal backing plates. Make sure to reinforce the area where the standoffs contact the hull, and use stainless hardware of sufficient size to resist the tremendous loads that the swim platform will have to bear.

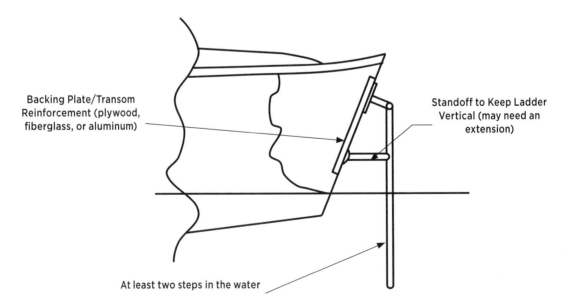

Backing Plate/Transom Reinforcement (plywood, fiberglass, or aluminum)

Standoff to Keep Ladder Vertical (may need an extension)

At least two steps in the water

In some cases, the transom will need to be reinforced with a backing plate inside the boat. If ladder standoffs are used, make sure that section of the transom is also reinforced.

QUICK RELEASE FOR A BOARDING LADDER

Another important consideration is how to deploy a hinged ladder from the water. You may have the best ladder in the world, but if you fall overboard and can't get the ladder down, you're still in trouble.

One of my boats sports a quick-release mechanism made from two rail clamps, a hitch pin, and a couple of feet of light line. The ladder is held up against the stern pulpit with a hitch pin passed through a rail clamp on either side of the ladder rung. The line is tied to the loop of the hitch pin and the base of the stern pulpit and hangs down almost to water level. A quick jerk on the line pulls the hitch pin free from the rail clamps and allows the ladder to drop. Just make sure you're clear of the ladder when you deploy it, or it'll knock you a good one!

This boarding ladder quick-release setup was made from two Helms Products rail clamps, a hitch pin, and a short length of line. The line is long enough to reach the water so it can be deployed from the water.

PAIN-FREE LADDER RUNGS

Nothing hurts worse than trying to stand on a round steel-tube ladder rung with bare feet. The solution to this problem is to add flat treads to the round rungs. In times past, several manufacturers offered teak or StarBoard treads and the hardware to easily mount them to round rungs. Alas, all but one of these suppliers seems to have dropped these products from their lines.

The one remaining manufacturer, C. Sherman Johnson Co., supplies only a half step that is just 5 inches long. It recommends bolting the steps to alternating rung ends—that is, the lowest one on the right-hand end of its rung, the next one up on the left-hand end of its rung, and so on, alternating from side to side for your convenience as you climb.

The good news is that it is simple to make your own treads from teak or StarBoard. I have teak steps on one of my boats but would recommend using StarBoard for a maintenance-free ladder. The teak treads require regular cleaning to keep them looking their best.

You can make either one from ¾-inch stock. After cutting the stock into 3½-inch-wide strips, you will need to cut them to length. For added security and less stress on the mounting bolts, I cut the treads long enough to notch into the side tubes on the ladder.

One method of cutting those half-round notches is to lay out several treads on the same strip. Make the length of each tread equal to the distance between the ladder's side tubes plus twice the radius of the side tubes. For 1-inch-diameter side tubes that are 13 inches apart, make the treads 14 inches long. Cut a 1-inch hole centered at the midpoint of each line separating adjacent

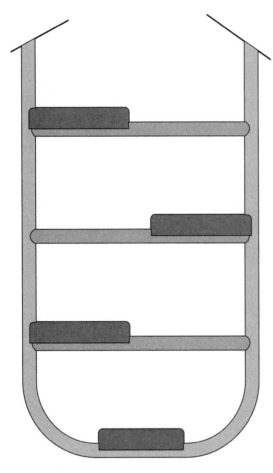

Treads alternate side to side

The C. Sherman Johnson Company makes ABS plastic treads for attaching to ladders with round rungs. The half steps, called Sole Mate Ladder Treads, require no cutting or modification to the ladder.

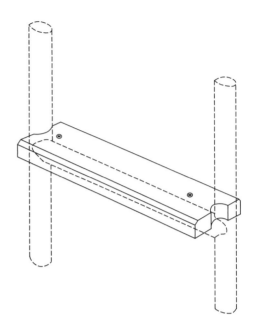

You can make your own full-width steps from teak or StarBoard.

treads in the layout, then cut out the treads. In each tread end you should have a smoothly radiused half-round notch that will fit over the side tube. If you measured right, the tread should fit tightly between the vertical tubes, which lock the tread in place and prevent it from trying to rotate around its rung.

If you have access to a heavy-duty ½-inch shank router and a 1-inch ball router bit, you can rout a slightly rounded groove on the bottom of the tread to fit around the ladder rung. Don't go any deeper than ¼ inch, however, or you'll weaken the tread.

To finish off the tread, chamfer the edges and round the corners to prevent scrapes. Cut three or four shallow grooves on the top surface to provide a little extra traction.

The tread can then be fastened to the ladder rung. I drill through both the tread and the rung, and then use a countersunk-head machine screw with a cap nut on the bottom side. I like cap nuts, as they present a smooth surface with no sharp edges to scratch or cut feet.

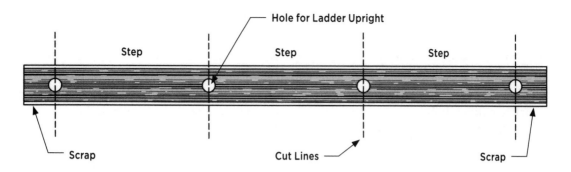

Drill holes, chamfer edges, and cut grooves before cutting steps apart

It's quicker and easier to make several treads at once from a single long piece of stock.

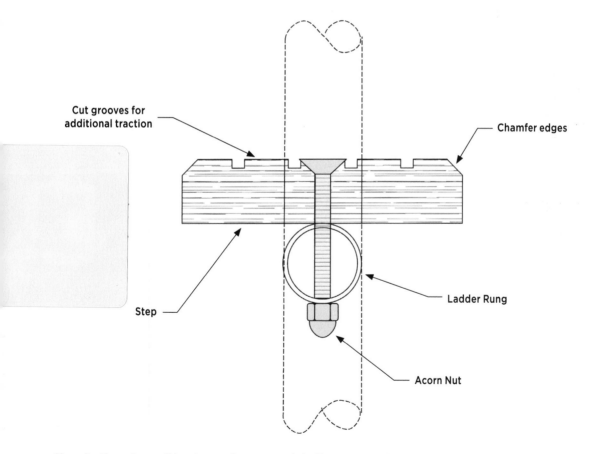

Chamfer the edges of the step and cut several shallow grooves for added traction. The steps are then bolted to the ladder rungs with acorn nuts on the lower side.

FIXING DECK DINGS

When you run into a dock with your bow rail, two types of damage are likely. If the rail itself is damaged, this will be only too obvious. Refer to Repairing Railings, Pulpits, and Pushpits later in this chapter. But take a close look as well at the deck around the stanchion bases—there's a good chance that you'll see damage to the fiberglass, perhaps in the form of a crescent-shaped indentation with one or more cracks radiating from it. With luck, you might be able to fix this without having to repaint the deck.

An indentation in the deck is a strong indication that the deck is cored. It's also not unlikely that the core was already damaged, quite possibly punky from water leaking into it through fastener holes for deck fittings, including the stanchion bases themselves.

The first order of business is to determine if the core is sound, and the only reliable way to do this is to drill into the core and look at it. A 1-inch-

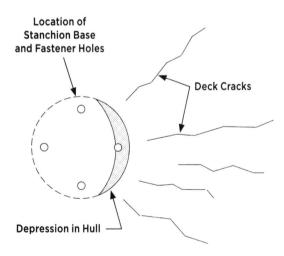

The damage that often results from the chance encounter of a bow pulpit with a dock.

Labels in figure:
Location of Stanchion Base and Fastener Holes
Deck Cracks
Depression in Hull

diameter holesaw can be used to drill through the top fiberglass skin and into the core. Make sure you don't go through the bottom skin. The hole should be centered under the stanchion base (which you will have removed) to hide it from view when the repair is finished. With a screwdriver, pop out the center plug left by the holesaw. Examine the sawdust (if the core is balsa or plywood), the center plug, and the sides of the hole; the core should be sound and dry and the top skin of fiberglass firmly bonded to the core. If the core material is wet, rotted, or delaminated, proceed to Repairing Cored Decks later in this chapter.

The second task is to determine how badly the deck itself is damaged. Look for broken fibers in the cracks. Look on the underside of the deck to see if there are any signs of cracks or bulges directly beneath the stanchion base. Any of these might indicate further damage to the deck, damage that would involve repairs that are more extensive. Oftentimes, visible cracks may be cosmetic stress cracks in the gelcoat only, resulting from the flexing of the deck.

Let's proceed on the assumption that you were doubly lucky—that you've found no damage to the underside of the deck, and that the core is still dry.

The core underneath the railing base needs to be removed. This should be done through the 1-inch-diameter hole you cut earlier. Use any tools that will get through the hole and clear away the core. Dremel tools, drywall saws, a bent wire—whatever works. Vacuum out all the debris as you go along.

Try to clear out the core from at least part of the area where the cracks in the deck skin appear. This is the first step in strengthening the weakened area and helping to support additional repairs in the deck skin above.

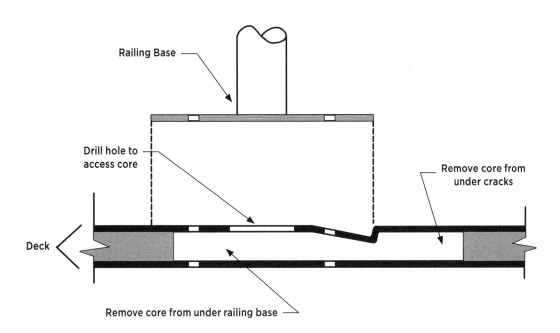

Railing Base

Drill hole to
access core

Remove core from
under cracks

Deck

Remove core from under railing base

The crushed core should be cleaned out so that the void can be filled with epoxy/filler for crush resistance.

With the core cavity cleaned out, make sure it is dry inside. A little acetone can be used to finish cleaning out the cavity. If the pilot bit for your holesaw penetrated the inner skin, tape off that hole (plus any other holes you see) underneath the deck. Be very careful to fully seal any openings; otherwise you may have epoxy-cicles hanging down from your overhead.

The next step is to apply a coating of unfilled epoxy to the sides of the cavity. This is to prevent the dry core from sucking the epoxy out of the epoxy/filler mixture you're going to apply next.

After the sealing coat of epoxy has begun to cure, mix up another batch of epoxy with a high-density filler. Use epoxy syringes or even a plastic cake-decorating bag to force the filler into the cavity. You want to fill the cavity, leaving no bubbles or voids.

Once the epoxy has cured, we can move on to the repair of the deck surface. There are two areas needing repair, the crescent-shaped indentation in the deck and the cracks radiating from it. The crescent-shaped depression can be filled using a marine polyester filler, which is easier to sand than filled epoxy. Available in marine stores, marine polyester filler is a lot like autobody putty (such as Bondo) but is made with materials compatible with the marine environment. It can then be sanded smooth and covered with gelcoat.

The cracks might be simple stress cracks in the gelcoat, or they might indicate fractures in the underlying fiberglass laminate. Some exploratory surgery should tell you. To repair a cosmetic stress crack, widen it to a shallow V to provide more bonding area for the gelcoat repair material you will use. (This material too is available from

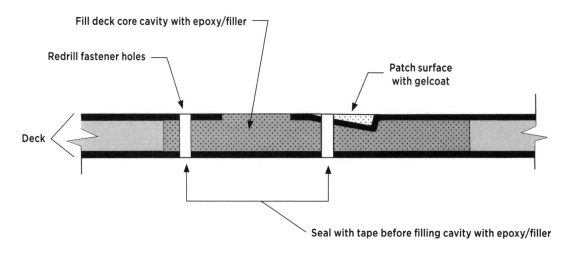

The void is primed with epoxy and then filled with epoxy that has been thickened with high-density filler. Make sure to eliminate any air spaces when filling.

marine stores.) A good tool for this is a sharpened "church key," the old-fashioned bottle or beer can opener.

Follow the gelcoat putty application directions carefully; some require a covering of plastic wrap or polyvinyl alcohol (PVA) to cure properly. The cured gelcoat can then be sanded and polished.

If a crack is structural, the laminate should be reinforced. Sand the crack to create a shallow V-shaped cross section, the vertex of which will probably be in the core material, sloping up from there through the top skin and the gelcoat with approximately a 12 to 1 slope. Thus, a ⅛-inch-deep crack will need a 1½-inch-wide slope on either side of its center, for a total sanded width of 3 inches. Use 80-grit sandpaper to give the surface some "tooth" for the repair to grip. Build up this depression with small pieces of glass mat or cloth wetted with polyester resin. I recommend polyester rather than epoxy resin here because gelcoat, which is a polyester material, does not stick well to epoxy. Once the repair has hardened,

sand and fill with marine polyester filler as necessary to fair it.

Finally, apply gelcoat resin over the area. (Refer to Repairing Molded Nonskid later in this chapter.) When this has cured, sand and polish the repaired area to bring out the shine.

The railing base can now be repositioned and the mounting holes redrilled. The new holes will be going through solid epoxy/filler and should be considerably stronger than the original installation.

Be sure to follow good rebedding practices: tape off the deck and base, use plenty of sealant, and don't overtighten the fasteners and squeeze out all the sealant. You can come back after the sealant has cured and retighten the nuts from below. Don't turn the screws or bolts from the topside, however, as this will break the sealant bond around the fasteners and lead to further leaks.

With any luck, the repaired area won't be noticeable and will certainly be better than the original. Now just don't hit the other side!

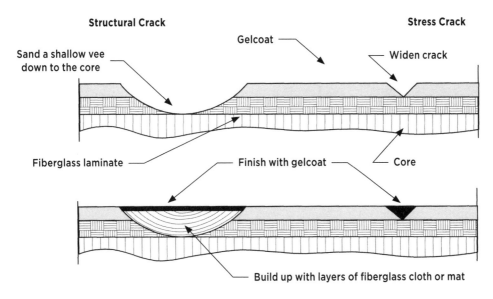

Structural Crack

Stress Crack

Gelcoat

Sand a shallow vee
down to the core

Widen crack

Fiberglass laminate

Finish with gelcoat

Core

Build up with layers of fiberglass cloth or mat

Cracks will need to be widened or ground out to effect a long-lasting repair.

Strategies for Sealing Deck Hardware

You may not think you need a "strategy" for sealing decks—perhaps you're confident your deck isn't leaking. Well, you may be right, but your deck may well be leaking below your feet without your knowledge. Deck leaks can be insidious, going on for years before manifesting themselves in drips from the overhead and a damp interior.

Most decks are cored, with upper and lower fiberglass skins bonded over a core material of plywood squares, end-grain balsa, paper or plastic honeycomb, or one of several types of plastic foam. This "sandwich" is stronger and stiffer than the equivalent weight of solid fiberglass. The voids between adjacent pieces of core are supposed to be filled with resin, but this doesn't always happen.

When the lamination is complete, the boatbuilder starts installing hardware, ports, and hatches in the cored deck by cutting out the open-ings or drilling mounting holes. Then the hardware is installed using a marine sealant to guard against leaks.

Very likely all will be well for several years. Then the sealant begins to break down and allows water to start seeping into that inner core. There, it can start rotting plywood or balsa or break the bonds between the fiberglass skins and the core material. Finally, when the core is saturated, water may start dripping below through the mounting holes.

Given the high labor cost of repairs, nothing lowers the resale value of a boat quicker than a spongy, wet deck. Hence, the need for strategies for sealing deck hardware.

The first step in sealing a deck is to deal with that core material. If your deck core is dry, you can proceed directly to sealing the core. If it is wood of some type and is wet, however, you will need to

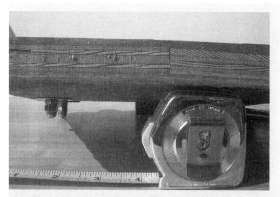

This is an actual piece cut from a cored deck. The ⅜-inch-thick plywood core is sandwiched between the outer, gelcoated fiberglass skin and the inner fiberglass skin. The gelcoat is so thin (just 0.015 inch or so) relative to the laminate of the upper skin that it isn't visible in this sectional view.

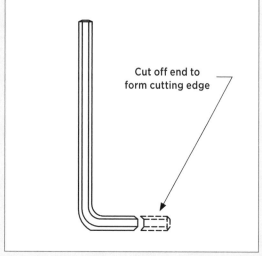

Cut off end to form cutting edge

A sawed-off Allen wrench chucked into an electric drill makes a good tool for cleaning out core material from the edges of a hole.

remove the wet wood and replace it before sealing the opening, as covered in the section Repairing Cored Decks later in this chapter.

Assuming for the moment that the core is dry, remove the core material from around the hole or opening. A modified Allen key in a drill is effective in removing the core around a hole. For ports and hatch openings, a Dremel tool or router can be used. The core needs to be cut back about ½ inch around the opening for best results. Fastener holes should be drilled out oversize, filled with epoxy/filler, and redrilled.

The cavity is then filled with an epoxy/filler mixture, using a filler such as WEST 404 High-Density Filler or fumed silica. (The fumed silica reduces the tendency of the epoxy to sag and run.) Epoxy syringes are effective when filling the cavities around fastener holes.

When the epoxy/filler hardens, the mounting hole can be redrilled. This time the hole passes through solid epoxy, and the core is thus protected from water intrusion.

The first thing to consider when installing deck hardware is the type of sealant to be used. There are at least four basic types:

- Silicones
- Polyurethanes
- Polyethers
- Polysulfides

Silicones are not ideal adhesives—and thus are best used under compression in conjunction with self-sufficient mechanical fasteners—but they are chemically benign and don't attack some plastics the way the other sealants can. Polyurethanes, such as 3M 5200, are terrific adhesives as well as sealants—so terrific, in fact, that hardware installed with polyurethane is difficult to remove. Polyethers, such as 3M 4000, are new and have very

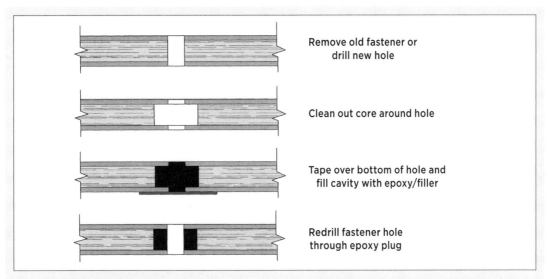

Remove old fastener or drill new hole

Clean out core around hole

Tape over bottom of hole and fill cavity with epoxy/filler

Redrill fastener hole through epoxy plug

Once the core is cleaned out, the void can be filled with epoxy/filler and the hole redrilled. This illustration appears with a half-dozen projects in this book because this step is critical.

good UV resistance. Polysulfides, like 3M 101, are both good adhesives and good sealants.

The most common mistake people make when installing deck hardware, besides not sealing the deck core, is to apply too thin a layer of sealant. They apply sealant to the hardware, then tighten down the hardware and squeeze out all the sealant.

A thin sealant layer doesn't have the ability to move with the expansion and contraction between the deck and the hardware. In a short time, the sealant fails and leaks begin.

There are two effective methods of maintaining a decent sealant thickness when installing hardware. The first—as mentioned several times previously in this book—uses neoprene washers placed on the fasteners under the hardware. When the fastener is tightened, the hardware bottoms out on the neoprene washer while allowing an adequate thickness of sealant elsewhere under the hardware.

The second method is a little more difficult to get right but still seals well. The edges of the fastener hole are chamfered slightly. A rubber O-ring is then placed on the fastener, sealant is applied, and the fastener is tightened. The O-ring seals the fastener opening and at the same time acts as a spacer to provide the needed sealant thickness. The trick is getting the right chamfer in connection with the appropriate size O-ring. Start with a small chamfer and trial-fit until you have a chamfer just large enough to provide about a $1/16$-inch clearance between the fitting and the deck when the O-ring is compressed.

The time to think about cleanup is before you start spreading sealant around. A little prep work will make cleanup easy. First, tape around the deck where the part is to be installed with blue tape 3 to 4 inches around the item. Temporarily locate the part and trace around it. Remove the part and cut away the tape from underneath where the part will go.

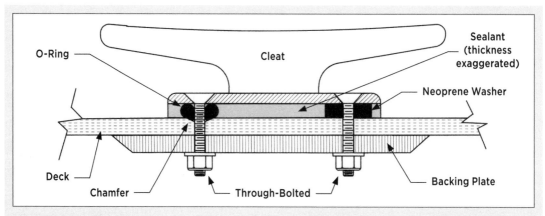

Here are two different options for sealing a fastener and maintaining a proper sealant thickness.

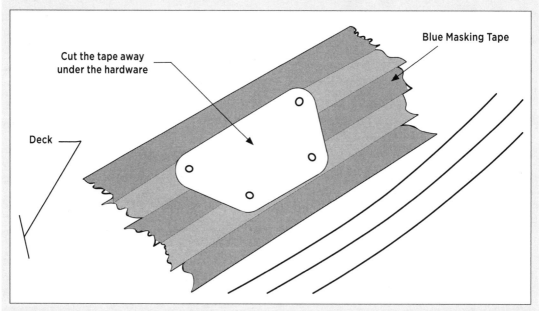

Painter's blue masking tape (not ordinary household or classroom tan masking tape) is your friend. It is a lot easier to remove the tape than to clean sealant off the deck.

Then tape around the edges of the part or fitting. Place the neoprene washer or O-ring on the fastener and apply a generous layer of sealant. Use more than enough, because you don't want any voids or air bubbles in the sealant.

Locate the part and tighten down the fasteners. *Don't overtighten*! The excess sealant will squeeze out from under the edges of the hardware; clean this up with tongue depressors or Popsicle sticks with their ends cut square. Once the excess sealant is cleaned up, let the sealant harden for a short time, then remove the tape. If you were neat and taped everything properly, your cleanup is finished.

If you want to further tighten the fasteners, wait until the sealant has fully cured. Have someone hold the fastener immobile on deck with a wrench or screwdriver, and tighten the nut from below. Don't turn the fastener from the deck side or you'll break the sealant bond around the fastener, creating a sure source for leaks.

If done properly, the hardware installation should be good for five years or longer with no leaks below or water intrusion into the core. After that, start thinking about rebedding with new sealant.

To protect your investment in your boat, start executing your deck sealing projects now. You don't have to tackle them all at the same time. Take a fitting or a port at a time. Just make sure that you get to them all sooner rather than later.

REPAIRING CORED DECKS

No words strike more terror in the hearts of boat buyers and sellers than *wet decks*! The boatowner sees his investment going down the drain; the buyer sees that his dreamboat has fatal flaws.

Is core rot curable, or is it the end of the line? The answer is a firm maybe. I'll discuss some of the causes, preventions, and cures for core rot. Armed with this information, you'll be better able to judge for yourself.

Of the two main types of core problems, the simpler to repair is core delamination. The bond between the fiberglass layer and the core material breaks from impacts or simply overloading the deck. This allows the deck to become springy, and the structure is weaker. As long as the core remains dry, however, repairs are possible. The second and far worse scenario is when water penetrates the core. The wet core material breaks away from the fiberglass skin and eventually rots or turns to mush. This is the more complex to solve and, unfortunately, the more common.

If your cored deck or hull is tight and dry, count your blessings. But don't expect to lead a charmed life forever. This is a perfect example of an ounce of prevention being worth a pound of cure. Inspect your vessel and be prepared to eliminate all sources of water intrusion. In some cases this water intrusion is due to poor construction practices. In other cases it is due to poor maintenance.

Common areas of water leaking into cores are around ports, deck hardware, and stanchions. In no case should anything—bolt, screw, or whatever—penetrate the actual core! Rebedding fittings without properly sealing the opening only postpones the inevitable. Fortunately, it is relatively easy to fix these problems as long as the core is still dry. Follow the advice in the previous project (Fixing Deck Dings) and the sidebar Strategies for Sealing Deck Hardware, earlier in this chapter, for proper bedding procedures.

But what if it's too late for preventive measures? Can the boat still be fixed? Back to our firm answer of maybe. If the boat has a cored hull and it is saturated, your best bet is probably to run, not walk, away from the boat. Repairing a saturated hull core could be a thankless and expensive task even if possible. If your core rot problem is limited to the deck, it may be repairable. The problem here is that a professional repair job to an extensively saturated deck might easily exceed the value of the boat!

If you are willing to tackle the job yourself, however, all is not lost. There are three major types of repairs: deck delamination with a dry core, small areas of core rot or wet core, and major deck saturation and delamination. We'll tackle them one at a time.

In all cases, the first step is to define the extent of the problem. Tap the deck with a plastic mallet or small hammer. A delaminated area will return a different sound—softer, hollower, duller, less ringing—than a solid deck area. (This is a case where the services of an experienced surveyor might be well worth the expense.) Mark the areas to be repaired. You want to do this job only once, so thoroughly check every area. Nothing is more disheartening than to fix one area and find out later that an area right next to it also needs repair.

In the case of a simple deck delamination with a dry core, the repair can be as simple as drilling a grid of holes, about 5 to 6 inches apart, over the area of delamination and filling those holes with epoxy and filler mixed to a ketchup consistency. Using a plastic syringe, fill the lowest hole first, injecting epoxy until it comes out of the next higher hole. Proceeding from low to high will avoid trapping any air bubbles under the skin. Take time to cover the surrounding areas with drop cloths to catch the epoxy drips.

A word to the wise—don't assume that the core is void-free! Boatbuilders are supposed to fill all voids between pieces of core when molding a deck, but sometimes this isn't done, and open channels remain between adjacent pieces of core. This is also why deck leaks can be so hard to trace: water enters at one point, runs down a channel, and drips somewhere else. Before injecting large quantities of epoxy, try injecting a solvent like acetone or alcohol first. Go below and look for any telltale leaks. The solvent will simply evaporate, and that's a lot better than a leak of epoxy that will cure to a rock-hard lump down the back of your bookshelf!

If you find such a leak, inject a small amount of epoxy around the periphery of the area to be repaired. That should seal the area around the delamination so you can continue filling the holes with epoxy.

In the remaining scenarios, you must decide whether to do the repair from below- or above-decks. Both approaches have advantages and disadvantages. If you elect to repair from below, you will preserve the look and integrity of your deck, and the interior headliner will cover the repairs neatly. The disadvantage is that you will be working overhead with the attendant epoxy drips and spatters and the complication of holding things in place. You may also have to remove some of the interior joinery to get to the overhead.

Working from above will provide much easier access, but will require replacing nonskid areas and repainting. If your nonskid is worn or your deck already needs painting, your decision will be an easy one.

Once you have determined the areas to be repaired and the direction of the repair (up or down), it's time to gather materials and tools. Even though the deck was probably built using some form of polyester resin, epoxy is the only material to consider for the repair. Only epoxies will reliably form a secondary bond to cured polyester. As we've discussed elsewhere, there are several major suppliers of epoxies to the boating market. Visit your local boating store or the epoxy manufacturer's website to gather information about their products. Invest in the epoxy pumps, as they will soon pay for themselves!

You will need the epoxy resin and hardener, pumps, mixing tubs, fillers and additives, fiberglass cloth and/or tape for reinforcement, plus safety equipment like gloves, safety glasses, and respirators if working inside. Don't scrimp here, because developing an allergic reaction to epoxy will end your boat repairing days quickly.

If the area to be fixed is relatively small, I use a Dremel tool and cutoff wheel to cut back the fiberglass skin. You want to cut back only the top or bottom skin, not both! In larger areas, a circular saw with a carbide-tooth blade can be used to cut back the skin, but be sure to set the blade depth just slightly deeper than the fiberglass skin. If you are working near the edge of the deck or the cabin side, leave a narrow strip of the surface in place. If you are making the repair abovedecks, you can often save the deck surface and re-epoxy it in place over the new core, thus greatly mitigating the chief downside of an abovedeck repair.

With the core exposed, you can cut away the saturated material. Dig the core out from under the edges of the exposed area, making sure you've excavated back to good, solid core around the entire perimeter. Clean up the area where the core material was, sanding with coarse-grit sandpaper for a good bond. Grind a taper on the edges of the deck opening and on the piece of deck you cut out (if you can reuse it). If the deck is ⅛ inch thick, taper back about an inch or so.

It's now time to install a new core. Plywood, foam, and honeycomb are all possibilities for larger areas. Smaller areas may simply be filled with an epoxy/filler mixture. The most common replacement core is plywood. Use as good an exterior grade as you can find and afford. A good choice is MDO plywood, which is formulated for exterior use in things like highway signs. If the area you are repairing has any curvature to it, you will need to cut the core material into squares; about 4 to 6 inches should be small enough. It should be the same thickness as the original core.

Dry-fit the squares in place, fitting them under the edges of the repaired area and cutting them to shape where required. Plan on leaving

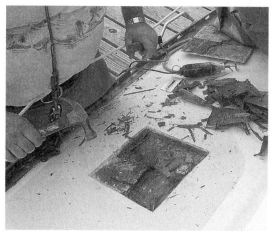

This wet and rotted core needs to be completely removed.

Here the replacement core has been epoxied in place. Make sure all voids are filed with epoxy/filler.

⅛ inch or so between the squares. Number the squares or lay them out on a surface where you can easily identify which piece goes in next. Don your safety equipment and begin mixing your epoxy. Follow the manufacturer's suggestions for a heavy adhesive mixture. Spread a generous layer of the epoxy in the opening and begin pressing the core squares in place.

If you are working on the underside of the deck, you will need to get creative to keep the squares in place. Spring-loaded shower rods, for example, work wonders in situations like this. Be sure to add colloidal silica to your epoxy, because it makes the mixture thixotropic—that is, resistant to sagging or dripping.

Let the epoxy begin to harden. You don't have to wait until it's fully cured, just until it's stiff enough to keep things in place while you continue. If you are able to reuse the section of deck you cut out, clean it up and grind the bonding surface with a coarse sandpaper to ensure a good bond. Dry-fit it in place to make sure it will be at the right height. If it is higher than the surrounding deck surface, you will need to sand down the new core. If it is too low, you will need to add more filled epoxy over the new core.

Remove the deck section and apply a layer of epoxy to the core surface, again following the manufacturer's suggestions for a thick adhesive mixture. Be sure to fill all the voids under the edges of the repaired area and between the core squares. Place the deck section on the epoxy and hold it in place with weights, shower rods, or even screws. If you use screws, don't overtighten them and squeeze out all the epoxy. Clean up any ooze around the edges.

Once the epoxy has cured, sand the tapered area between the existing deck edge and the replaced section. Then laminate several layers of glass tape in place, using 1½-inch or 2-inch-wide tape. Sand level and fill with epoxy/filler if needed. You can then repaint the deck and/or apply new

In this case the removed deck section could not be reused, so a new laminate is built up using squares of fiberglass cloth with epoxy resin. Cut each successive layer of cloth a little larger than the one before so as to lap the beveled edge of the repair.

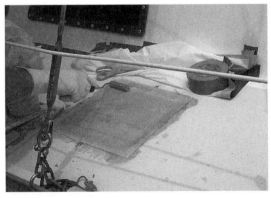

Here the top layer of cloth is applied. From this point, you can finish the repair flush with the surrounding deck surface using thickened epoxy. Had I been able to save the original deck section, I could have epoxied it back in place and faired in the seams.

nonskid as described in the following project (Repairing Molded Nonskid).

If you were unable to save the section of deck you cut away, you have a little more work to do. Once all the core squares are bonded in place, you need to apply a layer of epoxy/filler over the squares, being sure to fill all voids. You then build up a new deck surface using layers of 9-ounce or 10-ounce fiberglass cloth. Be sure to lap the cloth over the tapered edges of the opening. Once you've built the surface up to almost the original height, you can use epoxy and filler to fair the surface into the existing deck level. Then it's time to paint and apply nonskid.

Well, that's the process. Is it practical and doable? Yes, in many cases it is. It all depends on your abilities. Is it economical? If you do the work yourself, it can be. Done professionally, you will have to evaluate whether the investment is worth it or not. If you don't have any core rot now, get after those deck penetrations and make sure you'll never hear those dreaded words!

REPAIRING MOLDED NONSKID

One of the most difficult cosmetic repair jobs on a boat is repairing damaged nonskid. Trying to match an existing design is difficult, and replacing all of the nonskid is an expensive, time-consuming solution.

One of the impediments to a universal solution is that nonskid comes in so many different forms and applications. Many production boats have their nonskid molded in as part of the deck molding. Other boats have the nonskid applied after the deck is molded, using paint or another medium for applying it. Still other boats use thin sheet goods—rubber or vinyl—in which the nonskid pattern is molded. This material is cut to shape and fastened to the deck with some form of adhesive. We discuss repairs to molded nonskid in this project and cover other types in subsequent sections.

Gibco Flex-Mold is the chief manufacturer of nonskid rubber or vinyl sheets in a variety of patterns for boatbuilders. The builder cuts this material to shape and glues it onto the plug used to make the deck mold. Gelcoat is sprayed onto the plug, the deck mold is laminated in place, and when the plug is removed, the molded nonskid pattern is in place in the mold tooling. Thereafter, parts pulled from the tooling have the nonskid pattern molded into their surface. This is one of the simplest ways for a production boatbuilder to incorporate a nonskid pattern into a deck.

The usual sort of problem with this style of nonskid is that some of the edges get chipped or damaged from things being dropped on them. Other problems arise when a section of the deck containing the nonskid has to be replaced. Damaged areas stand out like a sore thumb against the regular pattern of undamaged nonskid. They can also telegraph that repairs have been made and scare off potential buyers.

The technique for repairing this style of nonskid requires a mold of a section of undamaged nonskid. Gibco supplies molds of the patterns used on many production boats. You can contact them to see if a mold for your boat is available. If not, you will have to make your own mold from latex or room temperature vulcanizing silicone rubber, known as RTV. Kits of these molding materials can be found online or at your local craft supply store. The kits contain the RTV or latex mold compounds, mixing tubs, stirrers, and gloves. (See HobbyCast in Appendix B.)

Once you have found a section of existing, undamaged nonskid with the required pattern and orientation, clean the deck of all dirt and grease. Follow the directions in the molding kit for making the mold. This involves mixing the two molding compounds and then applying it to the nonskid area in a uniform thickness of about ¼ inch or so. When it has cured, you should be able to peel the mold off your deck. The following instructions will then apply whether you bought your mold or made it.

Thoroughly clean the nonskid area to be repaired. If you have to, use a toothbrush to get off all of the dirt and grease. Remove the nonskid from the area that needs to be repaired by sanding or grinding—only to the thickness of the nonskid—and then taper the edges of the affected area. Wax around the area to be repaired with several coats of nonsilicone wax and buff it out, but do not get any wax in the area to be repaired. The purpose of the wax is to allow any squeeze-out to be easily removed.

If you made your own mold, coat the nonskid surface of the mold with PVA mold release and let it dry. The Gibco molds come with PVA mold release already applied. Place the mold over the area to be repaired, making sure the nonskid pattern of the mold meshes with the deck nonskid. Tape one edge of the mold and roll back the other edge to expose the repair area.

You will need gelcoat of the appropriate color to complete the repair. If your gelcoat is white, you can purchase it at any marine store. Colored gelcoat is another matter. In some cases, you can buy small amounts from the boatbuilder. In other cases you may need to buy a gelcoat kit with tubes of pigment in primary colors. These are mixed with the base gelcoat to achieve the desired color. This is extremely difficult to get right unless you have a good eye for color. An artist's color wheel, available from art supply stores, will give you an indication of what primary colors to use to achieve a specific gelcoat color.

Apply the catalyzed gelcoat to the area to be repaired with a disposable brush. Make sure there is enough to fill the repair area and a little more. Carefully unroll the flexible mold back over the repair area, pushing excess gelcoat ahead of the roll and forcing out any air bubbles.

Once the mold is flat and meshed with the existing nonskid pattern, firmly squeegee the back of the mold to evenly distribute the gelcoat. Let the gelcoat cure, then remove the mold. The excess gelcoat can be removed from the waxed areas outside the repair perimeter with a hardwood stick or similar hard but nonscratching item.

The repaired area should be indistinguishable in its pattern from the surrounding deck. Be aware, however, that gelcoat ages at variable rates, and the color of the new gelcoat may not match the old gelcoat after a period of months. Hopefully the difference will be subtle enough to live with, since your only alternative is to redo the entire deck.

PAINTING NONSKID

Many boatbuilders apply nonskid using a granular material suspended in a paint or resin mixture. Matching these repairs takes a little detective work to find out what the original material and method of application were. Ask the boat's manufacturer or try online owner groups. If neither of these approaches pans out, you may have to go the trial-and-error route.

Several paint manufacturers supply nonskid paints with the nonskid additive mixed in with the paint, and most also supply the nonskid additive separately for use with their other paints. Before buying a large amount of paint for a repair, buy a small container of the nonskid additive, pour it in a small can of paint, and decide if the resulting pattern matches your deck.

Another common nonskid additive is beach sand, which is sprinkled on top of a layer of wet paint. Once the paint has dried, excess sand is vacuumed off. The resulting surface has a lot of similarities with sandpaper and may be painted with an additional coat or two of paint.

A third method is to sprinkle coarse salt or sugar into the wet paint. After the paint has dried, water is used to dissolve the salt or sugar, leaving small pits in the paint that act as nonskid.

Once you have determined the proper nonskid additive and paint mixture, clean off the area to be repaired. Use a fiberglass dewaxer and a solvent such as alcohol or acetone to remove any traces of grease. Sand the area smooth and apply the nonskid paint. Some skill and practice are needed to properly blend the new nonskid into the old. Have rags and thinner ready to clean off the area if you don't match the edges on the first try.

SHEET NONSKID

Sheets of rubber or vinyl nonskid material are available from several manufacturers, including Treadmaster and SeaDek. These materials come with a nonskid pattern molded into the upper

This Treadmaster nonskid material comes in sheets and is epoxied in place. This cockpit locker cover is over ten years old and still in good condition.

surface. Treadmaster's product is designed to be bonded in place with epoxy, while SeaDek's has a pressure-sensitive adhesive on the underside.

I have not heard of any successful repair for these types of materials other than peeling off the old material and applying new. The good news is that, being flexible, they are very hard to damage. I have had this material installed on a boat for over ten years with no sign of fading or damage. Wear seems to be uniform across the surface, and when the nonskid pattern is gone, I'll just replace the whole piece.

Start the installation process by laying out the design of your nonskid. A drawing of the deck will make the layout easier. If you already have old nonskid in place and like the layout, make paper patterns before you remove the old nonskid. If the nonskid is molded into the deck, you will have to sand it flush with the rest of the deck. If the nonskid is a sheet material, try heating it with a heat gun and scraping it off with a putty knife. Painted-on nonskid will have to be sanded smooth. Be careful to confine your sanding to the nonskid, or you'll create a new job for yourself of repainting the entire deck.

Clean any dirt, sanding dust, or grease off the area where the nonskid will be bonded. Interlux 202 Fiberglass Solvent Wash is a good choice.

Nonskid areas are separated by areas of smooth fiberglass anywhere from 2 to 3 inches wide. These allow water to drain from deck areas and divide the nonskid panels into sections that efficiently use standard sheets. Rounded corners on the panels yield a much more professional look and are less likely to peel than sharp corners. Most nonskid sheet goods can be easily cut with a good pair of scissors or small shears.

Once the deck is cleaned and ready, cover the area where the nonskid material will be placed with blue tape. Place a panel on the deck exactly where you want it installed. Trace around the panel, then remove it and cut away the tape under the panel. Place the panel in the correct location and firmly tape one edge.

Fold the panel back along the tape hinge. Most sheet goods can be bonded in place with epoxy, but I have used 3M 5200 with good results.

Apply the adhesive to the deck. Then, starting at the taped edge, slowly roll the nonskid panel onto the adhesive. This rolling motion forces out any air that would otherwise be trapped under the panel. After the panel is in place, roll the surface with a linoleum seam roller or a rolling pin to ensure good, uniform contact.

REPAIRING RAILINGS, PULPITS, AND PUSHPITS

No matter what boat you have, it is probably equipped with some sort of railing. Railing struc-

This is what a Zamak fitting looks like after some saltwater exposure and a few years on the boat.

tures go by several names according to their locations, including pulpits, pushpits, stern rails, side-deck railing, and so on. All are commonly made from lengths of metal tubing, sometimes bent to shape, that are mounted to the boat using a series of cast metal sockets and brackets. Over time, these components can become bent, corroded, or scarred. Fortunately, they are made from a limited range of easily found components.

Aluminum and stainless steel tubing are both in common use. Aluminum is lighter and cheaper and bends easier. Stainless polishes better, is stronger but more expensive, and doesn't corrode (much).

The most common tubing outside diameters are ⅞ inch and 1 inch. You occasionally see ¾-inch tubing, but aftermarket components are hard to find for this size. The ⅞-inch and 1-inch sizes are stocked in most marine stores and come in 6-foot lengths. Longer lengths are available by special order (and price!).

Most boat stores and boating equipment catalogs have a selection of fittings from manufacturers such as TACO, Perko, Suncor, and Whitecap.

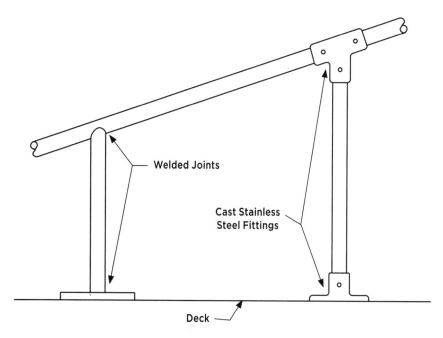

Welded Joints

Cast Stainless
Steel Fittings

Deck

Bow and stern rails can be mounted and joined with fittings cast from stainless steel or Zamak, or they can be welded.

Fittings are usually available in stainless steel and chrome-plated Zamak, a common alloy of zinc, aluminum, copper, and magnesium used in high-production casting and also known as "pot metal."

Stainless tubing is often bent to shape, notched to fit, and then welded. This practice avoids the use of tee fittings at the stanchions and, given neat welds, is very clean looking. The stanchion bases can stand in stock fittings or welded mounting plates.

Stainless steel fittings are strong and have high corrosion resistance. They are heavier than other alternatives and generally more expensive. Zamak has many sterling qualities, but corrosion resistance isn't one of them.

Most base fittings have round or rectangular baseplates with three or four countersunk holes for mounting bolts or screws. The tubing is locked in place in these fittings with setscrews. In some cases, replacing the setscrews with self-tapping stainless screws will make a stronger installation. Be sure to drill a pilot hole in the tubing for the self-tapping screw.

Base fittings are available in numerous configurations, common among which are 90-, 60-, 45-, and 30-degree angles. In addition, there are several streamlined styles in various sizes and shapes. These match many common railings or allow you to develop your own railing style.

Railings and fittings suffer from two common types of problems: impact damage and corrosion. Zamak fittings used in conjunction with stainless steel tubing in a saltwater environment will certainly corrode. Corrosion will happen in a freshwater environment, too, but not as quickly.

Aluminum tubing will corrode when used with stainless fittings.

If the tubing is bent, it may be possible to straighten it to its original shape by carefully clamping it between blocks of wood. However, severe bends or kinks may have collapsed the tubing. In these cases, the tubing will need to be replaced, as the kink would forever weaken it. Aluminum, in particular, can work-harden, making it prone to cracking.

Another problem with bent tubing is simply being able to apply enough force to straighten it. Remember, it may have been bent when several tons of boat hit the dock. Trying to apply enough force may well crack the base fittings or even the fiberglass deck to which they are fastened.

In some cases, the tubing may have been bent to its final shape after a fitting has been placed on the tube, making removal of the fitting almost impossible. Further complications arise from the fact that many manufacturers install the railings on the deck units before mounting the deck to the hull. After the deck is placed on the hull, the hull/deck joint may be covered with several layers of fiberglass cloth and resin. This makes access to the fitting's mounting bolts impossible without grinding away some fiberglass.

Scope out the repair before attempting it. Are the fittings still available? Will the tubing need to be replaced, and if so, will it need to be bent to shape? Depending on the answers, it may be more practical and cost-effective to take this job to a professional marine metal fabricator.

In some cases it makes sense to have the original fittings repaired and rechromed. This is especially true if replacement fittings cannot be found and the fitting is a unique design that represents a recognized feature of the boat. Look for metal refinishers who do work for automobile restorers: they are used to this type of repair.

Let's consider an actual repair. The example boat was a 20-footer with a pushpit (also known as a stern rail) consisting of stainless steel tubing and Zamak fittings. The Zamak fittings were pitted and corroded and of questionable strength. There were four round base fittings, one for each end and one for each of the two intermediate stanchions. The stanchion tops required two tee fittings.

Investigation revealed that the same fittings were available in stainless steel, the tubing was in excellent shape, and the fasteners for the fittings were all accessible. The only complication was that the rail ends had been bent forward after the tee fittings had been installed, and the fittings simply could not be slid off the rail ends.

The solution was to cut the tubing at the tee fittings. This allowed the old, corroded fittings to be removed and new ones slid on, but it left the pushpit railing short.

The next step was to bed the new base fittings. The new fittings had the same hole pattern and dimensions as the old, so I didn't have to fill the existing holes and drill new ones. Even though the deck in this area wasn't cored, I did seal the edges of the mounting holes with several coats of epoxy so water wouldn't wick into the fiberglass.

Next I had to splice the cut tubing back together with no loss of its original length or strength. Salvaging a 12-inch length of tubing of the same diameter from a discarded pulpit, I cut out a lengthwise section. This allowed the split length to be compressed until one end fit tightly inside each of the two rail sections, the result being a 12-inch-long splice running through the tee-fitting. In place of setscrews in the tee, I used

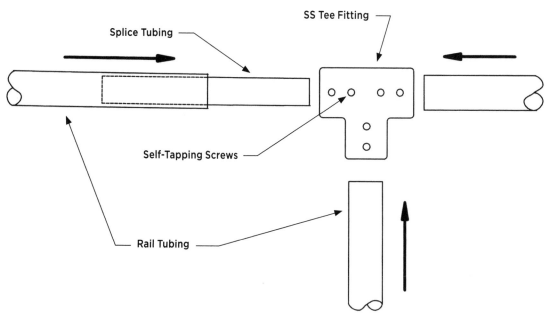

Rail tubing can be spliced by cutting a lengthwise slot in a short section, then compressing that section so that each end slides inside an end of the original tubing. In the layout shown here, the finished splice is hidden inside a tee fitting.

long self-tapping stainless steel screws, screwing them through the fitting, the railing, and the inner splice and restoring the rail to its original strength.

This type of repair is typical for units made of stock fittings and tubing. If your railing is stainless steel with welded baseplates, however, plan on going to your favorite local marine fabricator. Getting strong, good-looking welds in stainless tubing is almost an art and takes more than a little practice.

CHAPTER 5

Boat Canvas

I have often been told that the most important feature on a boat isn't its fuel economy, its ride, or even how good it looks. It's how well the occupants are protected from the sun. Indeed, I would not go boating nearly as often if I didn't have an effective system for sun protection. It's not just a question of comfort. As we now know, protection from overexposure to the sun is a matter of long-term health.

BIMINIS

One of the quickest ways to add effective shade protection to your boat is by installing an after-market bimini. These are available off the shelf in a wide variety of sizes, styles, and colors from marine supply stores and almost any boating catalog. If you measure your boat carefully and choose wisely, they work fine.

Most aftermarket biminis consist of a metal tubing frame with a fabric cover. Depending on the size, the frame will include two, three, or four bows. Obviously, the longer the bimini, the more bows it needs to have. Also included are mounting brackets for the bottom of the bimini and straps and clips to secure the bimini forward and aft.

A bimini can be attached to a flat horizontal surface such as the top of a gunwale, or it can be attached to a vertical surface such as the side of a cockpit. Most kits contain brackets for both styles of mounting, but check before you buy. Most biminis can be accommodated to a limited range of mounting widths by squeezing the uprights a little closer together or spreading them a little farther apart.

Once you've determined the width, you should figure out how high and how long the bimini should be. You probably want standing headroom beneath it, so figure how much height you'll need above the deck or gunwale mounting surface.

As for length, you can decide how much of the boat you want to shelter from sun (and rain). It's nearly impossible to manage a fishing rod from beneath a bimini, so you might want to leave part of the cockpit open.

Bimini frames are available in aluminum or stainless steel. Aluminum tubing isn't quite as strong as stainless steel and is not as corrosion resistant, especially if used with stainless fasteners. Stainless is more expensive.

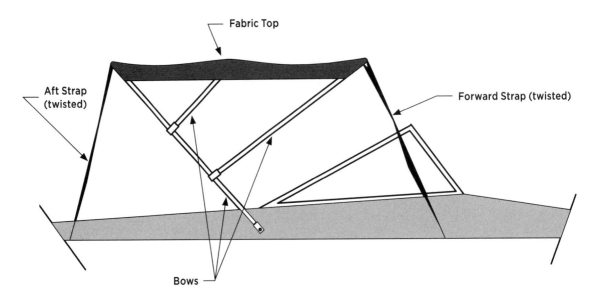

A typical bimini designed to be installed by the boatowner.

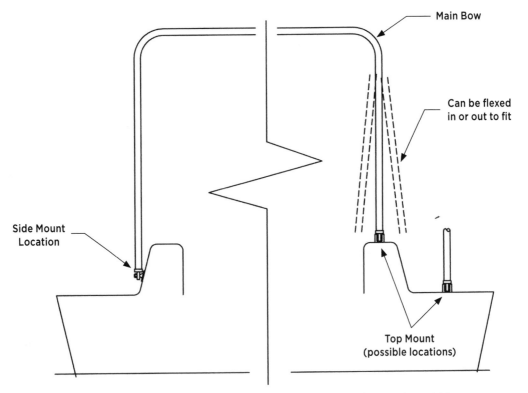

Bimini bows are flexible enough to accommodate a modest range of mounting widths.

The main fabric options are acrylic canvas, vinyl-coated fabrics, and some proprietary fabrics. Sunbrella is an acrylic fabric that has been widely used as boat canvas for years. It has high UV resistance and holds up well as long as it is sewn with UV-resistant thread. Vinyl-coated fabrics are also common and hold up well, although I find them slightly more susceptible to mold and mildew. Several manufacturers offer new, proprietary fabrics that don't fit readily into established categories but are reputed to offer such special advantages as low stretch.

Color is also a consideration. Sunbrella offers a wide range of colors, but not all have the same fade resistance. Vinyls are available in far fewer color choices, often only white or gray. Darker colors are hotter in the sun and transfer at least some of that heat underneath. They also seem to fade a little more. The standard color for Sunbrella biminis has long been the ubiquitous blue. I prefer other colors just to set my boats off from all the others.

The bows of an aluminum frame come in three sections—a center piece and two ends. The bows, fabric top, and webbing straps fit together in a definite sequence. It pays to lay out all the pieces on a flat surface to make the assembly process more obvious. With the fabric top lying upside down, you can see that the center section of each bow slides through a sleeve sewn in the fabric. The sleeves for the forward and aft bows each have two cutouts—one to port and one to starboard of the centerline—where straps are looped over the bows. As you slide the center section of the forward or aft bow through its respective sleeve, you must pass it through the loop end of a strap placed in each of those cutouts. Forget to do this and you will soon be disassembling the bimini top. Don't ask how I know that.

Once the center sections are in place, slide the end pieces on, completing the bows. In the aluminum frame these end sections are fastened to their respective center sections with short stainless steel screws. The bimini is now assembled but is upside down.

The bimini can now be placed on the edges of the cockpit where it will be installed. Make sure it is centered, then mark the location for the mounting screws and drill pilot holes. If the fiberglass has a wood or foam core, you will need to seal the sides of the holes in the usual manner to protect the core from water intrusion. The bottom brackets can then be affixed with stainless steel self-tapping screws and sealant. It is important to use the right size pilot drill. If the holes are too large, the self-tapping screws won't hold; if the holes are too small, the screws will crack the surrounding gelcoat and fiberglass.

The only remaining tasks are to locate the forward and aft strap eyes and attach the restraining straps. Twist each strap at least once when installing it. Although a straight strap looks nicer, it will oscillate violently and annoyingly in any amount of wind—that is, whenever you're under way. Twisting the straps breaks up the airflow and prevents the straps from vibrating.

Several years ago I installed a bimini on one of my boats. I selected an inexpensive kit with an aluminum frame and white vinyl fabric. It cost less than $300 and took less than a day to install. It held up well in the sun, rain, and snow for over four years, until a ferocious hailstorm ripped holes through the fabric. I don't think this was due to any failure of the fabric, however, since the same storm also totaled one of our cars and did more than $3,000 worth of damage to the other. I ordered a replacement fabric top and easily installed it.

AWNINGS

While an aftermarket bimini is quick to install and reasonably cheap to buy, it can't provide the total solution for all situations. The stern of my 20-footer faced the setting sun when in her slip. As the sun dipped below the aft edge of the bimini in the summer, the cockpit became an oven. I devised an aft awning to give me the required sun protection. While I couldn't use it under way, it became a real asset at the dock or anchored out.

I arrived at the design of the awning through trial and error. My first attempt revolved around a blue tarp from a local home improvement store. It held up for a while but then shredded. Besides, it looked ugly, and the available sizes were either too big or too small.

I then tried an off-the-shelf white canvas awning, which I held in place over a wooden bat-ten with bungee cords. It didn't shred, but again the stock sizes didn't work well. It also mildewed excessively and leaked a little.

The good news was that these experiments nailed down what I wanted in terms of length and width, and they provided some design ideas. I had a local canvas shop make up a vinyl awning to the design I drew, which showed the finished size and where I wanted the grommets located. The canvas shop did a first-class job for around $90 using the standard gray vinyl material they use for pontoon boat projects.

After installing this awning, I spent some time optimizing the support system. The front edge of the awning fit just under the aft edge of the bimini and snapped around a wooden dowel with an eyebolt screwed in each end. The eyebolts faced up and were tied to the aft bimini bow with Velcro strips.

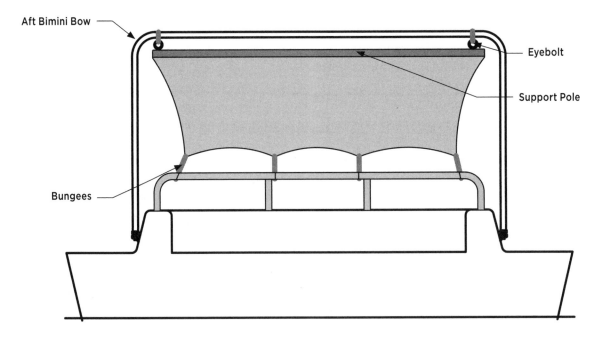

This awning provides shade when the sun is behind the boat.

A series of bungee cords secured the lower, aft edge of the awning to the stern pulpit. With the aft edge just above the pulpit, I had adequate room to look sternward under the awning when seated in the cockpit. I could watch all the goings-on at the fuel dock almost unobserved.

To strike the awning, I would simply remove the aft bungee cords and roll it up. I could leave it slung below the aft edge of the bimini or snap it off and store it below.

This awning provided ample shade when the boat was anchored or docked with the sun toward the stern. The total cost was less than $175, and the awning has lasted (so far) about eight years.

A bow awning provides shade forward when at anchor or at the dock. (Courtesy Taylor Made Products, Inc.)

SUNSHADES

Many boats have large hatches in the foredeck. When open, these hatches can provide a refreshing breeze below, but let the first drop of rain fall and the hatch must be slammed shut, cutting off the ventilation. This is just as annoying as the sun beating down directly into the open hatch. I have solved this problem on several boats with a bow awning, or sunshade.

A local canvas shop—which I found by asking around the dock for satisfied customers—made one to my design for less than $50. This roughly triangular sunshade is attached to the bow rail at the forward end and the windshield at the aft end. A loop of light line runs between the two points to help support the fabric. Bungee cords tie the sides of the shade to the lifelines or deck edge. With the sunshade in place, I can leave the foredeck hatch open in all but the worst weather.

CLEANING AND TREATING CANVAS

Sooner or later, no matter what the fabric, all boat "canvas" will require cleaning and possibly the application or reapplication of a water- or mildew-proofing treatment.

Sunbrella has a water-resistant, mildew-resistant, UV-resistant finish applied at the factory. The manufacturer does not recommend using a detergent solution to clean the fabric, because it breaks down the finish. Sunbrella recommends occasionally brushing dirt off the fabric and washing it with a mild, nondetergent soap solution such as Lux or Ivory Liquid.

Should your canvas be mildew stained, always proceed from the mildest treatment toward more aggressive ones, and stop when you have cleaned the canvas. Try to remove as much of the stain as possible by brushing. When that fails to produce any further improvements, switch to scrubbing with a weak solution of nonchlorine bleach such as Clorox II.

Only when all else fails should you switch to chlorine bleach or mildew removers. This treatment may damage the finish and the thread with which the canvas is sewn, so as soon as the stain has disappeared, flush the canvas with plenty of fresh water. Most marine stores have solutions for waterproofing fabric as well as applying a mildew-resistant finish. Keep an eye on the stitching, and have the item resewn if the thread starts to deteriorate.

Some canvas makers suggest spraying a 50:50 solution of white vinegar and water on the canvas after you wash the boat or after a heavy rain. The vinegar won't hurt the canvas, but mildew doesn't like it.

RESTORING ISINGLASS

Keeping the clear vinyl or isinglass (brand names include Isenglass and Stratoglass) in your canvas clean also has its dos and don'ts. The most important thing to realize is that salt crystals are abrasive and will damage the windows. Salt should be washed off with plenty of clean water. Do not use detergent or scrub the isinglass. After the salt is washed off, dry the isinglass with a chamois before attempting any other steps.

Once the salt and dirt are off, the vinyl can be polished with a soft cloth or chamois and a plastic cleaner. Do not use paper towels, as they are very abrasive. Boat stores usually have several brands of vinyl cleaner on the shelf from manufacturers such as 3M, Star brite, Meguiar's, and Davis. Do not use Windex or any product containing alcohol, as these will make the plastic surface sticky.

If this still doesn't get the plastic clear, you will need to switch to a vinyl scratch remover and then follow that up with a final polish. SIS, Inc., offers a two-part kit for removing stubborn scratches and restoring clear plastic. The full procedure is available at www.sisweb.com/micromesh/reference/clear-seas-vinyl.htm. Star brite and Meguiar's also offer plastic scratch removal kits. In general, these work by applying a mildly abrasive cleaner followed by a polish to protect the plasticizers that keep the vinyl flexible.

INSTALLING AN AFTERMARKET T-TOP

In times past, just about the only way to get a T-top on a center-console boat was to either buy the boat that way or have the top custom-made by a marine fabricator. Those are still options, but if you're willing to do the job yourself, you now have other choices.

One of these is from Taylor Made Products, a supplier of all sorts of marine products. Their Bimi-Tee Top isn't as large as some stock T-tops, but it does have the advantage of easy installation and may be ideal for smaller boats. Two sizes are available, 4 by 5 feet and 4½ by 6 feet.

The Bimi-Tee Top is a bolt-together product. There are a lot of parts, but the installation instructions are very complete. You begin by installing two forward vertical supports, or uprights. These attach to the sides of the console with special brackets, which need to be through-bolted, so be sure to check for back-side access before purchasing the kit. If the console is cored, you will have to protect the core from moisture intrusion. Refer to Adding Access Hatches in

A Taylor Made Bimini-Tee Top. (Courtesy Taylor Made Products, Inc.)

A typical T-top installed on a center console fishing boat. (Courtesy C. E. Smith, Inc.)

Chapter 2 for the measures you must take to seal the hole against water intrusion and provide solid epoxy through which the mounting bolts will pass.

Care must be taken to locate the two uprights even with each other, both fore and aft and vertically. The main horizontal bow is then attached to the tops of the uprights.

Once the two uprights are installed and checked for symmetry and the top bow is level, the rest of the top is assembled piece by piece. With the basic assembly complete, the top can be leveled and all connections properly tightened.

The complete installation instructions for the Taylor Made Bimi-Tee Top are available on the Taylor Made website. I suggest downloading the instructions and reviewing them before purchasing, so you can be sure the unit is suitable for your boat (www.taylormadeproducts.com/catalog).

Robust T-tops are also available from C. E. Smith (www.cesmithco.com) in larger sizes than the Taylor Made version. The uprights are sturdy 1½-inch stainless steel tubing, while the top frame is 1-inch stainless steel tubing. The unit comes

The adjustable feet on C. E. Smith's T-top uprights adjust to cambered decks. (Courtesy C. E. Smith, Inc.)

packed flat in two boxes and must be shipped by common carrier. One way to get around this shipping problem (since common carriers don't usually deliver to household addresses) is to purchase the unit through a local marine store such as West

Marine and have the packages delivered to the store for pickup.

The uprights and top come prewelded, while all other joints must be bolted together. The uprights mount directly to the cockpit sole via mounting feet that can turn and swivel to match any compound curvature in the mounting sur-face. These mounting feet also have a feature that allows the top to be quickly unbolted while leaving the feet firmly in place. This makes removing the T-top for winter storage a snap.

A large T-top, especially one loaded with accessories, can impose quite a load on the deck around the mounting feet. Care should be taken

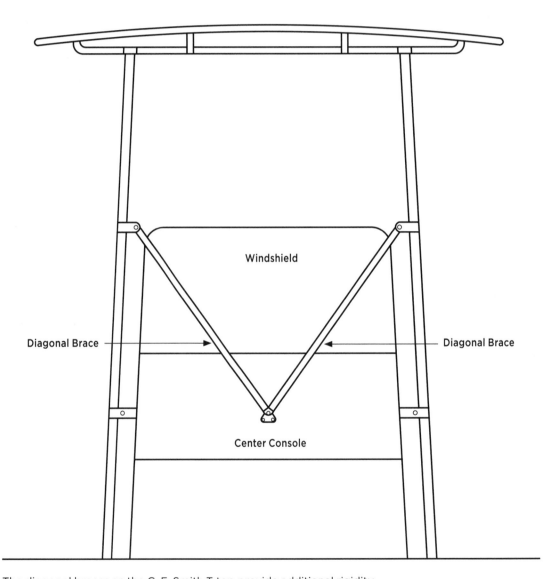

The diagonal braces on the C. E. Smith T-top provide additional rigidity.

to ensure that the deck structure is strong enough to handle the load. In some cases, backing plates may be needed under the deck. Through-bolting the mounting feet is always best. If the underside of the deck isn't accessible, consider using stainless steel toggle bolts. The last resort is to use stainless steel self-tapping screws. In any case, the mounting holes should be well sealed to prevent water from leaking into the core of the deck or through the deck.

The C. E. Smith website provides extensive installation drawings and instructions, among the best I've seen.

In addition to the mounting feet for the uprights, C. E. Smith offers a wide range of standoffs that attach to the sides of the console and brace the T-top. In addition to the standoffs, each T-top includes a set of diagonal braces attached to a center mount, and these provide additional stiffness to the assembly.

Installation time is reported to be on the order of four to five hours for a pair of handy boaters.

T-TOP ACCESSORIES

A T-top provides a platform for a wide variety of accessories. A trip to a local boat show will give you a host of ideas on how to customize your installation.

One popular option is the installation of an electronics box under the T-top cover. These can be used to house a VHF radio, fishfinder, GPS unit, or stereo in a protected place. Most such units are designed to fit specific T-tops, so check the dimensions before ordering. Many feature a fold-down and lockable acrylic cover. The aft face can be square or angled down for better visibility

This lockable electronics box fits against the underside of a T-top. (Courtesy Moeller Products Company, Inc.)

of the installed electronics. Typical sizes are on the order of 24 to 30 inches wide and 9 inches high on the inside. The box is clamped to the frame tubes with a bracket.

These units come with a blank panel to be cut out to fit your choice of electronics. Make sure any equipment you purchase for installation in one of these boxes has a flush-mount option.

The most difficult part of installing such a unit is the need to snake the various wires and cables through the upright supports. Power and transducer cables will have to be snaked through holes in the tubing. Most antennas will be mounted on top of the T-top and can be wire-tied to the support bars instead of being routed through the tubes. Be sure to use grommets in the tubing holes to protect the wires from chafe.

From bitter experience gained trying to fish wires through holes, I always make the access hole a little bigger than needed and pull a messenger line through along with the wires and cables. A messenger line is simply a string with both ends exposed and accessible. When the time comes to pull through the wire you forgot in your initial installation or the one you need for equipment added later, simply tie the end of the wire to the messenger line and pull it through the tubing run. Fishing a wire through the tubing any other way is next to impossible. When pulling that additional wire through, remember to attach another messenger line for the next addition.

External GPS and VHF antennas may need to be mounted on the T-top cover frame. Be sure to use a fold-down mount for that long VHF antenna

so you can pass under low-clearance bridges. Don't be tempted to mount the VHF antenna on the transom or the side of the console. The range of a VHF radio is purely line of sight. The higher the antenna, the greater the range it can provide.

One of the most popular options is rod holders, also known as rocket launchers when lined up in a row. They can be bolted onto almost any piece of available tubing on a T-top, be it vertical or horizontal. The number of rod holders you install on a T-top is limited only by your wallet and common sense.

Rod holders (rocket launchers) can be added to a T-top frame. (Courtesy C. E. Smith, Inc.)

CHAPTER 6

Hulls

Our boat hulls are where the "rubber meets the road," so to speak. The hull bears the brunt of the forces, from trailer to wave action to docking. More importantly, it keeps the water outside, where it belongs. The hull is also one of the first things people notice about our boats, and pride of ownership should motivate us to keep the hull in tip-top shape.

APPLYING ANTIFOULING PAINT

One of the least pleasant maintenance tasks is scraping and painting the bottom. Unfortunately, if you do your boating on salt water, especially warm salt water, it can also be an unavoidable annual chore. You should do it right to minimize the agony and get the most from your efforts. (If you use your boat on fresh water, or if you trailer it, you may be able to do without antifouling paint, thus avoiding not only the work but the paint's environmental impact.)

The good news is that you don't have to be a great painter to do a good job. The favored technique is to roll on the paint using a roller with a medium nap. Tight areas around rudders and such may require the use of a brush. In any case, the important criterion is to get a uniform coat of paint over all the bottom surfaces.

Before proceeding, read the sidebar Bottom Paint Choices later in this chapter.

In most cases, antifouling paint is not thinned. It is used just as it comes from the can. One of the hardest jobs will be to get all the copper compounds mixed into the paint, but this is key to applying a uniform coating of antifouling agent on your boat. If you have purchased paint well before you plan on using it, be sure to turn the can over regularly to keep all the solids loose and in suspension.

A paint mixing paddle in a corded electric drill is the preferred method of stirring the paint. Forget about using your battery-powered drill—it doesn't have anything like the stamina required to mix antifouling paint. Keep a "manual stirrer" (a stick) handy, and mix the paint frequently as you work.

Often you will be lying on your back painting the boat overhead. Use a Tyvek "bunny" suit in conjunction with a painter's hood to keep paint out of your hair. Wear goggles to keep paint out of your eyes.

If the existing bottom paint is in good condition, you may want to just repaint the bottom with a maintenance coat. Prep the hull by pressure-washing the bottom. Do this—or have it done—when the boat is first pulled out and any bottom slime is still soft. Waiting until it has dried and hardened means increased work to clean the bottom.

Scrape off any loose paint, then wipe down the bottom with the recommended thinner to remove any traces of grease or oil. Then sand the bottom lightly with 80-grit sandpaper. Remove all traces of sanding residue. If there are any bare patches, coat them with bottom paint. Apply the antifouling paint and let dry. Relaunch the boat within the recommended time for the paint you use.

As mentioned in Bottom Paint Choices, ablative paints work by wearing away. Most paint manufacturers suggest applying three coats the first time this type of paint is used on your boat. The first coat should be of a different color than the last two, say black over red. That way, when patches of red start appearing, you know it's time to reapply the paint.

Unfortunately, ablative paint doesn't wear away uniformly. Areas of higher water flow wear away first, while other areas, where water flow is slow or near stagnant, remain in good condition. Recoat the areas where the base coat color is appearing before recoating the entire bottom. That will build up the paint film to an effective thickness. In fact, it won't hurt to give those areas a second or third coat, because this is where future wear will occur as well.

Bottom Paint Choices

There are hundreds of brands of bottom or antifouling paint on the market. There is also a great deal of hype about those products, making the choice of paint confusing.

Bottom paints by design are lethal to underwater organisms. Historically, the favored and most effective antifouling agent was an organic compound of tin called TBT (tributyltin). This biocide was found to have negative impacts on desirable forms of aquatic life such as fish and shellfish, however, and it was banned from use as an antifouling agent in 1990.

As a result, most antifouling paints today use some form of copper-based compound as the active antifouling agent. These paints can be roughly divided into two groups, hard and soft. While both contain copper compounds, they work in different ways.

Hard paints dry to a hard coat, with the copper compounds distributed throughout. The paint vehicle is designed to allow the copper compounds to slowly leach out of the film to perform the antifouling function. The hard film can be burnished or polished to form a smooth surface useful in racing boats.

When the copper compounds have leached out, the paint film remains behind. Applying subsequent coats of bottom paint to restore the antifouling function will result in a buildup of layers of paint, which can eventually add hundreds of pounds to a hull.

Another problem with hard bottom paint occurs when the boat is stored out of the water for an extended period. Contact with air causes the copper compounds to form an insoluble chemical, negating the paint's antifouling effectiveness. Paint manufacturers therefore specify the maximum time that can elapse between painting and launching for the paint to retain its effectiveness.

Soft bottom paints work differently. The paint film is softer and actually wears away, exposing new copper compounds in the process. The time between painting and launching can be longer, as the surface will wear away, or ablate, exposing new antifouling chemicals.

You can apply either hard or soft paint over a hard coat, as long as that base coat is solid and doesn't flake. Soft paint can be applied only over existing soft paint, however. Hard paint will simply peel away when applied over soft paint.

Like TBT, copper may not be entirely benign to the aquatic environment. While copper compounds have not yet been banned, certain areas in the United States are working on regulations to reduce the amount of copper entering the water. Sweden, the Netherlands, and parts of Denmark have already banned copper-based antifouling paints. So it's possible that an alternative to both hard and soft paints may someday be required.

The good news is that one alternative is already on the market. A small company, E Paint, based in Falmouth, Massachusetts, has developed a paint that, when immersed in water and subjected to sunlight, generates hydrogen peroxide. The hydrogen peroxide is an effective antifouling agent near the surface of the paint, but it rapidly dissipates in the water with no buildup of toxins. E Paint also adds a biocide to its paint to handle slime buildup.

The application of E Paint is different from that of typical bottom paints, so it's important to read the directions. As of early 2008, E Paints were not available at most boating stores, and most sales were via Internet orders. See http://www.epaint .net/index.shtm.

A final type of bottom paint is specially formulated for use on through-hull and transom-mounted transducers. For these, use a water-based antifouling paint identified as a transducer paint. These paints will not corrode transducers and can be used in salt or fresh water.

PAINTING A NEW BOAT BOTTOM

New boats or boats that have never had bottom paint applied present a slight challenge. If new, the surfaces will have traces of mold-release wax remaining from the building process. Older unpainted bottoms may also retain traces of this wax, along with dirt, grease, and oil contamination. This all has to be removed for an effective bottom job.

Start by thoroughly washing the bottom with detergent and water, then rinsing well. Most paint manufacturers offer a solvent wash or surface prep liquid. Wipe down the hull with the suggested product and follow up with a second wipe-down with the recommended thinner for the bottom paint you'll be applying.

At this point the gelcoat on the bottom of your boat will be shiny but clean. Now you have to remove that shine. Sand the bottom with 80-grit sandpaper until you achieve a uniform satin or matte surface. What you are doing is providing "tooth" so that the paint will adhere more effectively. Water lightly sprayed on the surface shouldn't bead up. If it does, keep on sanding.

The advice to use 80-grit sandpaper comes directly from the paint manufacturers. Before using it, though, check to see if you have a blister guarantee on your hull. If you do, sanding may void that warranty. In this case, contact the boat manufacturer for instructions on applying anti-fouling paint. Some suggest applying a barrier coat to the bottom of a new boat. Here again, I would seek the advice of the boat manufacturer before doing something to the boat's bottom that might void your blister warranty.

Clean off the sanded surface with solvent wash or thinner (use the products your paint manufacturer suggests) and let dry. Apply the bottom paint of your choice. Many boaters report that the first year's paint doesn't adhere well, and that the surface has to "age" for good paint reten-tion. Others counter that adequate surface prep avoids this problem.

antifouling paints might do to a small, enclosed freshwater body. Use your judgment and experi-ment. Less is more. If you can get away without antifouling paint, don't use it.

The question then asked is, "If not antifouling paint, then what?" Unfortunately, most other marine paints are not suitable for continued underwater use. If the bottom looks bad, say from a past antifouling job, you may want to bite the bullet and give the bottom a quick coat of the cheapest bottom paint you can find just to make it look good on the trailer. Off the trailer, in the water, only the fish will know.

The No-Bottom-Paint Option

The bottom paint discussion in this chapter is predicated on keeping your boat in salt water dur-ing the boating season. If you trailer your boat, or leave it in fresh water, or don't leave it in the water for extended periods, you may not need to apply antifouling paint. Depending on the area and the salinity of the water, leaving the boat in the water for up to several weeks may require only a good scrubbing when the boat is pulled. Considering the cost of today's antifouling paint, that repre-sents a considerable savings.

A boat left in fresh water for a full season may be subject to a buildup of slime and other soft aquatic growth, so if you leave your boat in a freshwater slip, you might be happier with a coat of bottom paint that includes a slime-killer addi-tive. I make this suggestion with reluctance, how-ever, because I hate the thought of what

REMOVING BOTTOM PAINT

If you are applying hard paint over hard paint or soft paint over either hard or soft, and if the bot-tom paint remaining on the hull is tight and in good shape, you need not bother removing it. But if you are changing from a soft, or ablative, paint to a hard paint, you will need to remove the remaining ablative, because hard paint will not stick well to soft. And a buildup of multiple coats of hard paint will likewise eventually need to be removed, either because the surface becomes rough or the accumulated weight of the paint affects the boat's performance.

A good, sharp carbide scraper can make quick (relatively speaking) work of removing old bot-tom paint. Be sure to get the kind of scraper with a knob over the blade: this allows a two-handed operation for increased pressure and faster scrap-ing. Careless or improper use of a scraper can

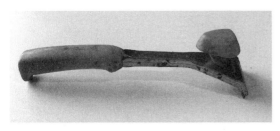

One method for removing bottom paint is to use a carbide scraper like this one. Be sure to get one with a knob near the head so you can apply additional pressure.

gouge the gelcoat, however, so round the corners of the blade with a file or a grinder before you begin. Mark any gouges you make so you can go back later and fill them in with an epoxy/filler such as Interlux Watertite Epoxy. One nice thing about scraping (as opposed to sanding) is that the chips of paint tend to be large and much less likely to blow into your eyes, nose, and hair.

If you choose to sand off the old paint, be sure to use a vacuum on the sander to control the dust. In fact, most marinas today require this, and many have the equipment available for rent. Start with 80-grit sandpaper on a 6-inch random orbit sander. In tough cases, you might have to start with 60 grit. Have plenty of sanding discs on hand, and change them often. Life is too short to use dull sandpaper. All in all, scraping is preferable to sanding for this job.

Another option is to use a paint stripper to soften the paint, and use a scraper to remove it from the hull. Some strippers are simply brushed on and left to do their work. Others require placing sheets of a special paper over the wet stripper. Once the paint has softened, it can be scraped off with a carbide scraper.

Whichever method you choose, you will have to deal with obstacles. The bootstripe should be protected by multiple layers of a good, long-life painter's blue masking tape that will hold up for the duration of the job. Whatever you do, don't use duct tape or the cheap tan masking tape used in classrooms. By the end of the job, it will have bonded itself to the hull. There are tapes designed for these types of outdoor applications. The main difference between the various types is the duration the tape can be left on the hull and reliably removed. Times vary by tape—from 24 hours to more than 80 days. Be sure to pick a tape that matches your expected timeframe. A good reference is the masking tape section of the West Marine catalog.

You will also have to remove bottom paint from around things like through-hulls, rudder bearings, and prop shafts. This is the perfect time to inspect those components and replace them if necessary.

Any of these methods requires measures for personal safety and pollution control. Use proper respirators, eye protection, "bunny" suits, and gloves. The respirator should be rated as a "toxic dust respirator" for sanding and scraping and rated for use with volatile organic compounds for stripping. You will be responsible for properly containing any dust or debris from your work site. Don't work in conditions that will spread that dust or debris. Place tarps under the boat to contain scrapings and dust and then properly dispose of them. Check with your marina or boatyard before starting in order to learn the rules for disposal. Some people "tent" their boats with tarps to contain the mess.

An alternative to sanding, scraping, and chemicals is blasting, in which an abrasive material is forced out of a nozzle with high-pressure air to abrade the paint from the hull. The process is quick and leaves a nice matte surface that has

The sensible setup for sanding a boat's topsides or bottom: "bunny" suit, eye and breathing protection, and a vacuum-equipped sander.

Sandblasting is one method for quickly removing bottom paint. It should be done only by a skilled blaster, though.

good tooth for painting. The downside is that it isn't for do-it-yourselfers. Improper abrasive blasting can ruin a hull, so hire a pro with experience in blasting boats. And it isn't cheap. I had a 35-foot boat blasted by my boatyard a year ago. The cost was $700, and it took a day to do.

The most common abrasive medium is sand. In the hands of an experienced operator, a sandblaster is a precision instrument, removing multiple layers of paint while leaving the gelcoat intact and ready for new paint. Another blasting medium is bicarbonate of soda, or baking soda, which is much less aggressive than sand and easier on the gelcoat.

An even newer process is dry-ice blasting. The very cold dry-ice pellets deliver a thermal shock to the painted surface as they strike it, and this aids in breaking up and removing the old finish. Best of all, the blasting medium sublimes into carbon dioxide gas, leaving only the paint residue to clean up.

The end result of any of these procedures is a clean hull with a matte finish that is ready for bottom paint. In extreme cases of blistering, the hull is ready for blister repair, as discussed in Fixing Blisters, later in this chapter.

RESTORING FADED GELCOAT

Eventually your pride and joy will begin showing signs of age. There are many products on boat store shelves to postpone that aging as long as possible, but even the best gelcoats eventually fade or chalk. Ultimately the gelcoat will probably require a paint job, but there are things you can do to extend the life of your gelcoat, ranging from mild to wild.

Gelcoat is the heavily pigmented layer of polyester resin that is first sprayed into the female mold in which the hull or deck of a production boat is laminated. It forms the shiny exterior surface of a hull or deck, but it is thin (15 to 20 mils, or thousandths of an inch), and overly aggressive sanding or compounding can eventually wear all the way through it. The first rule of restoring gelcoat, therefore, is to do the least aggressive treatments first, leaving the more aggressive ones for later years.

Fiberglass boats should be washed and waxed regularly, especially if used in salt water. As salt water dries on the gelcoat, small salt crystals form on the surface and can attract dirt and promote minute scratches. There are soft silicone- and carnauba-based waxes, which contain no rubbing compound, on the shelves of most boating stores. Look at your owner's manual to see if the boat's manufacturer recommends a specific type. Some builders recommend against using carnauba waxes, for reasons unexplained.

Once that new-boat gloss is gone, it's time to begin using a cleaner wax such as those from Star brite, 3M, Collinite, and Meguiar's. These one-part waxes contain small amounts of rubbing compound and will remove mild haze, light oxidation, and minor scratches. They can be applied with a cloth and then buffed out by hand or with a power buffer. Microfiber rags, available at most boating stores, work well for hand buffing.

When cleaner waxes no longer do the job, move up to a color restorer. Meguiar's, 3M, Star brite, and West Marine all offer comparable products. These compounds have a more aggressive abrasive than the ones in cleaner waxes and will remove a mild oxidation film and bring back the shine. They are also applied with a rag. Most often, this requires a four-step process: wash, apply the restorer, buff, and then wax.

If you are not satisfied with the results from using a restorer, it is time to move on to pure rubbing compounds. These are highly abrasive and wear away that chalky outer layer of oxidized gelcoat. Star brite and 3M are the most popular brands and offer the greatest number of different grades. Obviously you don't want to use them excessively; you'll literally be removing the gelcoat. Start with the mildest you can find.

While you can apply them by hand, a power buffer/polisher is most often used. Be careful and watch the state of the polishing pad. It is possible to grind swirl marks into the gelcoat. Keep several polishing pads available for your unit. Wash them and change them regularly. Whether buffing by hand or with a machine, try to maintain even pressure. Avoid pressing down excessively with fingertips or the edge of a buffer pad, as this will cause swirl marks.

Most rubbing compounds leave a satin finish that must then be polished to bring out the shine. One of the most popular products for this is 3M Finesse-It II finishing material. This liquid is applied by hand or by polishing machine and then buffed out. The result is a gelcoat as close to the original shine as possible. Finish with wax for more protection.

When a mild or medium rubbing compound won't do the job, move up to the heavy-duty products. These usually need to be applied using a polishing or buffing machine. Again, keep an eye on the pads and change them often to avoid leaving swirl marks. Following the heavy-duty rubbing compound, try going straight to Finesse-It to bring out the shine. If the surface is too rough, however, you may need to next use a mild rubbing compound, then the Finesse-It.

If all of the methods described here fail to bring back the shine, it's time for the last resort—sanding. Use wet-or-dry sandpaper with plenty of water. Put a few drops of dish detergent in the water to lower surface tension and clear off the suspended sanding dust. Wet-or-dry sandpaper is available up to as fine as 2,000 grit, but start with 600 and then move to 1,000 grit. Hand-sanding something the size of a boat is a daunting task, but it's the best way, so bring friends.

If you finish with the finer grits of wet-or-dry sandpaper, you might be able to go straight to Finesse-It polish, then wax. Otherwise, you may need to use a rubbing compound.

REPAINTING A BOAT

There comes a time in the life of every fiberglass boat when waxing, polishing, and compounding no longer do the job. The gelcoat has faded to the point of no return or is chipped and crazed. In any case, it is decision time. Is the boat worth an investment of time and effort, or do you simply take the course of least resistance and sell the boat?

A surprising number of folks decide, for reasons economic or sentimental, to keep the boat and repaint it. Such was the case with my family's vintage 1972 boat. I describe the details of that paint job, referring to specific brands and products, not because they are the best or only products on the market but simply because they were the ones I chose and am therefore familiar with.

Not all boatowners decide to do this job themselves. There are numerous competent shops out there that can handle painting projects with great skill. In fact, some finishes, such as Awlgrip and Imron, require professional applicators for a safe and effective job and aren't even available to the consumer. Nevertheless, there are plenty of two-part polyurethanes, single-part silicone-modified urethanes, and even traditional marine alkyd enamel paints that will provide a good owner-applied finish on a fiberglass boat. The job I did on my boat worked out well.

It has been said that proper preparation is 90 percent of a good paint job. It was certainly a challenge on my boat. The gelcoat had faded and been compounded (scrubbed with rubbing compound to remove stains, scuff marks, and oxidized gelcoat) several times. In addition, parts of the hull were crazed. (Crazing is an alligator pattern of shallow gelcoat cracks, reminiscent of those you sometimes see in dessicated mud. It isn't structural, but it looks terrible.) Heavy sanding would be required to get down to a firm base for painting, and most of the remaining gelcoat would be removed in the process.

The first step, however, was to dewax the hull. The hull had been laminated in a heavily waxed mold, and further coats of wax had been applied over the years. All this would have to come off for good paint adhesion. After a good cleaning with detergent and water, I dewaxed the hull with Interlux 202 Fiberglass Solvent Wash. I used plenty of clean rags and wiped in only one direction.

Then I began sanding, starting out with 80-grit sanding discs on a 6-inch random orbit sander. The going was hard on the old gelcoat, so I soon switched to 60 grit. My boatyard requires that all sanders be used with a vacuum attachment to control dust.

Once I finished sanding with the 60-grit discs, I went back over the hull with 180-grit discs to get

A random orbit sander sitting atop a shop vac, to which it is attached via hose. Most boatyards require that your sander be attached to a vacuum cleaner to control dust. Clean the filter often, as the sanding dust is very fine.

out the 60-grit scratches and prepare the hull for primer. I rolled on a coat of Interlux PreKote gray primer and let it dry. The PreKote instructions state that it should be sanded almost translucent, which I did with 220-grit sandpaper.

I then went over the hull and marked all remaining imperfections—chips, gouges, scratches, and pits. These I filled with Interlux Watertite Epoxy Filler. Once the epoxy had cured, I carefully sanded these areas flush with the surrounding hull, then rolled on the second coat of PreKote, this time adding a little topcoat to pre-color the primer. (This is especially useful when the primer color is light and the final coat is darker.)

After the primer had dried, I sanded it with 220-grit sandpaper, then wiped down the hull

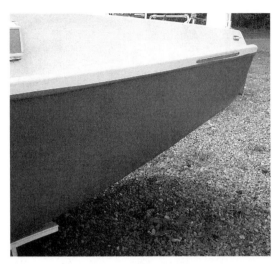

This hull has been painted with two coats of Interlux PreKote primer. The primer can be rolled on, as it will be sanded between coats.

The primer is sanded to translucence between coats.

with Interlux 216 Thinner to get all the dust off. The hull was finally ready for the topcoats.

The PreKote primer is formulated to work with Interlux's one-part polyurethane paint, Brightside. I applied the finish coats of Brightside using the "roll and tip" method. This technique works best with two people. The first person rolls on a thin coat of paint with a foam roller, while the second person follows behind and lightly strokes or "tips" out the paint with a dry foam brush. The tipping brush, used dry, simply smoothes out the rolled-on paint. Once the tipping brush picks up any significant amount of paint, it should be discarded or cleaned and a new, dry brush used. The two people work from one end of the hull to the other in 2-foot by 3-foot sections, with the roller beginning each new section before the trailing section loses its "wet edge." Properly done, a rolled and tipped hull looks as if it has been spray-painted.

One key to effective paint application is the proper thinning of the paint. Unfortunately, it isn't as easy as saying, "Add 5.5 percent thinner," because the proper amount varies with temperature, humidity, wind speed, and sunlight intensity. You have to use trial and error. I mixed a small amount of thinner into the paint, then rolled and tipped a small section of the hull. If the paint flowed smoothly and left no brush or roller marks, I was good to go. Otherwise, I wiped off the hull and tried a little more thinner. Alternatively, try the paint on old window glass before you use it on the boat.

Once the thinner ratio was right, it was off to the races. My wife, Pat, and I could roll and tip a coat of paint on the 20-foot hull in about an hour and a half. I rolled while my wife tipped. She went through about two foam brushes per side, throwing a brush away when it gathered too much paint

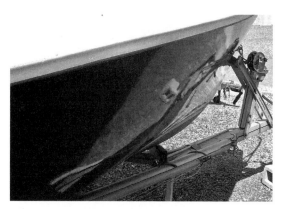

The finished hull with four coats of thinned Interlux Brightside single-part urethane paint.

to tip properly. If the paint became too thick due to evaporation in the paint tray, I added a little more thinner.

For best results, Interlux recommends wet sanding between each coat with wet-or-dry sandpaper. I did wet-sand after the first coat, but not after the remaining coats. I simply wiped down the entire hull with thinner before adding the next coat. Depending on the weather and our schedules, we waited as much as several days between coats.

Because I was applying a red topcoat over gray primer (and forgot to add some topcoat paint to the primer), I put on four coats of the topcoat. Don't try to substitute one or two thicker coats for three or four thin ones, because the paint will run and sag and will take forever to dry hard. I painted the hull in late fall and didn't launch the boat again that year, which gave the paint ample opportunity to cure to a solid, hard finish. Don't put your boat in the water before the paint has a chance to fully dry according to the paint manufacturer's recommendations.

The final finish had excellent gloss and smoothness. I would give it a "5" rating (looks good from 5 feet away), but then I'm biased. I didn't save every receipt, but I estimate that it cost $250 to $300 to paint a 20-foot hull. Not a bad price, considering the cost of a professional paint job.

FIXING BLISTERS

I knew I had a blister problem as soon as I pulled the boat in Tennessee in to prep her for hauling to the Chesapeake. Not a catastrophic problem, but a problem nevertheless. Maybe about two dozen large blisters on each side. It wasn't unexpected; she had been sitting in warm fresh water—the worst possible combination for breeding blisters in a fiberglass hull—for almost eight years.

Blisters typically develop between the gelcoat and the outermost layer of underlying fiberglass mat. Fiberglass is not as impervious to water as was once thought. Water molecules migrate through the pores of the gelcoat and find weak spots in the bond between the gelcoat and the mat. These weak spots can originate from a host of problems, including resin-starved laminations, improper resin mixtures, contamination of the gelcoat before the mat layup, and poor resin quality, to name a few. The water vapor mixes with styrene and other unreacted chemicals in the fiberglass and forms a potent liquid in the blister. That liquid is under pressure and forces the gelcoat away from the mat layer.

Many modern boats use vinylester resins below the waterline to prevent blister formation, quite successfully. Those of us with older boats, however, aren't so lucky. The blisters can range from a few on each side to massive numbers covering the entire bottom of the boat. In a few instances (certain models of Valiant sailboats, for

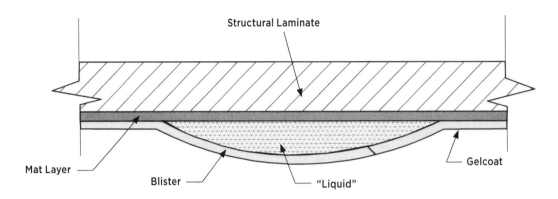

A cross-sectional view of a typical blister.

example), blisters may affect the topsides as well. Luckily, such cases are few and far between.

Mild cases of blistering can be fixed by repairing individual blisters. In a worst-case scenario, however, the entire gelcoat and outermost layer of mat must be removed by grinding or "peeling" (with huge machines), and then new fiberglass reinforcement must be applied. The reinforcement is needed to build the hull back up to its original thickness and strength. This is a huge job, best left to pros. My case, which wasn't so severe, represents a good example of the kind of blister problem that any determined boatowner can tackle on his or her own.

I started the repair as soon as the boat was out of the water and on jack stands. The blisters were evident as bulges in the hull, and I circled each one with a Magic Marker. It is important to mark them while the hull is still wet and the blisters are at their largest. As soon as the hull is out of the water, it begins to dry, and the blisters will shrink and become harder to spot.

I planned to remove the bottom paint, repair the blisters, and then apply a barrier coat to the hull. This meant the markings would disappear when the paint was removed. So once I had all the

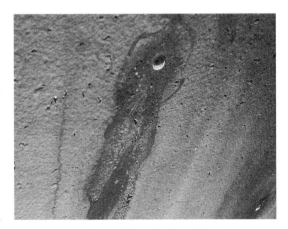

Immediately after pulling the boat from the water, I drew a circle around each blister, then drilled a hole into each to drain the liquid.

blisters marked, I drilled each one with a countersink bit in my battery-powered drill. This accomplished two things: it marked the location of each blister, and it opened up the blisters and allowed the liquid inside them to drain.

Be sure to wear eye protection when doing this. The liquid inside the blister is under considerable pressure and will spurt out. It is a nasty concoction, and you do not want it in your eyes. I let the blisters drain and start drying out. Actu-

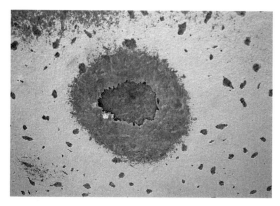

I had the person sandblasting my hull pay special attention to the blisters. Sandblasting opened them up and made them dry faster.

The final result was evenly sandblasted gelcoat, devoid of bottom paint.

ally, I let the boat sit for well over a year as other projects and life in general intervened. By the time I returned to the project, the blisters had drained and the hull was "smooth" again—with the exception of the countersunk holes.

I had planned to remove the bottom paint using paint stripper and scrapers, and actually did about 6 feet of one side of the hull before I came to my senses. Apparently the hull had never been stripped before, and it retained remnants of every coat of paint it had ever received. I decided to have the hull blasted to remove the paint, and I chose sandblasting as the most aggressive medium.

My boatyard assigned a skilled sandblast operator, who did small sections of the hull at a time. He initially worked on each blister in a section, concentrating on the countersink marks to open the blisters and clean them out. He then did the remainder of each section, leaving the gelcoat intact but with a smooth satin finish, ready for the barrier coat.

Not all the blisters were completely dry. A few still contained traces of the blister liquid. The high-pressure air forced the liquid out and restarted the drying process.

The next step was to grind out the blistered areas. I determined the rough size of each area to be ground out by rapping on the hull with a knuckle, small hammer, or plastic screwdriver handle. A hull in good condition will sound solid, while loose, delaminated gelcoat will sound hollow. I ground each blister into a dish shape with tapered sides. To make sure I had gotten rid of all areas in which the bond between the mat and the gelcoat had failed, I tried to insert a thin knife blade between the two at the edges of each ground area. Anyplace where I could insert the blade meant that I hadn't ground far enough.

I washed all the ground areas thoroughly with water and detergent to remove any remnants of the blister liquid. I then left the hull to dry completely, since any moisture is a sure recipe for a later renewal of the problem. I used a moisture meter to take regular readings of various parts of the hull until the readings stabilized. If you don't have access to a moisture meter, tape a square of plastic over each blister and let it sit. If there is still

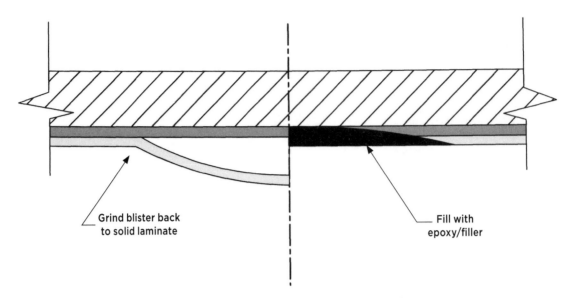

Grind blister back
to solid laminate

Fill with
epoxy/filler

Once blisters are opened up and dried out, they can be filled with epoxy/filler and faired.

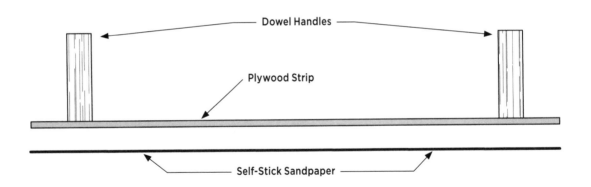

Dowel Handles

Plywood Strip

Self-Stick Sandpaper

A longboard can be used to sand blister repairs. The board should span a large enough area of the hull to conform to its curvature and ensure that your sanding fairs the repair into the surrounding surface.

water vapor, it will condense on the plastic. When no more condensation appears, proceed with the blister repair.

I gave the surface of the depressions a coat of epoxy resin. This sealed the fiberglass from further water intrusion. While that coat was still slightly tacky, I filled the depressions with an epoxy/filler mixture. My personal choice is Interlux Watertite Epoxy. Some of the deeper depressions took several coats to fill completely.

After the filled epoxy had cured, I faired the hull smooth (see the Using Epoxy sidebar in

Chapter 2). This process is best accomplished with a long, narrow piece of flexible plywood with sandpaper glued to one side and handles attached to the other side. The resulting tool is called, appropriately enough, a *longboard*. It spans the depressions and keeps you from sanding hollows or unevenness back into the hull.

After all the blisters had been faired, I gave the bottom a coat of epoxy resin to seal the filler from water intrusion and to establish a sound base for a barrier coat, as described in the next project, Applying a Barrier Coat.

APPLYING A BARRIER COAT

Why barrier-coat a hull? To seal the fiberglass laminate against the penetration of water, which causes blistering. Keep in mind that any damage to the barrier will negate its effectiveness. Repairs should be made whenever the boat is hauled and inspected. *NOTE*: Be sure to consult your boat manufacturer if you are intending to barrier-coat a new boat. In some cases, this may void the blister warranty on your boat.

The first prerequisite for barrier-coating a hull is that the hull be dry. A barrier coat applied over a wet hull is sure to fail, with the water vapor trapped under the barrier coat fostering new blisters. The hull should have been dry before patching any blisters, and the longer it dries out, the better. Three months or so isn't too long.

New hulls need to be thoroughly cleaned to remove all remaining traces of mold-release wax. Each manufacturer of barrier coats has its own recommended solvent wash or dewaxer. Follow the manufacturer's instructions. Do not sand before cleaning, as this simply drives the wax further into the pores of the fiberglass and will cause barrier coat adhesion problems.

Hulls previously bottom painted need to have the bottom paint removed down to the gelcoat. This can be done by chemical strippers and scrapers, by sanding, or by abrasive blasting, as described earlier in this chapter. Once the hull is cleaned, it should be sanded to a uniform matte finish with 80-grit sandpaper. Spray the sanded area with water. If the water beads up, keep sanding. Finish up by removing the sanding residue with the solvent recommended by your barrier coat supplier.

Probably the two most popular barrier coat systems are Interlux InterProtect and Gougeon Brothers WEST System epoxy. Both can be and are applied by boatowners all the time. Both are epoxy-based systems, each with additives to enhance the effectiveness of the coating. Each requires multiple coats to build an effective film thickness. It is this film thickness that provides the barrier to keep water from migrating into the fiberglass.

Refer to the sidebar Using Epoxy in Chapter 2 for guidance on this product. Remember to avoid contact with these products by using appropriate protective gear. Gloves, face masks, and bunny suits are wise precautions.

InterProtect is available in two forms: 2000E and 3000. Both are two-part epoxies formulated for application by do-it-yourselfers. There are some differences in application procedures, but the main difference between the two products is that 3000 is formulated for low VOC (volatile organic compounds) emissions.

Once the hull has been prepped, the two components of InterProtect are mixed together. Mix only as much as is needed for a single coat. The mixture needs to sit at least twenty minutes to let the two components react. The InterProtect can then be rolled or brushed onto the hull.

To be effective, the final barrier coat needs to be at least 10 mils (0.010 inch) thick. This means that about five or six coats of InterProtect are required. Additional coats can be applied as soon as the previous coat passes the "thumbprint test": Press your thumb into the paint, and when the paint is dry enough not to stick to your thumb yet still tacky enough to show a thumbprint, it is ready for the next coat.

InterProtect comes in two colors—white and gray. The manufacturer suggests applying alternating colors so you can get total coverage with no missed areas. The InterProtect instructions lay out a time line that will allow applying all five or six coats in one weekend. It is a bit of a stretch, but it can be done. Conversely, you can wait up to two weeks between coats. After that, you will need to sand the last coat you applied for best adhesion, which is counterproductive to attaining that 10-mil final thickness.

Once the final coat of InterProtect is sufficiently dry, the surface is ready for bottom paint. No further prep is required.

The Interlux website (www.yachtpaint.com) provides a great deal of information, including a twelve-page technical bulletin. Read this before attempting the project. Among other things, it has a chart showing the approximate amount of InterProtect needed for boats of various sizes.

The WEST System barrier coat comprises an epoxy resin (105) that can be used with several alternate hardeners—206 Slow, 205 Fast, 207 Clear, and 209 Extra Slow (Tropical)—of which the 205 Fast and 206 Slow are used most often. The resin and hardener are mixed in a 5:1 ratio, which is best done with the Gougeon Brothers'

calibrated epoxy pumps; one squirt of each provides the proper ratio.

Gougeon Brothers recommends a minimum of three coats of epoxy but strongly suggests six—a 20-mil (0.020 inch) thickness—for best protection. The first coat is applied without any additive, but for subsequent coats the company's 422 Barrier Coat Additive is mixed into the resin and hardener at the rate of 15 to 20 percent by weight. Each of these coats needs to be applied as soon as the previous coat has cured enough to accept it. Ideally, all coats should be applied the same day—a *real* stretch requiring several people to accomplish.

If you have to leave the epoxy on long enough to cure before applying the next coat, you have some work to do. The surface needs to be thoroughly scrubbed to remove any amine blush and then lightly sanded.

After the final coat has been applied, the cured epoxy surface will also have to be scrubbed and sanded before applying bottom paint.

Gougeon Brothers maintains an extensive website at http://www.westsystem.com with product descriptions and application notes.

REPAIRING CHIPS, DINGS, AND GOUGES

At the start of each new boating season, we start to notice all those little defects—gelcoat dings, cracks, scratches, and such—that didn't seem to matter the year before. Some defects may even be serious, suggesting structural damage to the underlying fiberglass laminate. (We cover structural repairs in the next project, Structural

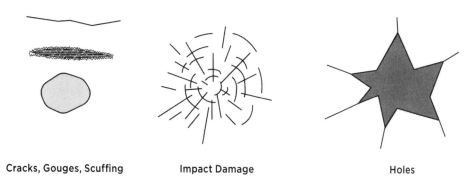

| Cracks, Gouges, Scuffing | Impact Damage | Holes |

Typical examples of the insults suffered by fiberglass boats.

Patches and Repairs.) In any case, interest in fiberglass repairs seems to peak in the spring, and it's a good idea to make the repairs before the boat goes back into the water. Last fall might have been an even better time for this, but that's life.

Cracks are common on older fiberglass boats. Since gelcoat contains no reinforcing fibers, overly thick gelcoat is necessarily brittle and prone to cracking. Even gelcoat of normal thickness can be subject to stress cracks over time from flexing of the underlying fiberglass laminate. One common area for this to occur is in the corner of a cockpit well, where the cockpit sides meet the floor, or sole. Other stress cracks can be caused by dropping a heavy object on a fiberglass deck surface. Cracks of this sort typically radiate outward from the point of impact.

Scratches can occur from a myriad of causes, including contact with docks and other boats. Trailered boats can suffer scratches while being launched from or recovered to the trailer. Other scratches can come from groundings or beachings, intentional or otherwise.

Gouges and dings commonly come from an impact that digs a chip from the fiberglass, but they can also occur on molded fiberglass edges where the gelcoat may be thicker than optimal. Again, gelcoat is brittle, and thicker accumulations on outside edges make it all the more vulnerable.

Earlier in this chapter, under Repainting a Boat, we discussed how to fill cosmetic scratches, gouges, and dings with epoxy after applying a primer coat of paint to a hull. When you repair a hull or deck surface that you do not intend to refinish, however, things get a little more complicated. You'll need to make the repairs using polyester gelcoat paste that matches the surrounding gelcoat surface.

The first step in repairing any cosmetic defects is to dewax the area. Most paint manufacturers have their own version of a dewaxing solvent. Use it liberally to remove any traces of dirt, grease, or wax from the surfaces to be repaired.

Cracks are too narrow to allow repair materials to penetrate, so they must be widened. This can be done with a Dremel tool if you have a steady hand. Another tool often used is the triangular point of a church key, or old-fashioned bottle opener. (If you don't know what a church key is, ask your grandfather or google it.) Sharpen the point and drag it down the crack to widen it to a vee. You have now turned the crack into a scratch, and we can proceed with scratch repairs.

After dewaxing the scratch, sand it with 80-grit sandpaper to provide some "tooth" for the repair material. Wipe the area clean with acetone to remove any traces of dirt, grease, or wax. The same process applies to gelcoat gouges and dings, which are a bit bigger than a scratch but otherwise pretty much the same.

Now let's look at the repair materials. There are two types of gelcoat paste, available in cans in most marine stores. Laminating paste does not cure tack-free in the presence of air, while finishing paste does. Laminating paste, therefore, is used to build up thickness in layers, while finishing paste is used for the final layer.

The most common color is white. Gelcoat color-matching kits are available, and these include several different pigments. The idea is that you should be able to match any nonwhite gelcoat you are trying to repair by mixing pigments. Good luck! Matching gelcoat colors is an art. If you are determined to try, go to an art supply store and purchase a color wheel. This gadget is like a circular slide rule and will give you the ratios of pigments needed to match a given color. Even if you do match your existing gelcoat color perfectly, however, don't expect it to match indefinitely, since the new gelcoat will fade at a faster rate than the old gelcoat that it's meant to match.

Styrene monomer is a thinner for polyester resin, the base ingredient in gelcoat. It's getting hard to find, but if you can find it, wipe it on the area to be repaired. This will aid in getting a good bond between the gelcoat paste and the fiberglass surface. Then mix the gelcoat paste with the recommended amount of catalyst and apply it to the surface to be repaired. This can be done with an epoxy syringe or a "pastry bag" made from a plastic baggie with a corner cut off. Overfill the area slightly, as the gelcoat will shrink upon curing. Be neat, and don't get gelcoat anywhere you don't want it. Keep a rag and acetone handy to wipe up any drips or smears.

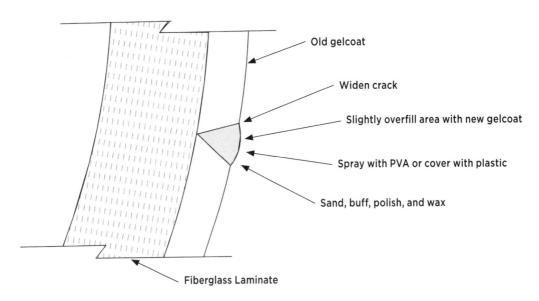

Old gelcoat

Widen crack

Slightly overfill area with new gelcoat

Spray with PVA or cover with plastic

Sand, buff, polish, and wax

Fiberglass Laminate

Scratches and gouges can often be repaired by the boatowner.

If you picked a laminating gelcoat, you have one further step at this point: You must seal the surface from air so the gelcoat will cure tack-free. You can spray a coating of PVA (polyvinyl alcohol) mold release on the surface or cover the area with a piece of plastic wrap. If you are using plastic wrap, make sure you apply it without wrinkles and as smoothly as possible, because you will have to sand out any imperfections. PVA is water soluble and can be washed off after the gelcoat has cured.

Once the gelcoat has cured, carefully block-sand the repair until it is even with the surrounding fiberglass. Don't oversand, as the gelcoat surface is usually only 10 to 20 mils (0.010 to 0.020 inch) thick. Continue wet-sanding with progressively finer grits of sandpaper. Go as fine as 1,000 or 1,500 grit, then polish the surface with a polishing compound (not rubbing compound!) such as 3M Finesse-It II. Then you can wax it and stand back and admire your handiwork. Take your time, follow the steps, and above all, properly dewax!

STRUCTURAL PATCHES AND REPAIRS

When the defect or damage you wish to repair extends well beneath the gelcoat and into the underlying laminate—when it's not just cosmetic but structural—gelcoat paste will not suffice. Structural repairs to a hull or deck, especially a hull below the waterline, need to be as strong as the original lamination. This requires both the right materials and the right techniques.

Although the hull or deck was more than likely made from polyester resin, polyester isn't the right resin for repairs. Polyester doesn't form

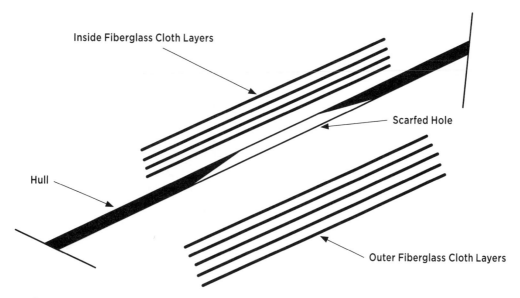

Anatomy of a patch. A proper scarf joint provides ample area for effective bonding of a fiberglass patch.

a good secondary bond with cured polyester. Epoxy resins do, and they are the right choice for structural repairs to fiberglass hulls and decks.

It is important to provide as much bonding area as possible for the epoxy. For this, a technique called scarfing is used. The edges of the hole to be filled are tapered, usually to a 12 to 1 taper. That is, a hole with a depth of ⅛ inch should be tapered back 1½ inches in all directions. Loose or damaged fiberglass should be cut back to sound fiberglass, and this edge is then scarfed. My favorite tool for grinding a scarf is a right-angle grinder with a 36-grit disc. Another choice is a diamond-coated tuck-point grinding disc, used to remove cement from the joints between bricks.

When you're repairing a hole through the hull, the scarf should face the direction of maximum pressure. Since water presses on the hull from the outside, this means that the scarf should face outward, not inward. Patches above the waterline may be subject to lower forces but still should be properly scarfed.

Some hulls and most decks are built with a balsa wood, plywood, or plastic foam core between the inner and outer fiberglass layers. Repairing this composite construction is a little more difficult than repairing solid fiberglass. If the damaged area is not large, the best repair method is simply to replace the damaged core with solid fiberglass laminations. The area should still be scarfed to give the maximum area for bonding the patch. If large areas of core are damaged, the repair should probably be referred to a fiberglass specialist—especially if the damage is below the waterline.

Typically, more of the repair laminations are applied to the outside of the hull than the inside, again to resist the force of the water pressing in. If the hole is big enough to require backing, the usual practice is to place something, such as a piece of cardboard faced with waxed paper or plastic, against the hole inside the boat. The fiberglass laminations are then built up against this surface. If the damaged area crosses a bulkhead or structural member inside the hull, you will need a temporary backing on either side of the interfering member.

As an example, let's look at a below-the-waterline repair that I recently did in a solid (non-cored) hull. (We've already talked about deck repairs in Chapters 2 and 4.) The boat had a through-hull fitting for discharge from the head that the owner wanted decommissioned and permanently sealed. After removing the fitting, my first step was to clean the repair site with a fiberglass dewaxer. Then I sanded the inside of the hull where the patch would go. I removed all traces of old paint and gelcoat until the glass fibers could be seen. On the outside of the hull, I cut the scarf with my angle grinder until I had the 12 to 1 taper.

The first step in any hull repair is to prep the area being repaired. Here the inside surface of the hull around the repair site has been cleaned and sanded.

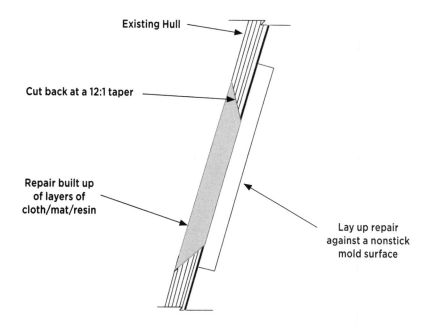

Existing Hull

Cut back at a 12:1 taper

Repair built up
of layers of
cloth/mat/resin

Lay up repair
against a nonstick
mold surface

If the hole being patched is large, a backing plate covered in plastic wrap may be necessary to support the first several layers of the patch until it cures. Although this diagram shows the scarf cut on the inside of the hull, I prefer to cut the scarf on the outside—at least for a below-the-waterline repair—so that water pressure will have no tendency to separate the patch from the surrounding hull surface.

I cut fiberglass cloth reinforcement for the inside of the hull. I used 9-ounce fiberglass cloth, but alternating layers of cloth and stitched biaxial mat would also have been a valid choice. Avoid using "regular" (that is, intended for polyester) fiberglass mat with epoxy, since epoxy won't dissolve the binder that holds the fibers together.

Some books tell you to cut circles of fiberglass cloth of increasing diameters for the patch (so that each successive patch adheres on its perimeter to solid existing hull laminate). I took the easy way and cut a series of squares out of the cloth instead, with each square about 5 inches across. I painted the area around the inside of the hole with epoxy and carefully placed the first piece of cloth over the hole.

For my repair of the hole left by a discarded through-hull, I laid down eight squares of fiberglass cloth inside the hull, wetting out each one with epoxy resin and turning it about 30 degrees from the square that preceded it. The hole was small enough that I didn't need to position a backer on the outside.

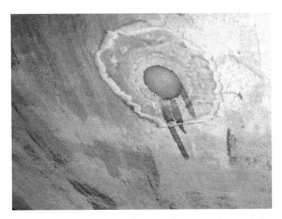

In this outside view of the repair, the inside patch is clearly visible through the hole. The outside of the hull has been sanded back to provide an ample bonding surface, and we're ready to apply fiberglass cloth and resin outside.

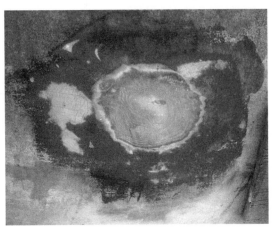

In this view of the finished repair, the fiberglass cloth and epoxy have been sanded smooth and faired into the rest of the hull. It is ready for bottom paint.

If the hole isn't large and you are careful not to push the cloth into the hole, you don't need to back up this first layer from the outside. If you aren't gentle with the cloth, however, you will need to tape a cardboard backing to the outside of the hull, covering the inside surface of the cardboard with waxed paper. After I had the first piece of cloth in place, I added the remaining layers, each at about a 30-degree angle to the one preceding. I used eight layers of cloth inside.

After the inside patch had cured, I returned to the outside of the hull and resanded the patched area and the exposed cloth from the inside patch. This ensured a good bond between the two layers.

I applied a coat of epoxy resin to the repair area and proceeded to apply the outside layers of cloth. I was, at this point, working on a slight overhead curve of the hull, so I added colloidal silica to the epoxy to reduce sagging. Otherwise, I used the same techniques as on the inside patch,

placing each cloth square at an angle to the previous one. I used a total of eighteen layers of cloth on the outside. That sounds like a lot, but it was what I needed to make the resulting patch as thick as the hull.

After the epoxy had cured, it took me just a few minutes with a belt sander to fair the patch into the hull and get it ready for bottom paint.

AN ABOVE-THE-WATERLINE HULL REPAIR

Here's another example of a hull repair with a few different twists. This one involved a cored transom more than an inch thick, and my objective was to patch a hole that had formerly been used to mount an engine exhaust fitting. The hole was normally above the waterline and was much smaller than in the previous example.

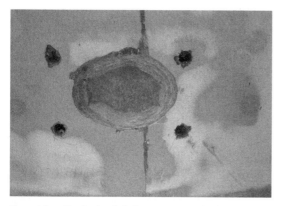

Repairing the holes left in a transom by a discarded engine exhaust fitting. The fitting and fastener holes have been reamed out and are ready for the repair to begin. Notice the blue tape backing up the central hole, and the exposed edges of plywood core.

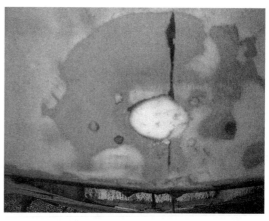

Here the repair has cured and has been sanded and faired with the rest of the transom.

Removing the fitting exposed the bare wood of the transom core. After the usual dewaxing, I tapered the edge of the hole with a cutter bit in my drill. A cutter bit looks like a very small pineapple and cuts quite aggressively. Given the above-the-waterline location and the thickness of the transom, I didn't need the full 12 to 1 scarf taper.

I placed several layers of blue tape over the hole on the inside of the transom, thus covering the hole and giving me something to laminate the patch against. I brushed a coat of epoxy resin on the exposed edges of the hole, paying special attention to the bare wood. I wanted the wood to soak up the epoxy resin to provide a good bond with the fiberglass laminations of the patch. I then began to build up the patch in the hole with multiple laminations of fiberglass cloth and epoxy resin, being careful not to push through the tape. After I had built up about eight layers of fiberglass cloth, I filled the remainder of the hole with epoxy fairing compound.

The exhaust fitting had been held in place with four screws. I drilled out these holes slightly oversize to clean them, then filled them with epoxy/filler, using a plastic syringe to fill each hole from the inside out, eliminating any air bubbles. After the epoxy cured, I sanded the patch fair with the transom.

TRANSOM REPAIR

A dock mate stopped by recently to ask about a project he was contemplating. He had been given an old Glastron outboard hull and was thinking about restoring it. One thing led to another, and he mentioned that water was leaking from several holes in the transom. Looking at it closely, we determined that the transom needed more than just a few patches. The transom core had disintegrated and would have to be replaced. Sometimes it pays to give a gift horse a thorough dental exam before letting him into your barn.

Replacing a transom core is difficult but possible for a boatowner to accomplish. Before you leap into such a project, make sure the boat is otherwise sound and that you like it enough to devote a lot of work to its repair. If you decide the effort is worthwhile, take your time and do it right; this is a job you don't want to do more than once.

Transoms tend to be among the most highly stressed parts of a hull, particularly of outboard and stern-drive boats, where they have to bear most or all of the weight of the drivetrain and resist its propulsive and steering forces. Boat manufacturers account for this by reinforcing the transom with extra layers of fiberglass and (usually) a plywood core.

As long as the plywood remains encapsulated in glass and resin, things are fine. But in stern-drive installations, a big hole is cut through the transom. Large outboards are often through-bolted. And on most boats—including those with inboard power—holes are drilled through the transom to mount swim ladders, transducers, and other accessories.

When the sealant fails around these holes, water begins to leak into the plywood core. After a while, the plywood begins to rot and delaminate, leaving the outer skins of fiberglass poorly supported. The transom becomes flexible, and the gelcoat and fiberglass begin to crack.

The first step in replacing a transom core is getting to it. You can do this from inside or outside the boat. The disadvantage of approaching it from the outside is that it will require removing the outer skin of the transom, necessitating extensive fairing and painting to return it to its original appearance. I therefore recommend doing the repair from the inside, even though this may

mean removing much of the interior, such as seats, tanks, and possibly other internal structures. If the boat is a stern drive, the drive unit and engine will have to come out. This is also a good time to look at the state of the decks and possibly replace them too. See Chapters 2 and 4 for deck repair and replacement procedures.

Once the interior surface of the transom is accessible, it is time to cut away that layer of fiberglass in a way that doesn't stress or crack the exterior fiberglass layers and gelcoat. An angle grinder with a cutoff blade works well. If the plywood is in bad shape, the fiberglass may just peel off at that point. Otherwise, judicious use of pry bars may be necessary. If you can remove this inner skin without damaging it, you can reuse it over the new core.

The plywood core can then be taken out. Some of it may be soft enough to scoop out with a spoon, but there will undoubtedly be firm sections that will still be bonded to the hull. These need to be carefully chiseled off, again without damaging the exterior skin.

Remove all traces of the old plywood, then sand and clean the inside surface of the exterior skin with 80-grit sandpaper. Be sure to sand the edges where the inner layers of transom fiberglass attach to the hull sides; this will make bonding the new transom in place much easier. Vacuum up the dust and wipe down the fiberglass with acetone.

The next job is to make a pattern of the inside of the transom so the new plywood can be cut to shape. A good choice for pattern material is artist's foam board. You can tape smaller pieces together with masking tape to get the sizes you need. Brown wrapping paper also works as long as you tape it in place so it doesn't slip around. The pattern (and the plywood cut from the pat-

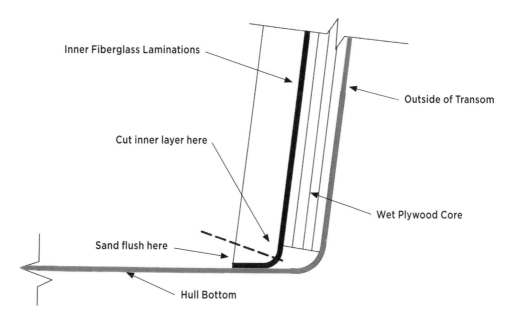

Inner Fiberglass Laminations

Cut inner layer here

Sand flush here

Hull Bottom

Outside of Transom

Wet Plywood Core

The first step in the repair of a plywood-cored transom is to remove the old, wet core.

tern) needn't fit precisely around the edges. In fact, the radius of the corners may well prevent a tight fit. Any gaps will be filled in when the plywood is bonded in place.

Let's talk about plywood before actually cutting any. Most transom cores are about 1½ inches thick. If there is any curve to the transom, this thickness is best made up of three layers of ½-inch plywood. You can use top-of-the-line marine plywood or lumberyard exterior ply. Marine ply is expensive and hard to get. Exterior-grade lumberyard plywood is much cheaper and readily available, but it is rougher and of poorer construction and probably has voids, which weaken the structure and provide a breeding ground for rot. Both types are made with waterproof glue.

MDO plywood is a better choice. This plywood is made with waterproof glue and is designed for use in exterior signs, has few or no voids, and has a smooth exterior surface of phenolic resin paper that accepts epoxy and paint very well. It is cheaper than marine plywood and much better than construction-grade exterior ply. It can be ordered at most good lumberyards.

You may have to make the new transom core in several pieces if fitting it back in the boat is a problem. If so, and you are using two or more layers of plywood, stagger the joints for maximum strength.

Coat the plywood on all surfaces with unfilled epoxy. Before it has completely cured, mix some more epoxy with a filler, such as WEST 404 High-Density Filler, and trowel it onto the inside surface of the exterior fiberglass skin. Do not use polyester resin, which isn't strong enough for this repair. A notched plastic squeegee will help you achieve a uniform layer of epoxy. It is better to use too much epoxy and clean up the squeeze-out than to use too little and risk voids or poorly

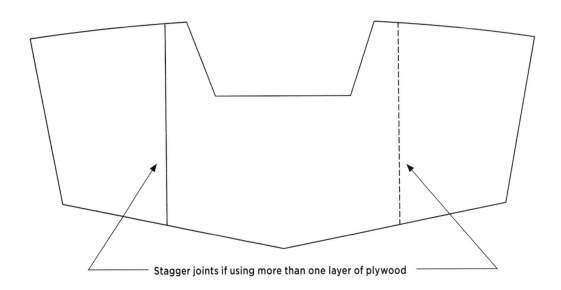

Stagger joints if using more than one layer of plywood

Replacement transom cores are usually made from three layers of ½-inch or two layers of ¾-inch plywood. If restricted access forces you to use two or three pieces in each layer, stagger the joints between pieces from one layer to the next.

bonded areas. Press the first layer of plywood into this epoxy bedding.

You will need to apply pressure to hold the plywood in place, seat it in the epoxy, and make it conform to any curve in the transom. One of the best ways to do this is to drill several holes through the plywood and the outer fiberglass skin and through-bolt it. Spray the bolts with a cooking spray so the epoxy won't stick. The holes will be filled in with epoxy and filler later.

Use any squeezed-out epoxy to fill voids around the plywood edges. Make sure you don't leave any drops or lumps of epoxy on the surface of the plywood, as this will cause problems when installing the next layer.

When the first layer has set sufficiently to hold itself firmly in place, but before it has completely cured, knock out the through-bolts and apply the

second layer of plywood in the same manner, using self-tapping screws to hold it against the first layer while the epoxy cures. If subsequent layers are required, remove the screws, fill the holes, and repeat.

Once the full thickness of plywood is in place, it can be covered with layers of fiberglass reinforcement and epoxy. You might be able to reuse the section you cut out originally, but in most cases you'll have damaged it beyond use in the removal. If you're building it from scratch, the reinforcement can be cloth, biaxial cloth with mat, roving, or a combination of all these. The intent is to build up a thickness equal to the one you cut out. Before you begin laminating, use a dewaxer on the adjacent areas of the hull, then sand and clean these adjacent surfaces to prep them for a good bond. Since you'll be working on

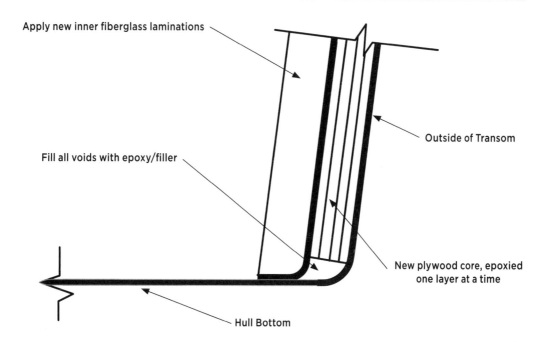

Apply new inner fiberglass laminations

Fill all voids with epoxy/filler

Outside of Transom

New plywood core, epoxied one layer at a time

Hull Bottom

Once the new core is in place, replace the inner fiberglass skin and tab it to the hull.

a vertical surface, mix a little colloidal or fumed silica into the epoxy to keep it from sagging. A grooved roller is an excellent tool for getting any air bubbles out of the fiberglass.

The fiberglass should lap over the inside of the hull all around the edges of the transom. This seals the plywood core and forms a strong structural bond to the hull. Once the epoxy has cured, it can be scrubbed with warm soapy water to remove any amine blush, then painted if desired.

On boats with a smooth interior surface, the repaired area should be faired in and sanded. Mix in an easily sanded fairing additive like microspheres to the epoxy before applying it. Several applications of filler and sanding may be necessary to get a smooth enough finish for priming and painting with a good marine paint.

If the boat is a stern-drive model, you will need to cut the opening for the outdrive as well as the necessary mounting holes. Use the outline of the opening in the exterior skin of the transom as a guide. Drill an access hole with a holesaw and then cut the opening with a jigsaw. The outside transom will also provide the location of the required mounting holes for transom-mounted equipment such as trim tabs or stern ladders, regardless of the drive system.

Unless you want to repeat this project in the future, you will need to take some care with all these holes, including the stern-drive cutout. All edges of any openings should be completely sealed with epoxy. In the case of fasteners, it is a good idea to drill the holes oversize, fill them with epoxy/filler, and then redrill the holes to the proper size.

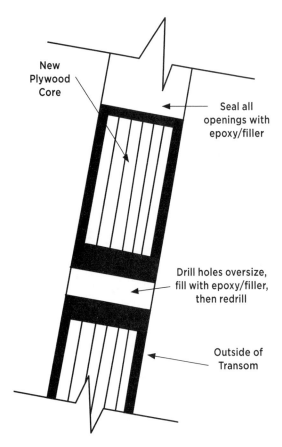

New Plywood Core

Seal all openings with epoxy/filler

Drill holes oversize, fill with epoxy/filler, then redrill

Outside of Transom

As in any wood-cored structure, it is critical to seal all the openings to keep water from saturating the new core.

SEALING A HULL/DECK JOINT

Of all the leaks aboard a boat, those at the hull/deck joint are probably the most persistent, hardest to find, and hardest to fix. By the nature of the joint, water can travel great distances before appearing as a leak belowdeck, making it difficult to identify the point of entry.

Let's look at the kinds of joints you are likely to find:

- **Box Joint:** In this type of joint, the deck molding has a downward flange like the lid of a shoebox around its perimeter. The flange fits over the hull, which has no flange.
- **Outside Flanges:** Both the deck and the hull molds terminate in horizontal flanges that mate with each other and are usually bolted, screwed, or riveted together, then covered with a vinyl or aluminum trim strip or rubrail.
- **Flange and Lid:** The flat deck edges are bolted or screwed down to an inward-facing horizontal flange on the hull.
- **"H" Joint:** In the dreaded "H" joint, a downward flange on the deck aligns perfectly with the upper edge of the hull, and the two meet in an aluminum "H" channel in which they are secured by screws, bolts, or pop rivets. *Do not try to remove an "H" channel!* The hull and deck were assembled in a jig. If you remove the channel, both parts will be unsupported and floppy, and reassembling them will be like putting toothpaste back in a tube.

There are other hull/deck joint configurations out there, but they are variations on these themes.

Fittings installed in, on, or over the hull/deck joint, including toe rails, rubrails, and chocks, may interfere with access to the joint and may have to be removed for complete access—which is itself a problem, as their fastenings may be hidden beneath several layers of glass cloth, mat, and resin inside the boat. This makes accessing the inside of the joint practically impossible.

Once you have an idea of what type of hull/deck joint you have, you can formulate a repair strategy. In some extreme cases, doing nothing while keeping all interior items protected from leaks may be an acceptable solution.

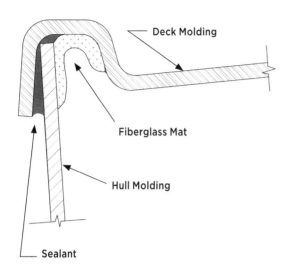

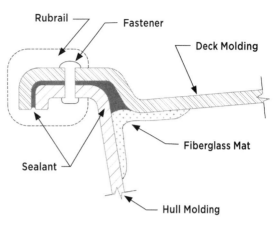

In a box joint, the deck molding fits the hull like a lid on a box.

An outside-flange joint is vulnerable to docking "incidents" even when well guarded by a trim strip or rubrail.

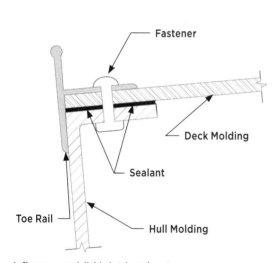

A flange-and-lid joint is robust.

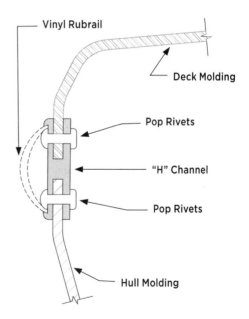

The "H" joint is probably the hardest type to seal. If you take the entire joint apart, you'll never get it back together.

You will often see boats with globs of marine silicone sealant smeared along the hull/deck joint. This looks terrible, ruins the gelcoat finish for any further painting, and rarely works for long (if at all), since silicone isn't a good adhesive and often hasn't been applied in such a manner as to actually penetrate the cracks or openings that are leaking.

If you want a simple solution, try an oddly named product, Capt. Tolley's Creeping Crack Cure, available in most marine stores. It is a thin liquid that penetrates fine cracks by capillary action and cures to form a flexible, waterproof seal. Several applications may be necessary to seal a joint totally. Do it slowly; don't try to seal everything in one go, as you may find that the liquid is just running down below. I have used this product on several occasions but can't offer any guarantees. In some cases it has worked well; in others, it didn't. I suspect that when it didn't, the cracks were bigger than I had realized.

Box joints usually have the space between the outside edge of the hull and the inside of the flange filled with a sealant. This is usually a dependable type of joint, but it may leak if the sealant fails. Reef out (remove) the old sealant with a thin tool such as a hacksaw blade, and replace with new. While I don't usually recommend 3M 5200 above the waterline, hull/deck joints are an exception. To do a neater job of applying the sealant, mask off the hull with blue tape. Fill the upper recesses of the joint completely, and leave no voids or bubbles.

Outside flanges and flange-and-lid joints are usually bolted or screwed together with sealant between. When this sealant breaks down, leaks start. For a long-term solution, the fasteners should be removed and the old sealant cleaned out. This means unfastening part of the joint at a time and prying the joint apart enough to clean out the old sealant. This may first require unbolting the toe rail or removing the rubrail.

The two parts must then be very carefully pried apart so you don't fracture the fiberglass. The joint can be held open with small wooden wedges. Work your way around the boat, doing a small section at a time, then replace the sealant and refasten. I didn't say it was going to be easy!

Pay careful attention when you reinstall the toe rails and other hardware, making sure to properly bed the fasteners in sealant. Nothing is more frustrating than going through this process and still having the joint leak. You did re-bed all the other deck hardware to eliminate them as a source of leaks, right?

Remember not to turn a bolt or machine screw once the sealant has cured. Tighten the nut from below or leave it alone. Twisting a bolt or screw in cured sealant breaks the sealant bond you just so carefully established and provides a convenient path for leaks.

The "H" joint is the hardest to fix. You can't really take it apart and expect to get it back together without a great deal of difficulty. Most joints of this type are fastened with pop rivets. Each fastener, as well as the deck flange and hull edge, is a possible leak source. Often the inside is glassed over, making access from the inside impossible.

The first step is to eliminate any leaks from the pop rivets. If they are still tight, you can try sealing the head of each one with 3M 5200. If they are loose, you can carefully drill them out and replace them with all-aluminum pop rivets with closed ends. Dab each rivet with sealant as you replace it.

The outside top and bottom edges are another potential source of leaks in this type of joint. You can try Capt. Tolley's Creeping Crack Cure, mentioned earlier in this chapter, if you feel lucky. Otherwise, clean the sealant out of the seam as well as you can. Use a thin blade to scrape out as much of the old sealant as possible. The edges of the fiberglass deck and hull won't be uniform, so the gap will vary from place to place.

Mask the edges of the channel and the deck or hull with blue tape and force sealant into the seam as effectively as you can. Clean off the excess sealant for a smooth seam, and wish yourself luck.

Cutting the channel and removing it a piece at a time is extremely difficult and only adds a number of additional joints to leak. If you can get at the entire joint from inside the boat, you could consider fiberglassing the joint. However, most boats have bulkheads and partitions that you can't get behind to fiberglass, and I'll guarantee that's where the joint will leak.

RUBRAILS

When slammed into pilings or dragged along rough dock walls and creosoted timbers, rubrails absorb a great deal of punishment, and they often show it.

Rubrails are made from a variety of materials. Flexible vinyl rubrails are the easiest to bend to shape; they come in long lengths. Rigid vinyl or aluminum rubrails with flexible inserts give better protection and last longer. Aluminum sections are available in 12-foot or 20-foot lengths and must be butted together to go around most boats. Rigid vinyl is available in longer lengths.

The rigid designs with flexible inserts have some advantages. If only the flexible insert is damaged or worn, you may be able to find an exact replacement that can be reinserted without changing out the rigid part.

Rubrails are commonly fastened to the hull with rivets or screws, and leaks through the holes are common. Often the insert must be removed to access the fasteners. Screws should be removed one at a time and the holes filled with a marine sealant.

Rivets are another matter. You can drill them out one at a time and rerivet the rubrail extrusion to the hull. Dip each rivet in sealant before placing it in the hole. You will need to find closed-end rivets. As the name implies, the ends of these riv-

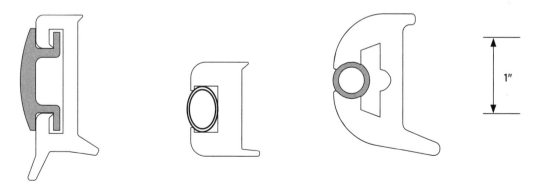

A few of the many styles of flexible vinyl rubrails (white) with inserts (shown gray) supplied by TACO Marine. Black and white are the most common colors.

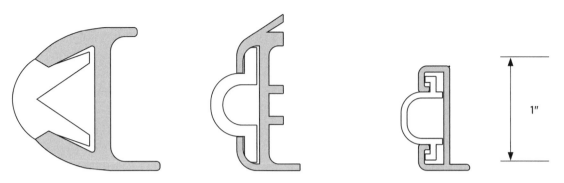

TACO Marine also supplies rigid aluminum rubrails (shown gray) with flexible inserts (white).

ets are closed, so water won't leak through. They are harder to find than the ones at your local home improvement store, but don't substitute here. Regular pop rivets have a soft aluminum body and a mild steel mandrel. The open end of the rivet is a sure source of leaks, and the mandrel will rust, staining the rubrail.

Where an entire aluminum rubrail needs replacement, plan your work so that butt joints are inconspicuous. Extrusions can be carefully

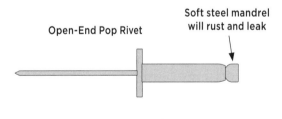

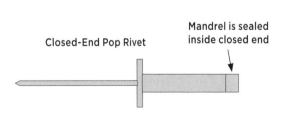

When riveting a rubrail or hull joint, be sure to use closed-end pop rivets.

bent around moderate curves such as at the bow. Transom corners usually employ end caps rather than bending the rubrail in such a tight radius. TACO Marine is a major supplier of replacement rubrails and offers most of the commonly used styles, along with the inserts and end caps. Seal all the old holes with epoxy/filler and predrill the new mounting holes to match the new rubrail.

A replacement length of rubrail consisting of a semirigid vinyl main piece with a flexible insert can usually be purchased in sufficient length to go from the center of the transom, around the bow, and back to the center of the transom. The vinyl will bend more easily around the bow radius and stern corners after a good soaking in hot water to make it more pliable. It is attached first to the bow while warm, and then stretched aft and around the corners of the transom.

After the outer rubrail is stretched and in position, it is screwed in place using stainless steel truss-head screws. Don't overtighten the screws in a vinyl rubrail, as this might pucker or wrinkle the vinyl.

The procedures for installing the insert in the rubrail vary, but generally speaking, a heat gun is used to warm up about 3 feet of the insert at a time; when it is softened, it is inserted in the rigid rubrail with help from a plastic putty knife and light taps from a rubber mallet if necessary.

Most replacement rubrails and rubrail kits are supplied by TACO Marine. Chances are they have the OEM (original equipment manufacturer) part for your boat, or an equivalent replacement or suitable substitute. The website for such kits (www.tacomarine.com/cat—Rub-Rail—rubrail. html) lists many production boats and includes drawings of the parts. If you can't find your boat in that list, they also have cross-references to rubrails based on material type.

FENDERBOARDS

Now that our rubrails are back in shape, let's take some steps to keep them and the rest of the topsides that way with a set of fenderboards. A fenderboard is a plank suspended from the side of a boat, with some sort of standoff—usually two or more fenders—to keep the plank away from the topsides.

The plank is usually common framing lumber in a size ranging from 2 x 4 to 2 x 8 or up depending on the size of the boat. Treated lumber could be used but really isn't necessary. Treated lumber is heavy, splintery, and unpleasant to handle. Make sure there are no knots or defects in the board to weaken it. Round the corners and edges with a sander or router so there are no sharp edges to bite you or dig into the deck. Drill mounting holes at each end and fasten drop lines in place with figure-eight stopper knots.

You can cover the outside face of the board with indoor-outdoor carpeting or trailer bunk padding, but remember that this face may well be in contact with some nasty surfaces covered with

creosote, tar, and slime. Bare wood will be easier to keep clean. If you decide to use carpet, tack it in place on the edges (not the face) of the board, to protect any surfaces you don't want to scratch—like another boat that you might raft up against.

Some boaters like to use solid wood standoffs on their fenderboards. The standoffs must be well padded. They make the board more difficult to store and heavier to deploy than fender standoffs, but if properly fastened, they stay in place. Fenders always want to roll out from behind the board unless you take special measures, which we discuss later in this chapter.

Cylindrical fenders should be large enough to keep the board from contacting the hull when compressed against another boat, dock, or lock wall. Two fenders are needed, although three is not out of the question, and bigger is generally better; you'd be surprised how much a fender compresses under pressure.

Fenders can be used loose or attached to the board. If you decide to leave them loose, you simply hang them behind the board on their own drop lines, which you tie off to cleats, stanchions, or any convenient piece of hardware. The danger is that fore-and-aft boat movement may roll the fender out from behind the board, allowing the board to contact and possibly scratch the topsides.

Simply tying the fenders to the board is not a good solution, as this leaves the line exposed on the face of the board and susceptible to chafe. Instead, drill a vertical hole through the board on either side of the fender location. Round the edges of the holes to prevent chafe. Pass a line through the holes and around the fender, top and bottom, in a continuous loop. Make sure that the knot is well removed from the portion of the fender that will rub against the hull. Tie the line in place with

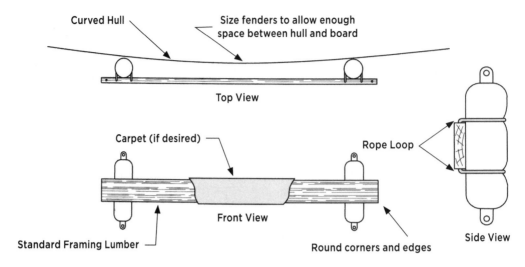

Fenderboards are highly useful when deployed against pilings and bulkheads or in locks.

the fender partly deflated, then inflate the fender to "bury" the line and lock it in place.

If you wish, you can add another set of drop lines to the fenders. This gives additional security at the cost of having to adjust four lines instead of two.

A fenderboard simply hanging from drop lines can move fore and aft, potentially moving away from where it is needed the most. By adding fore-and-aft steadying lines, you can keep the fenderboard exactly where you want it. This technique isn't often necessary, but keep it in your bag of tricks.

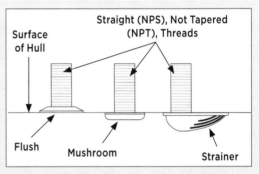

The three main types of through-hull fittings.

Through-Hull Fittings and Seacocks

I hear the terms through-hull and seacock used interchangeably, but they are, in fact, two different animals. According to the American Boat & Yacht Council (ABYC), a through-hull is "a fitting designed to accept pipes, hoses, or valves to allow the passage of water in or out of a vessel." A selection of three through-hull types is shown in the accompanying illustration.

A seacock, on the other hand, is a "type of valve used to control the intake or discharge of water through the hull giving a clear indication of whether it is open or shut." Notice especially the part about "giving a clear indication." That rules out using a standard plumbing gate valve as a seacock. (Gate valves are also fragile, difficult to operate and maintain, and liable to jam open or jam shut, and in general have no place on a boat.)

While the proper installation of a seacock involves threading it onto a through-hull, the two parts are distinct and not to be confused.

Through-hulls are available in a variety of materials, from Marelon plastic (a fiber-reinforced nylon from Forespar) to traditional bronze. They can be flush, mushroom headed, or equipped with a strainer, as the accompanying illustration makes clear. All have straight threads, and some come with nuts for fastening them in place.

Most modern seacocks have a stainless steel ball valve riding on Teflon seals and valve seats. Conbraco, one of the most popular manufacturers of this style of seacock, makes several varieties of these units. Make sure you get the marine unit with the stainless steel handles and valves.

Proper seacocks designed to meet ABYC specifications. The one on the right has an integral flange. The one on the left does not, which means that the through-hull must be secured to the backing plate with a flange nut.

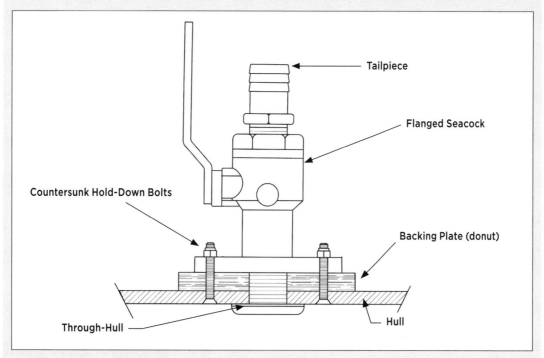

A flanged seacock installation.

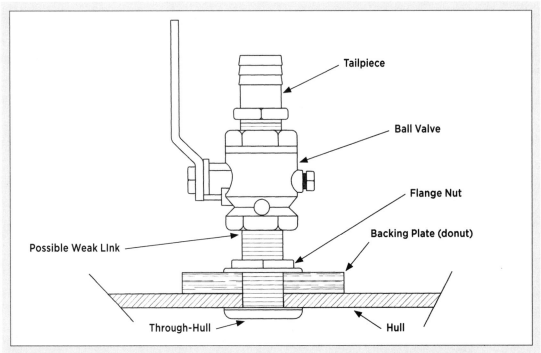

A nonflanged ball valve seacock installation is okay but not as robust as a flanged seacock.

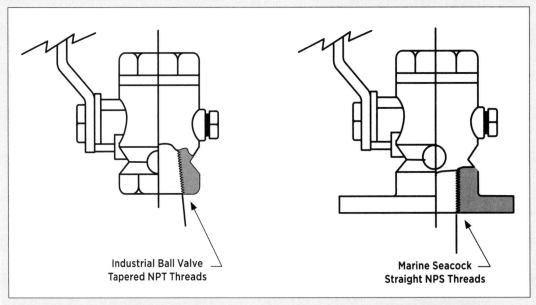

An industrial ball valve usually has tapered threads on both ends, while a marine seacock has straight threads on the bottom end.

The most common style of seacock includes a flange that is bolted to the hull once the seacock is threaded onto the through-hull. This flanged seacock, which is available only as a marine product, produces a very sturdy installation.

Another often-used type of seacock includes a ball valve threaded onto the through-hull, but it lacks the flange. In this installation the through-hull is fastened to the mounting pad and hull by means of a large nut on the inside of the boat. The ball valve is then threaded onto the end of the through-hull, and the hose barb is screwed onto the other end of the valve. A couple of turns of Teflon plumber's tape seals the threaded connection. This configuration may be found in home improvement and industrial supply stores as well as in marine stores, but don't be tempted by similar-appearing ball valves that are not intended for marine applications. These are not engineered to meet the ABYC standard for strength. (A seacock should withstand a 500-pound load applied to it for a period of thirty seconds.) Also, their handles do not necessarily swing through the specified 90-degree arc to indicate whether the cock is open or closed, and they are not made of materials that will survive in the marine environment. Sooner or later—probably sooner—they'll either freeze up or fall apart.

Most critical, however, is the design of the valve itself. Industrial-style ball valves have

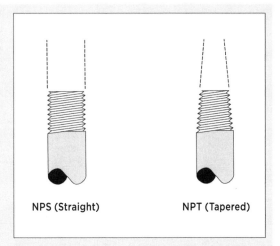

NPS (Straight)   NPT (Tapered)

A closer look at the difference between straight and tapered threads.

tapered NPT (National Pipe Thread) pipe threads on both ends, while marine seacocks have a tapered thread on the top end and an NPS (Nominal Pipe Size) straight thread on the flanged end. A ball valve with tapered NPT threads can't be screwed securely onto a through-hull with NPS straight threads. You might get three or four threads engaged, and if you use Teflon plumber's tape, it probably won't leak, but it won't stand up to the required load test and is a catastrophe waiting to happen. One day, when you go to turn the handle, the ball valve may come off in your hand, leaving a rather large hole in the bottom of your boat.

REPLACING SEACOCKS

Years of corrosion and numerous applications of a variety of sealants can conspire to keep a seacock and its associated through-hull fitting firmly attached to each other and to the boat's hull. But there are many reasons to remove and possibly replace either or both, ranging from alterations in the boat's interior accommodations to a desire to eliminate failing hardware. Before continuing, read the previous sidebar Through-Hull Fittings and Seacocks to learn the difference between the two and the importance of buying the right hardware.

The first thing to do is to try to remove the through-hull. Most have two tabs, or ears, more or less opposite each other in the through-hull's opening to the hull exterior. These tabs should be clearly visible when the boat is hauled out, and their function becomes apparent when you insert a through-hull step wrench into the exterior opening. The business end of this tool consists of a series of heads of diminishing diameter, perched one atop the other in wedding-cake fashion. Each head matches one of the standard through-hull inner-bore diameters, and you simply insert the tool into the through-hull opening until the head of appropriate diameter comes into play. Assuming for the moment that the through-hull does not have a flange nut on the hull interior, all you have to do now is clamp onto the other end of the step wrench with a pipe wrench and apply torque. The tabs in the through-hull opening will trap the corresponding slots in the step-wrench head, and if you're lucky the through-hull fitting will turn.

If you can't borrow a through-hull step wrench from your boatyard or a fellow boatowner, you can purchase one for about $32 or make a substitute.

In the case of a nonflange-mounted seacock, you will have to remove the seacock from the stem of the through-hull and remove the through-hull flange nut before you can remove the through-hull itself. This may be a two-person job—one outside the boat with a step wrench in the through-hull, and another inside the boat with a pipe wrench on the flange nut. Application of gentle heat from a heat gun may persuade the through-hull to loosen up.

If the through-hull won't loosen up, you will need to cut it out. The simplest method is to mount two holesaws on a common pilot drill. The inner holesaw should just fit inside the through-hull opening, while the larger holesaw should equal the outside diameter of the threaded through-hull stem.

A cast-iron through-hull removal tool (shown here inserted into a through-hull) will fit all common sizes of through-hulls. Sometimes called a step wrench, the tool is usually used in conjunction with a pipe wrench and breaker bar.

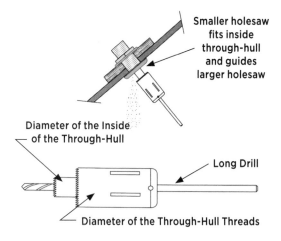

Smaller holesaw fits inside through-hull and guides larger holesaw

Diameter of the Inside of the Through-Hull

Long Drill

Diameter of the Through-Hull Threads

When all else fails, you may need to cut out a through-hull with this homemade tool.

The smaller holesaw keeps the larger holesaw centered as you cut through the outside flange of the through-hull and the hull laminate. With any luck you can cut away the stem of the through-hull without significantly enlarging the hole.

And speaking of that hole, the first step in reinstalling the through-hull and seacock is to inspect the hole. If the hull is cored, cut back the core around the hole and fill the exposed edges with filled epoxy. If the hull is solid fiberglass, give the hole edges a good coat of epoxy to seal against water intrusion.

The original through-hull was probably installed with a spacer, or donut, on the inside of the hull. This spacer serves as a backing plate but also mediates between the curved hull and the flat through-hull flange or flange nut. Its outboard face is shaped to the hull, while its inboard face is flat. It is usually plywood and may or may not have been protected with a resin coating. If the spacer is in good shape, seal it with epoxy and reuse it. In many cases, though, you will need to replace it. Use void-free exterior plywood sealed with several coats of epoxy. You can epoxy the donut in place or use 3M 5200. The important thing is that the seacock flange or through-hull flange nut fit flat against the plywood. If not, sand the plywood until it does.

Make a trial installation of the through-hull, seacock, and associated fittings without sealants. Make sure there is enough room to properly access the handle, flange nuts, hose clamps, and other components of the system. Trim the through-hull stem to the proper length if necessary.

Now apply plenty of polyurethane adhesive/sealant (such as 3M 5200) and bolt the flange of the seacock in place. Don't overtighten the mounting screws and squeeze out all the sealant. If you are not using a flanged seacock, apply a thick bead of sealant to the through-hull and have someone outside the boat hold the through-hull in place with a step wrench as you install the flange nut inside the boat. Use sealant under the flange nut, too.

If using a flanged seacock, give the underside of the through-hull a generous bead of sealant and screw the through-hull in place. Don't overtighten! Use Teflon plumber's tape when making threaded connections, such as the hose barb. After launching, keep an eye on the new seacocks and fittings, checking for any leaks.

The best thing about new seacocks with stainless steel ball valves and Teflon seals and valve seats is that maintenance is minimal. Regular opening and closing of the seacock is about all that is required. Exercise each through-hull at least once a month and you should enjoy trouble-free operation for years.

As an additional safety measure, invest in a set of tapered wooden plugs as found in the plumbing aisle of your marine store. Screw a small eye in the top of each one, and tie a plug of appropriate size to each through-hull. Keep a hammer where you can find it and make sure you have room to use it. While your through-hull may be marine rated and strong enough, the hose could fail. Having the plug ready to drive into the resulting hole might save your boat.

Bilge Pump Basics

It doesn't take a big hole in a boat to present a big problem. A hole three fingers wide near the waterline will allow 5,000 gallons of water to enter the boat in an hour. Poke a fist-sized hole through the hull 3 feet below the waterline, and you're looking at 19,000 gallons!

Two things are immediately apparent. First, the average bilge pump is only going to slow down the inevitable. Second, you don't have a lot of time to decide on a course of action.

We all see the units neatly packaged in marine stores with their capacities clearly marked in gallons per hour (gph). But manufacturers determine gph ratings under controlled conditions that don't closely reflect those you're likely to encounter in the real world. For starters, pumps are tested at 13.6 volts, while your battery is more likely delivering closer to 12 volts.

Then, too, the advertised performance numbers come from tests performed with "zero head," also described as "open flow." "Head" refers to the height above the pump that water must be pushed to expel it from the boat. Obviously, the higher the head, the lower the gph performance will be. The ABYC requires that bilge pumps be rated at zero head, 1 meter, and 2 meters, and the latter two additional ratings are usually found in the detailed instructions provided with the pump. Some studies indicate that each foot of head in a bilge pump installation reduces pump capacity by 5 percent or more.

Pump output is also affected by plumbing. Ideally the discharge hose should have a smooth interior; the corrugated hose commonly seen in bilge pump installations will reduce performance by increasing the turbulence in the discharge flow. Restrictions encountered in through-hulls and other fittings also reduce performance. A single through-hull fitting can add the equivalent resistance of several feet of hose.

Electric bilge pumps come in three types: diaphragm, impeller, and centrifugal.

A diaphragm pump has one or more chambers fitted with a flexible diaphragm. As this diaphragm is pushed into and pulled out of a chamber, intake valves open and close, sucking water into the chamber through one valve and forcing it out again through the second valve.

One of the best features of diaphragm pumps is that they are self-priming to a vertical intake distance of 10 feet. In other words, they will lift water from up to 10 feet *below* the pump intake. This means they can be mounted above the bilge in a dry, protected area, with an intake hose that passes into the bilge. Diaphragm pumps can run dry with no problems and are relatively good at handling debris in the water. On the downside, they are large, somewhat noisy, and pricey.

Impeller pumps utilize a finned or vaned rubber wheel turning inside an eccentric housing. As the rubber fins alternately bend and straighten, they suck water through the pump. These pumps are fairly good at handling small bits of debris and can lift water 4 feet or so, but running them dry will cause rapid failure. They need to be mounted in a protected and dry space with the intake passed down to the bilge.

In a centrifugal pump, an electric motor spins a disc with curved vanes on its surface. The water is sucked in through a central hole around the hub and is spun out around the periphery of the disc, collected by an outer casing, and directed out a discharge port. Centrifugal pumps can be submerged in the bilge, and the familiar red, white, and blue Rule pumps, as well as Attwood pumps, are in this category. These pumps are very quiet and can run dry without damage. They are susceptible to clogging from debris and are usually equipped with a built-in strainer. Some are automatic, having the ability to sense water and turn themselves on and off, while others require a separate switch.

BILGE PUMP INSTALLATION

It takes more than just a pump to make a successful bilge pump installation. So before we grab the tools, let's consider the other elements of a good installation.

- **Hoses:** A smooth interior wall will reduce friction and increase pumping efficiency. If a hose is to be used as a suction line between the pump and the bilge, it should be a reinforced, noncollapsing type, but avoid the common corrugated hose often sold for bilge pump applications. If your hose barb has room for two stainless steel hose clamps, use them. Otherwise, one will do.
- **Strainers:** If your pump requires a suction hose placed in the bilge, put a strainer on the end of the hose. A heavy bronze one is best. Make sure there is enough slack in the hose to allow the strainer to be raised high enough to clean it. Centrifugal bilge pumps usually come with a strainer base. The strainer can be removed from the bottom of the pump by pinching two plastic ears together. Some bilge pump switches likewise come with strainers or have one available that fits them.
- **Pump Discharge Through-Hulls:** These are usually plastic, either nylon or Marelon, although bronze ones are available. These need to be located at least 8 inches above the boat's heeled waterline to prevent back-siphoning of water into the bilge. They are usually barbed to make a firm seat for the pump discharge hose.
- **Switches, Controls, Counters, and Alarms:** The simplest bilge pump control is a manual switch to turn the pump on and off, but of course this requires human intervention to activate. Most bilge pump installations include a switch of some sort to sense rising water levels. These switches can be part of the bilge pump or a separate piece of equipment. Rising water will trip the switch, turning the pump on. When the water level falls, the switch turns the pump off.

There are control panels for pumps with separate float switches as well as one for pumps with built-in switches. The panels include a three-position switch, a fuse holder, and an indicator light. The indicator light comes on only when the pump is actually running in either automatic or manual mode. The three switch positions are automatic, off, and manual. In automatic mode, the pump has power available and will switch on when the float switch tells it to. In many cases, the manual switch position is a momentary one—that is, the switch returns to the "off" position when you release it.

Some people like to place a counter in the pump circuit, especially if the boat is left unattended for any period of time. The counter records the number of times the pump turns on, giving the owner an idea of how much water has come aboard and the amount of electrical draw required to keep the pump running.

Another option is an alarm that sounds when the water reaches a certain level or a backup bilge pump kicks on. The audible alarm gives a warning to people outside the boat that something is amiss and needs to be checked out.

- **Wiring and Fuses:** Bilge pumps should be wired with marine-grade tinned wire. The manufacturer's instructions will specify the required gauge wire. The circuit needs to be protected by an in-line fuse, and all connections should be sealed with adhesive heat-shrink tubing to keep water out, but connections are best kept well above the expected water level in any case.
- **Check Valves:** These prevent water from flowing back down a hose. Some folks like them; some don't because they are prone to jamming open

from debris. I cover them in more detail later in this chapter.

In planning an installation, the location of the pump is the first consideration. If you're using the common centrifugal pump, it should be located in the deepest part of the bilge. The typical Rule pump with a removable strainer base has holes in the bottom of the strainer that can be used to screw the pump in place. If you are attaching the pump to the hull itself, first bond a plywood pad to the hull and then screw the pump base to that. Be sure to completely coat the pad with epoxy to protect it from bilge water.

The pump can then be wired following the guidelines described earlier in this section. If the pump is not automatic, it should be wired to a float or other type of water-sensing switch and to an on/off switch or bilge pump control panel. Some recommend an athwartship mounting for the float switch, but I prefer to mount it fore and aft. Some manufacturers provide a bracket to mount the float switch right on the pump, but I find the brackets flimsy and prone to breakage. I mount float switches on a plywood pad, sealed with epoxy and glued to the bilge with 3M 5200.

The discharge hose from the pump should be routed up the side of the hull to the discharge through-hull fitting. That discharge location should be at least 8 inches above the waterline. I like to install the through-hull just below the toe rail. It is a good idea to loop the discharge hose above the through-hull fitting and then back down to it as a guard against back-siphoning.

There is a critical interrelationship between the volume of the discharge hose—that is, its length and inside diameter—and the location of the float switch. When the float switch turns off the pump, the hose is still filled with water. That

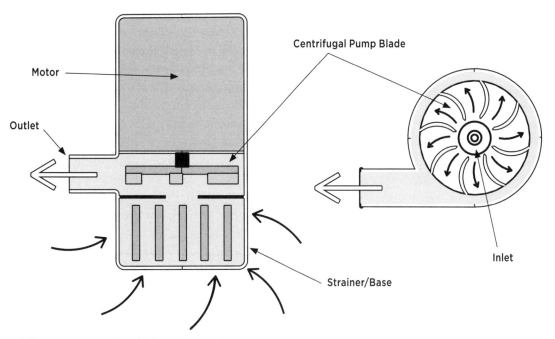

A Rule-style centrifugal bilge pump and strainer.

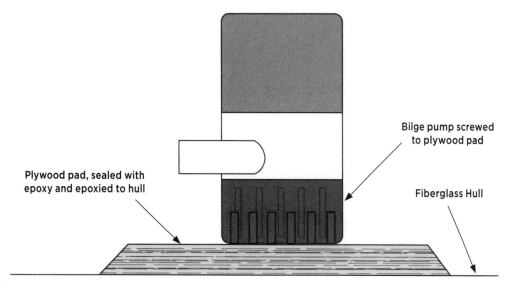

A bilge pump mounted on a plywood pad.

Bilge pump screwed to plywood pad

Plywood pad, sealed with epoxy and epoxied to hull

Fiberglass Hull

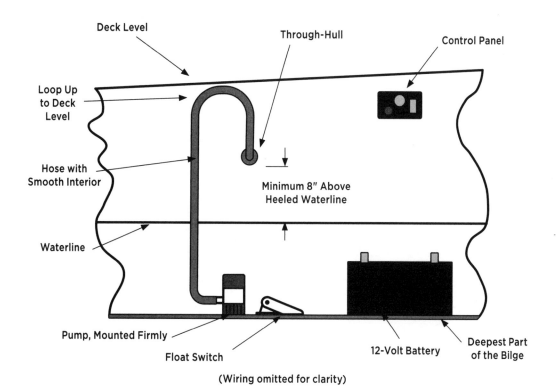

Deck Level

Through-Hull

Control Panel

Loop Up to Deck Level

Hose with Smooth Interior

Minimum 8" Above Heeled Waterline

Waterline

Pump, Mounted Firmly

Float Switch

12-Volt Battery

Deepest Part of the Bilge

(Wiring omitted for clarity)

Recommended bilge pump layout with discharge hose loop.

water then flows back down the hose, through the pump, and back into the bilge. If the float switch is located too low and the volume of water that just came back is too high, the pump will turn back on, pushing the water back up the hose. This cycle will continue until the water evaporates or the battery runs down.

This condition is what prompts some to install a check valve in the discharge line. The check valve prevents the water in the discharge line from flowing back into the bilge. You will still need to verify the proper height of the float switch, as the check valve could very likely jam open with debris. Neither is a check valve an adequate substitute for a proper antisiphon loop in the discharge hose. Don't bet your boat on a component that is likely to jam in an open position.

If you could choose a diaphragm or impeller pump as a bilge pump, it will be mounted somewhere other than the bilge. A float switch will be required, as will a suction hose with a strainer on the end. Make sure the hose you use for this appli-cation is collapse-proof, as you don't want the pump to suck the hose flat.

Compartmentalized bilges, with separate sections that don't drain into a common bilge, require a pump for each section. If your bilge does have limber holes to drain each area into a central sump, periodically check those holes to make sure they are clear of debris.

A COUPLE OF "PUMPSTICKS"

One of my boats had a bilge that was only a couple of inches deep—too shallow for a regular bilge pump installation. In addition, it had two stern lockers that I could not get to seal properly, even after many tries. These were constantly filling up with rainwater.

Needing a way to pump out these areas, I invented the "portable pumpstick," which I offer for your use royalty-free. I obtained a small,

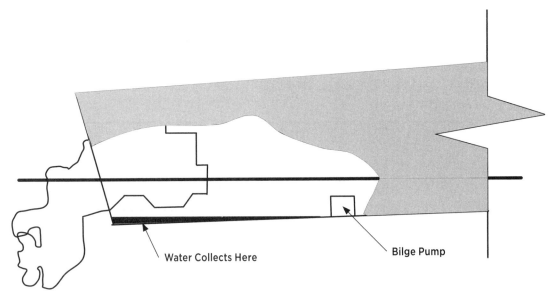

The problem: water pooling aft of the midships bilge pump in a hard-to-reach area beneath the engine.

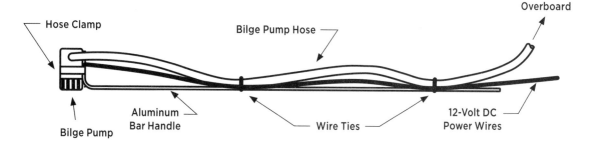

Hose Clamp

Bilge Pump Hose

Overboard

Aluminum
Bar Handle

Bilge Pump

Wire Ties

12-Volt DC
Power Wires

The solution: my portable pumpstick (no patent pending), which can be used to insert a Rule pump in restricted spaces.

360-gph bilge pump, available for about $16 in most marine stores, and fastened it to a piece of aluminum bar stock with a couple of hose clamps. I then bent the top of the bar stock to form a convenient handle and secured the pump wires and discharge hose to the aluminum shaft with wire ties. The wires and hose were long enough to reach anyplace on the boat, and on the end of the wires I placed an automotive cigarette lighter-style plug.

With the pumpstick plugged into the boat's cigarette lighter socket, it was quick work to pump the bilge and stern lockers dry. I also made up a pigtail with alligator clips on one end and a female cigarette lighter socket on the other. This allowed me to hook the pump to any 12-volt battery, on or off the boat.

A friend had a boat with a slightly stern-low attitude that caused bilge water to flow aft and collect under the engine. He had bilge pumps aboard, but they were located in front of the engine. The only way he had of draining the water was to send the crew to the "pointy end" of the boat so the water would run forward into the bilge pumps.

I adapted the pumpstick concept by turning it on its side and using an aluminum bar long enough to push under the engine to the stern of the boat. The hose was long enough to reach overboard, and a couple of alligator clips provided a connection to a 12-volt battery.

Although this setup could be permanently installed, my friend decided to leave it portable, which made it easy to access in order to clear a clog or move to another location.

CHAPTER 7

Boat Electrics and Electronics

Almost any boating magazine you pick up will include at least one article on installing and setting up the latest electronic doodad. These articles almost invariably end with a statement like, "Simply connect the unit to 12-volt power and you're finished!" But after two or three iterations of this sort of ad hoc gadget installation, your wiring system becomes an unreliable and undocumented mess. It's bad enough when *you* try to work with this setup; imagine what the next potential owner will think. You should always document what you do to your boat and keep the documentation current, and that admonition applies most of all to wiring diagrams.

This chapter deals primarily with your boat's 12-volt DC system, which runs off the boat's battery or batteries. For work on shore power, generators, inverters, and the like, I recommend hiring a competent marine electrician, since mistakes on the 120-volt AC system can prove fatal.

Maintaining Your Boat Information

I occasionally work in a local boating store, helping boaters find parts and equipment for their boats. All day long I field questions like "I have a 1976 XYZ boat. What oil filter do I need?"

That seems a simple, straightforward question until you realize that the world of boats isn't like the world of automobiles. Boat engines are generic in the sense that many different models can be—and often are—installed in any given model of boat. A 2002 Corvette engine probably won't fit anything but another Corvette of about the same age, but a 17-foot Whaler could have an engine ranging from 25 to 200 horsepower or so, of any year, from any engine manufacturer. Likewise with accessories and fittings—hardly any of these are made by the boatbuilder, and hardly any can be considered "standard." To further complicate matters, boatbuilders and parts suppliers go out of business much more frequently than auto makers.

All of this makes it important for you to collect and organize all the technical information about your boat. Doing so will make my job in the marine store easier, make your life simpler, and possibly save you some money.

You can organize some of the information on a computer. Several boating software packages—for example BoatExec, MyShipLog, BoatNotes, and Bosun's Buddy Electronic Log Books—have a database function that allows you to enter information about your boat. Be sure the software allows you to print out the information so you can keep it on the boat or take it with you when you need parts or service.

But a computer isn't necessarily the best way to keep track of things, since you will also need to collect owner's manuals, receipts, wiring diagrams, and other information in hard copy. Buy a good three-ring binder, some vinyl sheet protectors, a couple of vinyl pocket pouches for the binder, and a package of 8½-by-11-inch heavy paper or card stock.

Start filling your binder by locating all the information you currently have about your boat. Brochures, bills, instruction manuals, and installation diagrams should all go in there. Put receipts in one of the vinyl pouches. Most boat stores have a liberal return policy—as long as you have a receipt.

Go through the existing equipment on the boat and identify it. Part numbers, model numbers, and serial numbers should all be entered in your book. This is especially important for inboard and stern-drive engines. Whenever you install a new piece of equipment, make sure the information goes into the binder, including serial numbers.

You may want to start a separate sheet for each major piece of equipment aboard, with all the information for that equipment in one place. These sheets can also be used to track important service information: oil and filter changes, windlass servicing, and so on. I use heavy paper or card stock for these sheets, as they get a lot of handling.

Even if you don't plan to turn your own wrenches, it is highly worthwhile to purchase the service manual for your engine/outdrive combination, because it will contain specifications for spark plugs (if applicable), quantities and type of oil required, service intervals, and a hundred other details. You can also use it to help understand what your mechanic is telling you.

If a parts manual is available, buy that too. Parts shops can cross-reference OEM part numbers to parts they have on hand, including aftermarket parts that are often as good as the originals but much cheaper. Ask the parts person what these alternative numbers are and write them down in your binder. It will give you options and probably save you money the next time you're in need of that replacement part.

Another area of your binder should deal with contacts. If you ever go boating away from your home territory, cut out the list of store locations and phone numbers from the flyers you receive from the major boating chains and paste them in your book. Don't forget to add BoatU.S., your insurance agent, your towing service, and other key contacts.

Once you have gathered all this information, remember to take it with you on the boat or on the way to your favorite boating store. It will help you find your part quicker and get you back on the water.

There is yet another advantage in having all this information gathered and organized: proper documentation of services and maintenance should increase the value of your boat. When you sell your boat, this binder will go a long way toward convincing potential buyers that the boat has been well maintained and properly looked after.

MARINE WIRING BASICS

Marine wiring is subject to a great deal of vibration, and all wire installed aboard a boat should therefore be of marine grade—which is to say stranded copper wire. Stranded wire is more flexible than the solid wire used in household wiring and will stand up to vibration without fatiguing and breaking.

You are also well advised to use tinned wire—that is, stranded wire in which each copper strand has received a coating of tin to prevent corrosion. Take a look at old wiring on a boat—especially nonmarine or untinned marine wiring—and you will see green or black corrosion. This corrosion is especially dangerous around connectors, as it gradually raises the resistance in the connection. The result can be extra heat developed across the connection and, in a worst-case scenario, fire. Marine DC wiring is available in most marine stores and online.

It is also available in the form of duplex safety wire. Duplex wire consists of two conductors—one with red insulation and one with yellow—carried inside a protective sheath. This matches the ABYC recommendation that DC negative conductors be yellow rather than black in order to avoid potentially deadly confusion with an AC current-carrying black wire. Duplex wire is a good choice for installation in an open cable chase or where a cable chase or conduit is impractical. And when making long or difficult runs, it's easier to pull one wire instead of two.

The size or gauge of the wire needed for a new circuit depends on the current carried and the length of the circuit. Since the length of the circuit is the round-trip length from the positive supply to the device and back to ground, I show the ground wire in my circuit diagrams. Armed

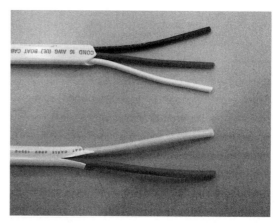

American duplex wire for DC systems (bottom) uses red insulation for the positive wire and yellow for the negative. In triplex wire for AC systems (top), the colors are black, green, and white.

with the current draw and the circuit length, you can go to a wire sizing chart to determine the size of wire required. The tables for voltage drop in 12-volt systems are shown later in this chapter. (For systems of 24 or 32 volts, see Ed Sherman's *Powerboater's Guide to Electrical Systems*.) The tables are also available in various suppliers' catalogs, including those from Ancor Wire and West Marine.

A 10 percent voltage drop can be tolerated by such devices as lights and DC motors. Electronics, on the other hand, should stick to the 3 percent wire sizing. To simplify things I usually use the 3 percent scales exclusively.

Older boats are usually wired with red for DC positive and black for DC negative. The problem arises when a boat is also wired for AC power. AC wiring utilizes white, black, and green wires. As mentioned earlier in this chapter, it is potentially deadly to confuse a black DC negative wire with an AC black wire. For that reason, the American

CONDUCTORS SIZED FOR 10% VOLTAGE DROP

Length of Conductor from Source of Current to Device and Back to Source - Feet

TOTAL CURRENT ON CIRCUIT IN AMPS

12 Volts - 10% Drop Wire Sizes (gauge)   -   Based on Minimum CM Area

	10	15	20	25	30	40	50	60	70	80	90	100	110	120	130	140	150	160	170
5	18	18	18	18	18	16	16	14	14	14	12	12	12	12	12	10	10	10	10
10	18	18	16	16	14	14	12	12	10	10	10	10	8	8	8	8	8	8	6
15	18	16	14	14	12	12	10	10	8	8	8	8	8	6	6	6	6	6	6
20	16	14	14	12	12	10	10	8	8	8	6	6	6	6	6	6	4	4	4
25	16	14	12	12	10	8	8	8	6	6	6	6	6	4	4	4	4	4	2
30	14	12	12	10	10	8	8	6	6	6	6	4	4	4	4	2	2	2	2
40	14	12	10	10	8	8	6	6	6	4	4	2	2	2	2	1	1	1	1
50	12	10	10	8	8	6	6	4	4	4	2	2	2	2	2	1	1	1	1
60	12	10	8	8	6	6	4	4	2	2	2	2	2	1	1	1	0	0	0
70	10	8	8	6	6	6	4	4	2	2	2	1	1	1	0	0	0	2/0	2/0
80	10	8	8	6	6	4	4	2	2	2	1	1	0	0	0	2/0	2/0	2/0	2/0
90	10	8	6	6	6	4	2	2	2	1	1	0	0	0	2/0	2/0	2/0	3/0	3/0
100	10	8	6	6	4	4	2	2	1	1	0	0	0	2/0	2/0	2/0	3/0	3/0	3/0

CONDUCTORS SIZED FOR 3% VOLTAGE DROP

Length of Conductor from Source of Current to Device and Back to Source - Feet

TOTAL CURRENT ON CIRCUIT IN AMPS.

12 Volts - 3% Drop Wire Sizes (gauge)   -   Based on Minimum CM Area

	10	15	20	25	30	40	50	60	70	80	90	100	110	120	130	140	150	160	170
5	18	16	14	12	12	10	10	10	8	8	8	6	6	6	6	6	6	6	6
10	14	12	10	10	10	8	6	6	6	6	4	4	4	4	2	2	2	2	2
15	12	10	10	8	8	6	6	6	4	4	2	2	2	2	2	1	1	1	1
20	10	10	8	6	6	6	4	4	2	2	2	1	1	1	0	0	0	0	2/0
25	10	8	6	6	6	4	4	2	2	2	1	1	0	0	0	2/0	2/0	2/0	3/0
30	10	8	6	6	4	4	2	2	1	1	0	0	0	2/0	2/0	3/0	3/0	3/0	3/0
40	8	6	6	4	4	2	2	1	0	0	2/0	2/0	3/0	3/0	3/0	4/0	4/0	4/0	4/0
50	6	6	4	4	2	2	1	0	2/0	2/0	3/0	3/0	4/0	4/0	4/0				
60	6	4	4	2	2	1	0	2/0	3/0	3/0	4/0	4/0	4/0						
70	6	4	2	2	1	0	2/0	3/0	3/0	4/0	4/0								
80	6	4	2	2	1	0	3/0	3/0	4/0	4/0									
90	4	2	2	1	0	2/0	3/0	4/0	4/0										
100	4	2	2	1	0	2/0	3/0	4/0											

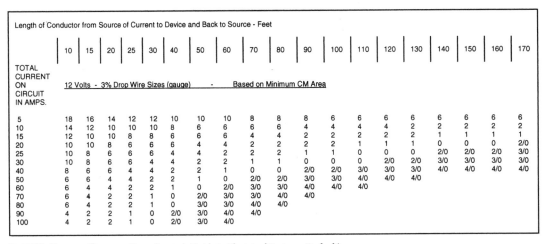

(©ABYC, Courtesy Sherman, Powerboater's Guide to Electrical Systems, 2nd ed.)

Boat & Yacht Council (ABYC) has established yellow as the new color for DC negative wires.

Wire Terminals and Markings

Wires need to be terminated to connect to devices. On one end, most DC wires are connected to a distribution panel or ground. The other end is connected to either a bus bar or a DC device. The integrity of those terminations has much to do with the reliability of your installation. Use only tinned connectors approved for marine use. That usually means buying them at a marine store.

Use a wire stripper that you can set for a fixed length of wire to be stripped. These are a little more expensive than a pliers-style stripper but will save you time and money in the long run. While you're at it, buy a ratcheting crimper of good quality to securely fasten connectors and terminals to the wire. This style of crimper also does a more reliable job of crimping than a pliers-style crimper.

Inevitably, the question of soldering connections crops up. Some say the ABYC does not recommend solder, but what the organization actually says is that solder should not be the *sole* method of terminating a wire. The reasoning behind *not* soldering connections is that solder will wick down the wire and form a hard spot that can lead to the strands breaking. A crimped terminal will remain slightly flexible. If you decide to solder your wires as well as crimp them, use a heat sink right behind the crimp connector to prevent solder from wicking past the connector.

A popular method of terminating wires is to use a crimp connector with adhesive heat-shrink tubing. Slip the tubing over the wire and push it out of the way. Crimp the connection, then slide the tubing over the joint between the connection and the wire and apply heat from a heat gun to shrink the tubing and activate the adhesive inside. The result is a strong, waterproof connection that also affords some strain relief to the wire and connector.

Often two wires need to be connected to each other end to end. In a house, this type of connection is often made with a wire nut, but *wire nuts should never be used aboard a boat*. They will eventually work loose or short out. I prefer using a butt connector with adhesive heat-shrink tubing. Properly crimped with the tubing heat shrunk and the adhesive activated, they provide a secure connection. You can even find step-down connectors with one wire size on one side and a different one on the other side.

Marking the wires and keeping good records will save you untold grief. I use the books of wire tags found in most home improvement stores to mark wires. The tags are small adhesive strips

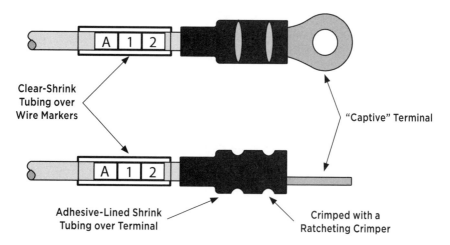

Clear-Shrink Tubing over Wire Markers

"Captive" Terminal

Adhesive-Lined Shrink Tubing over Terminal

Crimped with a Ratcheting Crimper

Do yourself a favor and label each wire, then record the labels on a wiring diagram.

with a number or letter on them. Wrap one around the end of a wire next to the terminal to identify what it is, cover it with a short length of clear heat-shrink tubing to protect the marking, and note the wire ID on your wiring diagram.

Wiring Aids

The two most common wiring aids are bus bars and terminal strips. Bus bars allow you to connect multiple outputs to one input conductor. Bus bars are often used for negative grounding. There are a host of negative ground wires in most boats' DC systems—too many to connect to a single grounding stud. Instead, a bus bar is connected to the ground with heavy-gauge wire, and the dozens of smaller negative ground wires from various circuits are connected to the bus bar.

Another handy option is a unit that has two bus bars, one positive or "hot" and the other negative, mounted on a single mounting board. These dual bus bars come in five- and ten-conductor versions. On one of my boats, I installed one of these units on either side of the boat, aft of the V-berth. That allowed me to run a single duplex wire to the bus bar and then connect the lights and fans to that bus bar. This was far easier than running individual wires back to the electrical panel.

Terminal blocks are another handy wiring device. These consist of an insulating molded strip with a series of conductors running across the strip. Each end of a strip has a mounting screw. Wires can be attached to either side, completing a circuit across the strip. This gives you a convenient place to disconnect things without cutting a wire. If you want to connect one wire to multiple wires, jumper strips are available that connect adjacent connectors to each other.

A bus bar is a convenient way of connecting a single main circuit to multiple branch circuits. (Courtesy Blue Sea Systems)

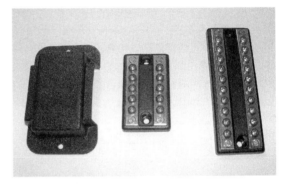

A dual bus bar combines positive and negative bus bars in a single unit. The use of a cover protects the circuits from accidental shorting. (Courtesy Blue Sea Systems)

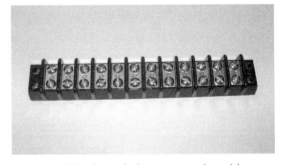

A terminal block can help you organize wiring and provides a convenient point at which to disconnect a portion of a circuit without the need for a connector. (Courtesy Blue Sea Systems)

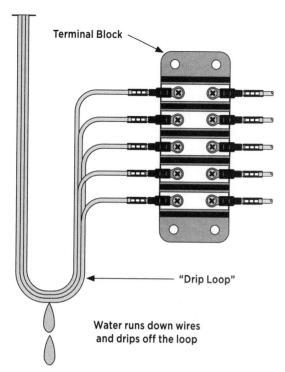

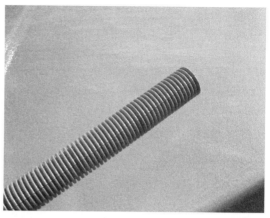

This blue corrugated conduit is available at most home improvement stores and can be used to contain and protect wiring aboard a boat.

A drip loop helps keep water out of panels and distribution boxes.

Since water frequently finds its way into inconvenient places on boats, drip loops should be installed in the wiring approaches to devices such as bus bars and terminal strips. Loop the wiring down below the device and then back up to make the connection. Any water running along the wire will drip off the bottom of the loop instead of running onto the bus bar or terminal block.

Cable Chases and Conduits

Cable chases are channels to carry wires. These make a convenient way to organize and protect wiring. Cable chases can be built into a boat or added later. Conduits, which are enclosed pipes

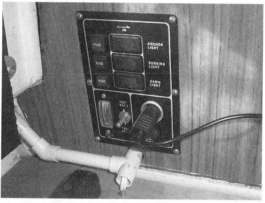

I used common PVC plumbing components to build this conduit system on a 20-foot boat. The inner liner was bonded to the hull, so the conduit had to be exposed inside the boat.

through which wires are run, are another option. Conduits can be as simple as PVC pipe and pipe connectors. Many home improvement stores carry blue corrugated conduit in a variety of sizes at relatively low cost. Any conduit should have small holes in the bottom to drain any water that finds its way in. Conduits need to be adequately supported through their length. Wire outside a conduit should be supported at least every 18 inches.

One of my small boats had an inner liner glassed to the hull and cabintop, leaving no room to install wiring between the two. When I needed to add wiring, I assembled a simple conduit using off-the-shelf PVC pipe and connectors and installed it on the inner liner. It looks neat and protects the wiring.

Circuit Protection

Circuit protection can be provided by either a fuse or a circuit breaker. The ABYC specifies where in a circuit a protective device should be, as well as the rating of the device. These specifications are longer than can be spelled out here, so I recommend you purchase a copy of Nigel Calder's *Boatowner's Mechanical and Electrical Manual* and refer to it before beginning any wiring project. Another good bet is *Boatowner's Illustrated Handbook of Wiring*, by Charlie Wing.

Fuses come in a variety of styles. The small glass fuses are common, as are automotive ATO/ATC-type fuses. There are also fuses designed for high-current, heavy-duty applications such as battery connections and windlasses. Each heavy-duty fuse requires an associated mounting block with studs for attaching wires.

Often your choice of distribution panels will determine what style of circuit protection you have. Fuse-style panels allow you a wide choice of amperages simply by switching fuses. A panel with circuit breakers, on the other hand, will

Heavy-duty ANL-style fuses are used when a fuse of higher amperage is required. Typical applications include main battery or windlass fuses. (Courtesy Blue Sea Systems)

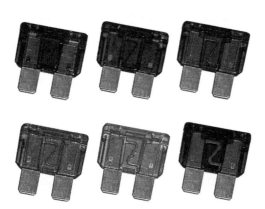

ATO/ATC automotive-style fuses are becoming more popular, replacing older glass fuses. They are available from 1-amp to 30-amp ratings. (Courtesy Blue Sea Systems)

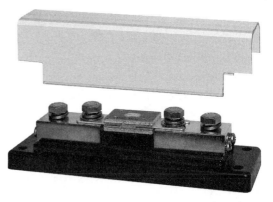

Each ANL-style fuse requires a heavy-duty fuse block. The use of a cover is highly recommended. (Courtesy Blue Sea Systems)

A DC distribution panel using ATO/ATC-style fuses. Note the weatherproof toggle-switch design for flybridge or open-cockpit installation. (Courtesy Blue Sea Systems)

A DC distribution panel using circuit breakers instead of fuses eliminates the necessity of carrying spare fuses. The breakers can be toggle (as here) or rocker-switch style. Note the push buttons for circuit reset. (Courtesy Blue Sea Systems)

require that the circuit breaker be swapped out for one of a different rating.

Distribution Panels

Distribution panels are where a good deal of the wiring ends up. Power from the battery or batteries enters a panel, and wiring to the various items requiring power goes out. These panels usually house the circuit protection, either fuses or circuit breakers. They can also include test meters for determining battery power levels, accessory sockets, and the like. They range from simple units with three or four fuses to elaborate ones costing one or more boat units. (For those of you unfamiliar with this term, a boat unit is a monetary unit that varies with the size of the boat. It may be $100 for a 12-foot fishing boat or $1,000 for a tricked-out center-console boat. Its proper context should be clear in the following example: "Honey, it will only cost one boat unit, I swear!")

In some cases, several panels might be required to get the combination of features and circuits you need. On one of my project boats I used a main panel with three circuits, a test meter, and an accessory socket in combination with an auxiliary panel with eight more fused circuits.

It's best to clearly segregate AC electrical systems from DC systems, as shown in the photo of the electrical panel I built for a 26-footer from

Distribution panels come in all sizes. This panel provides a main disconnect for DC power along with twenty branch circuit breakers. (Courtesy Blue Sea Systems)

The simple main panel I installed on a 20-footer includes a battery test meter, a 12-volt accessory socket, and three fused circuits. I wired it in combination with an eight-circuit auxiliary panel.

In this electrical panel I built for a 26-footer, the AC distribution panel is at far left, the DC panels are center, and the battery selector switch is at right.

StarBoard polymer lumber. The AC circuits were mounted on the far left of the panel, while the DC systems occupied the right-hand side.

The good news is that mistakes with DC systems are rarely fatal. Take your time, do your homework, follow proper procedures, and you should be fine. Document what you do for your own future reference and for future owners, who will be much easier to find when the time comes and who will thank you for having made their lives easier.

30 Tips for Better Boat DC Electrical Systems

1. Old DC electrical systems used red for positive and black for ground. The new ABYC (American Boat & Yacht Council) code uses yellow for DC ground. This is to keep from confusing the DC ground wire with the black AC "hot" wire. The AC wiring is black/white/green. The black wire carries current to AC appliances, white is AC neutral, and green is AC ground.

2. Identify each end of a wire. Self-adhesive electrical markers are available at most home improvement stores. Record the wire number on your wiring diagram, and slip a piece of clear heat-shrink tubing over the markers and heat shrink it to make them permanent.

3. Wire terminals should be crimped with a good-quality ratcheting crimper. If you decide to also solder the terminals, use a heat sink to keep the solder from wicking up the stranded wire. Solder in the strands, outside the connector, can form a hard spot prone to fatiguing and breaking the wire. Do not use solder only, since an overheated connection could melt the solder and loosen the wire.

4. Use a piece of adhesive-lined heat-shrink tubing over each terminal. This keeps out water and reduces potential corrosion.

5. Always use tinned stranded marine wire in a boat. Tinned wire more than repays its modestly higher cost with enhanced corrosion resistance. Similarly, use tinned marine-grade crimp connectors. All terminals need to be of the "captive" style so that they won't come off a terminal screw should it loosen.

6. Do *not* use wire nuts in any part of a boat's electrical system! Similarly, do not place a twisted wire under a terminal screw. *Always* use a crimp connector.

7. Do not cut and attempt to shorten GPS antenna cables, radar cables, transducer cables, or marine network cables. Coil the excess length and secure it where it will not uncoil or be snagged.

8. Bilge pumps should be wired directly to a battery with an in-line fuse, bypassing the master battery selector-on/off switch. You don't want to leave your boat with the bilge pump turned off.

9. Form a drip loop in wiring where it approaches bus bars or terminal strips. A drip loop sheds water before it can reach a terminal block or bus bar.

10. Protect wire and wiring bundles from chafe where they pass through bulkheads or other chafe-prone spots.

11. Always cover bus bars and terminal blocks, especially if they are in lockers where stowed equipment could fall against them and short them out. Make sure the components you buy have covers available with them. If they don't, switch brands!

12. Always install an appropriately sized fuse between the battery or batteries and the master battery selector-on/off switch.

13. Use strategically placed dual bus bars to reduce the number of wires going to and from the master panel or panels. For example, run a large-gauge duplex safety wire (red/yellow in a sheath) from the master panel to a dual bus bar in the V-berth area, then wire V-berth DC accessories to the dual bus bar. The wiring from the panel should be large enough to supply current to all items wired to the bus bar. The fuse or breaker on the main panel should be sufficient to limit the current to the capacity of the wire.

14. Do not place more than four wires on any bus bar or terminal block screw.

15. Always run wiring as high as possible in the boat, and definitely not through the bilges.

16. Conduits or wire chases are nice, but be sure to include extra messenger lines in case you need to pull additional wires.

17. Do not mix AC and DC wires in the same bundle or conduit unless both are sheathed cables.

18. The AC outlets should be protected with a properly installed and tested GFCI (ground fault circuit interrupter) outlet.

19. If you don't use conduits, bundle wires with spiral wrap or support them with wire ties and clamps every 18 inches.

20. The DC electrical circuits can generate heat in wires. Don't bundle an excessive number of wires in a single conduit or wire bundle. The ABYC standards spell out the allowable current that a number of wires in a bundle can carry. This means that you must reduce the current carrying capacity by 30 percent for up to three wires, 40 percent for four to six wires, and 50 percent for seven to twenty-four wires.

21. Wire sizing charts are available online or in the West Marine catalog. Usually two charts are provided, one for a 10 percent voltage drop and one for a 3 percent voltage drop. I always go with the 3 percent chart.

22. Standard flooded-cell lead-acid batteries still provide the best value per amp-hour if properly maintained. Check the electrolyte levels regularly, don't discharge below 50 percent of capacity, and don't overcharge. Gel and AGM (absorbed glass mat) batteries are more finicky about charging. Some 95 percent of batteries returned as defective have actually been damaged by improper chargers or charging practices.

23. Top up batteries *only* with distilled water.

24. Batteries should be fastened down with a battery hold-down system or, preferably, in a well-secured battery box.

25. Never turn your master battery selector switch (1-2-Both-Off) through "Off" while your engine is running unless the switch is wired for AFD (alternator field disconnect). If you're not sure, don't do it, or else the popping sound you hear may be the diodes in your alternator burning out—an expensive development. Lacking an AFD, you can safely switch between batteries or battery banks only under the following conditions while the engine is running: (1) you switch from "1" to "2" or vice versa only through "Both," not through "Off"; (2) there are no dirty or corroded points that could cause an ephemeral interruption in the alternator circuit during switching. (Since you can never be completely sure of fulfilling the second condition, you can instead wire an inexpensive Zap-Stop or snubber from the alternator output stud to ground. This will conduct any fleeting current spikes during switching to ground.)

26. Buy, and learn to use, a good multimeter for testing circuits and troubleshooting electrical problems.

27. If your zinc anodes suddenly start disappearing faster than normal, have the marina check out the dock wiring. It or a nearby boat may be experiencing a wiring problem, and the resulting galvanic corrosion can waste a propeller shaft or through-hull with startling speed.

28. Nigel Calder's *Boatowner's Mechanical and Electrical Manual* is an excellent reference work for all things relating to marine electrical systems.

29. If you don't feel comfortable with any of this, hire a marine electrician.

30. Draw up a wiring diagram for your boat. Note the wire IDs on the diagram and keep it up to date. Any future owner or potential buyer of your boat will certainly appreciate it.

CHOOSING AND USING MARINE BATTERIES

Judging from the feedback I get from friends and customers, marine batteries are among boaters' biggest sources of frustration and problems. Before getting into specific projects, therefore, let's try to reduce the level of confusion by spending some time discussing battery types and specifications.

There are three general types of marine batteries: AGM (absorbed glass mat), gel cell, and flooded cell. We'll discuss each separately below, but for now, it's useful to understand that they all rely on a lead-acid chemical reaction. Lead is immersed in an electrolyte consisting of sulfuric acid diluted with water. As current flows from the battery, lead turns into lead sulfate and the acid is broken down into water. The lead is formed into plates, and sets of plates are grouped into cells. Each cell provides 2.1 volts, so a six-cell battery provides 12.6 volts. For simplicity, we call this a 12-volt battery.

The great thing about lead-acid batteries is that the chemical process is reversible. The charging current turns the lead sulfate back into the original form of lead and new acid is produced, bringing the electrolyte solution back up to strength. This is a grossly oversimplified description of the process, but it's sufficiently accurate for our purposes.

AGM Batteries

In an AGM battery, the electrolyte is captured by microporous glass separators. This makes the battery spill-proof and reduces internal resistance, allowing faster charging than with flooded-cell batteries. The AGM batteries are considered maintenance-free, requiring no water to be added during the life of the battery.

Although AGM batteries are more expensive than flooded-cell batteries, they have a very low self-discharge rate, meaning they hold a charge very well. They also recover well from deep discharge (below 50 percent). A properly sized AGM can be used as a combined starting and deep-cycle battery, described later in this chapter.

Gel-Cell Batteries

The electrolyte in a gel-cell battery is (as you have probably guessed) in the form of a gel. This pro-vides a battery that is maintenance-free and spill-proof and recovers well from deep discharges. Like AGMs, gel cells also have a very low self-discharge rate. Properly sized gel cells can function as combined starting and deep-cycle batteries.

Gel-cell batteries are more expensive than flooded-cell batteries and require more careful charging than either AGMs or flooded cells, with the charging voltage maintained between 13.8 and 14.1 volts. This requires a charger specifically designed for charging gel cells to avoid damage.

Flooded-Cell Batteries

The most common type of marine (and automotive) battery in use today is the flooded-cell battery (also known as the wet-cell or liquid-electrolyte battery). The electrolyte in these batteries is in liquid form, posing a spill hazard if the battery is overturned. And a potentially dangerous amount of hydrogen gas can be produced if the battery is seriously overcharged. These batteries also have higher maintenance requirements than the other types of batteries. Electrolyte levels must be checked regularly and water added if necessary. The batteries require proper charging and discharging and should be kept clean and corrosion-free. Still, flooded-cell batteries are the most cost-effective choice when measured on the basis of dollars per amp-hour capacity.

Battery Applications

In addition to the fundamental differences between batteries, they also differ according to the applications for which they are designed.

Starting an engine requires a strong jolt of electricity for a brief time. *Starting batteries* thus have many thin lead plates in order to maximize their reactive surface area and provide the highest possible starting current. Once the engine has started, the alternator recharges the battery and the battery thereafter just loafs. Unless the engine refuses to start, the battery will not be deeply discharged, and it is not designed to withstand repeated deep discharging. Discharging a starting battery deeply and repeatedly will reduce its life.

Deep-cycle batteries are built with fewer, thicker plates, which provide power for longer periods of time at a lower rate. The charge in these batteries can be slowly drawn down deeply and repeatedly without reducing their useful life, but they are not so good for the quick burst of energy needed to start an engine. With their reserve capacity, deep-cycle batteries are ideal for long-duration, low-draw electrical loads such as trolling motors, fishfinders, lights, radios, and radar.

Dual-purpose batteries represent a compromise solution and are able to start an engine on the one hand and run marine accessories on the other. They don't provide as quick a burst of energy as a true starting battery or last as long as a true deep-cycle battery, but the technology is constantly improving, making a better case for dual-purpose batteries for some applications.

In a perfect world you would have a starting battery for starting your engine and a deep-cycle battery to run all the electronics and accessories. Things aren't often perfect, however, so compromises are necessary. For light to moderate starting loads and accessory use, choose a dual-purpose battery. For heavy accessory use, choose a properly sized deep-cycle battery. If you have to use a single deep-cycle battery for both starting and accessory use, make sure it is larger than the equivalent size starting battery to obtain suffi-cient cranking amps. Flooded-cell batteries are available for starting, deep-cycle, or dual-purpose applications, depending on the number and thickness of lead plates. A properly sized AGM or gell-cell battery is a good choice for a dual-purpose battery.

PROPER CHARGING

Decent battery life depends on proper charging practices. Batteries should not be left in a discharged state for any period. The lead sulfate is at its weakest then and can flake off and reduce battery capacity or even short out a cell.

On the other hand, overcharging will break down the water in the battery to oxygen and hydrogen, a potentially explosive mixture. If nothing else, it reduces the electrolyte level and exposes lead sulfate on the battery plates. Once the lead sulfate hardens, it becomes very difficult to convert back into its original lead form, thus reducing battery capacity.

Generally speaking, lead-acid batteries should not be discharged below 50 percent. It takes almost as long to charge a battery from 85 to 100 percent as it does to charge it from 50 to 85 percent.

A proper battery charger charges in three stages. The first stage is the *bulk phase*, taking the battery rapidly from 50 to 85 percent. Beyond 85 percent, the resistance from the battery increases, and the battery will accept smaller and smaller charging currents. This declining charging rate is called the *absorption phase* and is adjusted by the battery charger, which is usually equipped with some sort of microprocessor.

Once the battery is fully charged, the charger shifts into its third stage, a *maintenance* or *float stage*, designed to keep the battery fully charged without overcharging.

There is a wide variety of marine battery chargers on the market. Some charge only one bank; others will charge two or three banks at a time. Make sure the charger you choose will handle the type of battery you have (gel cell, AGM, or flooded cell). Temperature also has an effect on charging rates, and better battery chargers have temperature compensation circuitry.

Enough book-learning! Let's get out our tools and do some projects.

BATTERY MAINTENANCE

Always remember to wear eye protection when working around batteries. Batteries can explode, and the sulfuric acid can cause burns or even blindness. If you should get sulfuric acid in your eyes, flush immediately with water and get medical help fast.

All batteries need to be kept clean and cool with their terminals free from corrosion. If you notice corrosion, loosen and remove the cable clamps and use a terminal brush or steel wool to clean the terminals. Clean up any steel wool slivers from around the battery posts, as they can cause a short. Replace and retighten the clamps, then coat with petroleum jelly or a terminal protection spray. Check for loose or damaged cables and replace if necessary.

Flooded-cell batteries should be checked regularly for proper electrolyte levels. Remove the battery caps and use a flashlight to look into each cell. Add distilled water only—not tap water—to raise the level to the mark on the inside of the battery. Never add acid to a battery.

Beyond that, the most critical maintenance item is proper charging. More batteries are killed by undercharging or overcharging than by any other cause. You can tell the state of battery charge with a DC voltmeter or by measuring the specific gravity of the electrolyte with a hydrometer. Hydrometers can be purchased at most automotive stores. They look like a small turkey baster with an indicator float inside. Suck up some electrolyte from a battery cell, and the float will indicate the state of charge against markings on the outside of the hydrometer. Float hydrometers are more accurate than the old floating ball types. Still, I prefer a voltmeter simply because it is easier and doesn't require dealing with the acid. AGM and gel-cell batteries can be tested only with a voltmeter. The accompanying table shows the percent of charge at various voltage and hydrometer readings.

BATTERY CHARGE BY SPECIFIC GRAVITY

Specific Gravity	Battery Voltage	State of Charge
1.265	12.6	100%
1.225	12.4	75%
1.190	12.2	50%
1.155	12.0	25%
1.120	11.8	0%

Source: Exide Battery Co.

As mentioned, a lead-acid battery should never be discharged below 50 percent, and you will rarely raise the battery's charge to more than 80 percent of capacity through engine alternator recharging. Thus, the usual effective charge range of a lead-acid battery is between 50 and 80 percent. Charging to 100 percent takes plenty of time and is best done with a charger connected to shore power. It takes longer to charge from 80 to 100 percent than to charge from 50 to 80 percent because, as the battery heats up from charging, it can accept less charging current without boiling the electrolyte (battery acid).

Battery Safety

- Always disconnect the positive battery cable when working around batteries to avoid shorting out the battery.
- Follow the ABYC (American Boat & Yacht Council) established standards for wire sizes and circuit protection (fuses or circuit breakers).
- Be sure to keep all terminals and connections clean and free from corrosion. Corroded terminals will increase resistance and could cause a fire.
- Wear safety glasses when working around acid-filled batteries. You should also have a source of fresh water to wash out eyes or flush skin.
- Be careful with metal tools. Dropping one across battery terminals will short the battery, creating a lot more excitement than you bargained for.

INSTALLING A SECOND BATTERY IN PARALLEL

Why install a second battery? If the boat came with a single battery, the builder must have known what he was doing, right?

A starting battery does fine for starting the engine and for occasional use of the navigation lights. But then we start adding electronics: a GPS, VHF radio, maybe a stereo, fishfinder, and radar. Finally we add electric downriggers and a windlass, and the battery keeps going flat and needs frequent replacing. At this point a second battery is needed.

It's important to consider where and how to mount a new battery. Batteries are heavy and might affect the trim of your boat if installed off-center or too far forward or aft. The location of a battery will also determine the length of the cables required to connect it to the electrical system. Closer to the existing battery is usually better.

The one exception might be if you are installing a dedicated battery for a windlass. In that case it might make more sense to install the battery forward, near the windlass, to reduce the length of the heavy DC cables required to power a windlass. Relatively small wires can then be run to charge the battery.

Batteries should be installed in battery boxes, which should be firmly anchored so they can't shift or overturn. The battery box top will also protect the battery terminals from accidentally shorting, so make sure it is installed.

In the simplest possible upgrade, a second battery may be installed in parallel with the first. Batteries connected in parallel, negative post to negative post and positive post to positive post, double the battery capacity while keeping the voltage the same. The installation is as simple as adding a second battery and battery box and connecting the batteries with two short battery cables.

Most marine retailers offer premade battery cables with terminals already installed. The cables

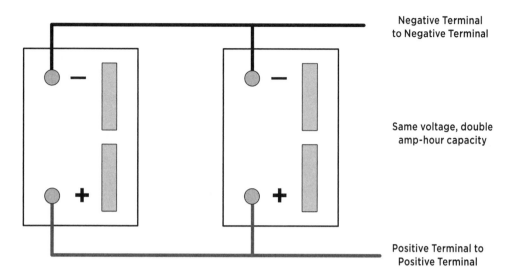

Negative Terminal
to Negative Terminal

Same voltage, double
amp-hour capacity

Positive Terminal to
Positive Terminal

Paralleling two batteries of equal voltage and capacity doubles their combined amp-hour capacity while keeping the voltage the same.

need to be correctly sized. Refer to the table on page 180 for the correct gauge of wire required for a given length and current.

All batteries charged from the same source should be closely matched in type, age, and size. Trying to charge two poorly matched batteries from a single source is a sure bet to cook one battery or the other. For best results, consider installing two new dual-purpose batteries. This will give you adequate starting power while providing the power necessary to power electronics and other 12-volt DC equipment.

INSTALLING A SECOND BATTERY BANK

More complex than a second battery installed in parallel, but better in many ways, is the addition of a second battery "bank." A bank can comprise a single battery or several connected batteries, though the former is more common in small-boat installations.

A dual battery bank provides a dedicated engine starting battery (a *starting bank*) and a deep-cycle battery for electrical loads such as marine electronics or other 12-volt appliances (a *house bank*). By splitting your two batteries into banks, you can select the battery that is best suited for its job.

In order to determine an appropriate rating for your deep-cycle house battery, you must first find the amperage ratings of all the DC devices it will power. You can find these on the specifications plate or in the owner's manual for each device. (If amps are not listed, you can determine the number by dividing the listed watts by 12 volts.) Estimate the amount of time that each device will be used between battery recharges and multiply that time by the current draw to obtain *amp-hours*. For example, a device that draws 10 amps for thirty minutes consumes 5 amp-hours of electricity between battery recharg- ings. Add all those figures and you will arrive at your energy budget. Remember that a battery should not be discharged below 50 percent, so the battery's amp-hour rating should be double your energy budget. If your energy budget is 50 amp-hours, you need a deep-cycle battery rated at 100 amp-hours.

Make sure your charging source, especially if it's from a smaller outboard motor, has enough output amps to fully charge both batteries in a reasonable time. A useful rule of thumb is that the actual alternator output should be at least 25 percent of the rated battery amp-hour capacity. Note that I said the *actual* alternator output, not the rated output. Alternators seldom produce their rated output. Use a multimeter to check.

(Most boats less than 35 feet in length run around with undercharged batteries much of the time, due to the ever-increasing size of outboard motors coupled with the ever-greater electrical loads from accessories and electronics installed on so many boats. If you trailer your boat or have access to dockside power, you may want to add a battery charger to keep your batteries fully charged under normal use. However, on an extended trip away from shore power, you may still gradually discharge your batteries beyond your alternator's ability to charge them.)

The two-bank solution creates some problems in charging two different battery types. One solu- tion is to install a 1-2-Both-Off battery selector switch. This switch allows you to connect one bat- tery or the other to the charging source. You can also briefly connect both batteries together in case of a weak starting battery.

Charging the batteries is accomplished by selecting Battery 1 to charge one bank or Battery

A multiposition battery selector switch allows the choice of one of two battery banks or the selection of both banks if needed—in the case of a weak starting battery, for example. (Courtesy Blue Sea Systems)

2 to charge the other. This requires a certain level of awareness, however; failing to switch batteries might result in one battery not getting charged, while leaving the battery switch set to "Both" could drain both batteries or damage one or the other. A battery voltage meter installed on the DC panel provides an easy way to check battery voltage and thus the state of charge. If your panel doesn't include a meter, consider installing one.

There are other solutions to the charging dilemma. One is to install a battery isolator in the circuit. This allows each battery to be charged independently and prevents the battery with the higher charge from discharging into the lower- charged battery. A battery isolator suitable for one charging source and two battery banks costs about $90.

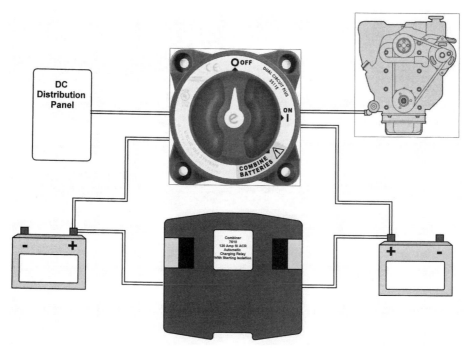

Blue Sea Systems' convenient Add-A-Battery kit for adding a second battery includes a battery selector switch as well as an automatic charging relay (ACR). (Courtesy Blue Sea Systems)

Automatic charging relays (ACRs) perform the same function, but instead of relying on diodes to control the charging current, as in a battery isolator, ACRs employ mechanical relays and a circuit that senses the battery's state of charge. For around $150, West Marine sells an Add-A-Battery kit that includes both the battery switch and the ACR unit.

Battery Switching Warning

When purchasing a master battery selector switch of the 1-2-Both-Off type, make sure it is equipped with an alternator field disconnect (AFD). An AFD works only on alternators with external regulators. The wire from the alternator to the regulator is cut and wired to the AFD terminals on the battery switch. This eliminates the possibility of blowing your rectifier diodes by inadvertently switching batteries with the engine running. This feature can be distinguished by two smaller terminals on the back of the switch.

Turning a non-AFD battery selector switch through the OFF position while the engine is running usually results in some faint popping sounds. These sounds are the diodes in your alternator blowing out. Install an AFD-equipped battery switch or be very careful not to switch batteries without shutting off the engine first. (You can switch a non-ADF selector from one battery to the other through BOTH while the engine is running, but don't do this. Sooner or later, you'll forget and switch through OFF—and once is all it takes.)

INSTALLING A SOLAR CHARGER

I've been known to kill a battery or two through neglect. My outboard-powered 20-footer doesn't have a charging circuit on the engine, so I have to regularly hook up the battery to a charger. I didn't do well with that even when I kept the boat at a dock with power at the slip.

My present slip doesn't have shore power, so I knew when I moved there that it would be only a matter of time before I killed yet another battery. That's why I decided to bite the bullet and install a solar-powered battery charger.

Looking through the boat store, I found a number of choices, ranging from a small solar panel (2 watts, $34.95) adequate for keeping a single battery topped up, to a medium one (6 watts, $89.95) designed for a medium-size deep-cycle battery, to a large one (18 watts, $159.95) intended for larger battery banks. The two smaller sizes were designed to charge the battery directly, without any sort of charge controller. The large panel required the use of a charge controller to prevent overcharging batteries and boiling off electrolyte.

I decided the small panel/charger would be just the ticket for the small battery I have aboard, which is used only for navigation and cabin lights, and not very often at that. The charger came with two charging cords. One is terminated with alligator clips to connect the charger directly to the battery terminals. The other has an automotive cigarette-lighter-style plug that allows you to plug the charger into a 12-volt power receptacle.

It just so happened that the new electrical panel I installed has an accessory socket for that style of plug, so the initial installation was dirt simple: I laid the solar panel on deck and plugged it into the

My solar panel battery charger simply plugs into the 12-volt accessory socket in the electrical panel.

socket. Electrically, this worked fine. It kept the battery topped off and didn't overcharge it.

Operationally, however, it was less successful. If I placed the solar panel in the cockpit, it was often either in the shade or in exactly the spot where I wanted to step. I never actually tested the durability of the charger by stepping on it, but I came close. On the other hand, whenever I placed the solar panel on the curved cabintop, it would eventually slide off. I would come back to the boat and find it hanging over the side, luckily out of the water.

In neither location was the charging cord long enough to plug into the electrical panel without the help of a 12-volt extension cord. This wasn't a big problem, but it wasn't neat or tidy either. I finally decided that the charger worked well enough to deserve a permanent installation.

The solar panel had four mounting tabs that could extend from each corner. The problem was that the place I wanted to mount the panel was curved in two directions, while the panel, although flexible, would bend in only one direction.

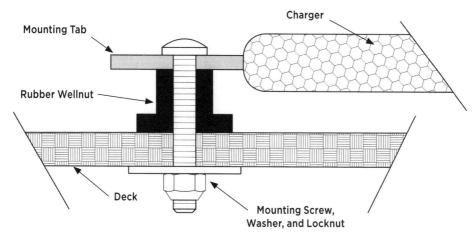

Charger

Mounting Tab

Rubber Wellnut

Deck

Mounting Screw,
Washer, and Locknut

A flexible rubber standoff at each corner of my solar panel provides an easy way to accommodate a curved deck.

Another stroll through the boat store provided the solution, a piece of hardware called a Wellnut. These are rubber spacers with a flange at one end and an internal threaded metal insert in the other. A machine screw inserted through a mounting tab and a Wellnut could then be fastened through the deck. Tightening a locknut on the screw, I reasoned, would compress the Wellnut's rubber spacer (flange end down) enough to accommodate the curvature of the deck and provide a secure mount for the solar panel.

After drilling the four through-deck mounting holes oversize, I filled them with epoxy/filler. After the epoxy had hardened, I redrilled the holes through the filler. This eliminated any chance of water leaking into the deck core and delaminating it. When bolting the assembly in place, I used plenty of polysulfide adhesive/sealant (3M 101 or BoatLIFE Life-Calk) on the bottom of the Wellnuts and on the machine screws.

I used a device called a CableClam as a leakproof method of bringing the charging cable through the deck. The first step was to drill a hole

The Blue Sea CableClam provides a leakproof method for leading an electrical cable through a deck or cabintop.

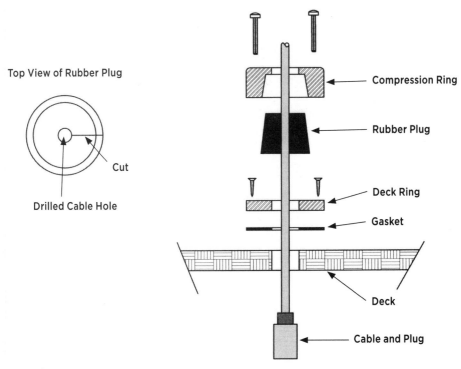

Top View of Rubber Plug

Cut

Drilled Cable Hole

Compression Ring

Rubber Plug

Deck Ring

Gasket

Deck

Cable and Plug

This CableClam schematic shows how easy it is to install. (Courtesy Blue Sea Systems)

through the deck large enough for the end of the charger cable to pass through. I likewise filled this hole with epoxy/filler to seal it, then redrilled it.

The CableClam has four parts. The first part, the deck ring, is screwed to the deck with self-tapping screws directly over the through-deck hole. Beneath the deck ring is the CableClam's second part, a rubber gasket, which should be augmented with plenty of sealant to keep water out. The third part of the CableClam is a tapered rubber plug. I drilled a hole through this plug exactly the same size as the wire used in the charging cable. I then used a sharp knife to cut through the plug wall on one side. This allowed me to force the cable into the plug's drilled center hole.

I then positioned the plug on the deck ring; placed the final piece of the CableClam, the compression ring, over the rubber plug; and screwed the compression ring to the deck ring. This compressed the tapered rubber plug and provided a waterproof through-deck seal for the charging cable. It takes longer to explain than to install and hasn't leaked a drop.

My battery now stays fully charged between uses and thanks me every time I step aboard. The panel stays in place and out of the way at all times. The location I chose was close enough to the electrical panel that I no longer need an extension cord. Life is good and my battery is happy.

INSTALLING ELECTRONICS

Most marine electronic devices can be installed either flush-mounted or in brackets, but check

My solar battery charger is mounted on the cabintop, out of the way of foot traffic.

before you buy. Some GPS/chartplotters with external antennas can't be installed in a flush mount, and many units have special requirements for ventilation. If the unit can be flush-mounted, be sure that the flush-mount hardware is either included or available; some flush-mount kits are available by special order only.

Bracket Mounts

Bracket mounts are the easiest to install. Not only that, they often have quick-release connectors and knobs that allow you to pop the unit off its bracket and take it home.

Don't rush into mounting the bracket. Play around with different placements. Have someone hold the unit in place while you view it from your preferred positions and under various lighting conditions. You wouldn't want to mount a display where glare makes it unreadable, for example.

Once you've found your preferred location, verify that you will be able to get power to that

location and that you will be able to snake any cables to it (from a fishfinder transducer, radio antenna, or radar, for example). Having access to the underside or back side of the mounting location will make mounting the bracket and snaking the cable much easier.

The next step is to bolt the bracket in place. I like through-bolt brackets with nylock self-locking nuts underneath. This makes for a secure mounting. As a last resort, you can mount a bracket with stainless steel self-tapping screws. If you do so, however, remember to check them periodically to make sure they are still tight. A bead of sealant around each fastener will keep water from leaking through the fastener holes.

Once you have the bracket mounted, you can drill holes for the cables. Many of the cable ends will already have connectors on them, requiring a larger hole than the cable itself requires. In situations such as this, I like to use a CableClam, as described earlier in this chapter, to seal the hole and provide a secure connection for the cable.

Flush Mounts

Flush mounts are a little more difficult to install than bracket mounts in that you need to cut a hole for the unit in a console, dashboard, or bulkhead. Every flush-mounted device I've seen includes a template for cutting the mounting hole. If you do not have a template, contact the manufacturer for one or make one from cardboard, fitting it by trial and error.

Before cutting, verify that there is enough room behind the mounting surface for the device and that you have sufficient access for feeding wiring and cables.

Flush-mounted devices are either fastened to the instrument panel from the front side (usually with screws through a bezel) or require a flush-mount bracket. The manufacturer's template will include the position and size of mounting holes for a front-mounted installation, and there should also be a rubber gasket to fit between the device and the mounting surface. Flush-mount brackets must usually be assembled from the back side when the unit is in place. Dexterity and small fingers are very helpful.

Once you are sure everything fits and you have run the required cables, remove the unit from the instrument panel and pull the wires and cable through the mounting hole. It is always easier to connect the cables in the open air, where you can see and manipulate them, rather than trying to find a hard-to-reach connecter in the back of a mounted unit. While you have the device out of the panel, you might want to briefly power it up so you know that all the connections are correct and live. Then put the unit back in and tighten everything up.

Electronics Boxes and Enclosures

Real estate on small boats is limited, and there often isn't enough room to install all the goodies the average boater would like. Several styles of marine enclosures have been developed to address this problem.

Smaller units can accommodate a single item, such as a VHF radio, and are designed to be bracket mounted to the overhead, on top of the dash, or below it.

Large units are designed to mount against the overhead or be hung from a T-top. These units run from 24 to 36 inches wide and about 9 inches deep and can house several devices, such as a GPS/chartplotter, a fishfinder, a radio, and even a radar display. Given the weight of the enclosure

A small enclosure like this one can be mounted on the dashboard and is often used to house marine AM/FM radios. (Courtesy Poly-Planer)

and the systems installed in it, mounting one of these units requires sturdy fasteners and a strong support structure.

While planning your installation, verify your ability to snake wires and cables between the devices, power sources, and transducers and antennas. Sometimes this is more difficult than actually mounting the unit and installing the electronics.

This lockable electronics enclosure fits snugly up under a T-top. The electronics are out of the sun and protected from spray and rain. (Courtesy Moeller Products Company, Inc.)

If you lead wires through holes in metal frame tubes or fiberglass, provide chafe protection at the entry points. When you pull wires through, add a messenger line—a string pulled through with the wire. A messenger line makes it easy to pull the next wire through—possibly one that you forgot. And when you do at last pull that wire, pull *another* messenger line. You never know when the *next* one will be needed.

SELECTING AND INSTALLING A VHF RADIO ANTENNA

Before installing a VHF antenna, it's necessary to make sense of the host of choices available in the electronics section of most marine stores. The first criterion is the antenna's decibel (dB) or gain rating, which describes the antenna's ability to suck in radio waves of certain frequencies. The higher the dB rating, the better the antenna accomplishes that. Typical ratings for VHF antennas are 3, 6, and 9 dB.

Based on that, why would anyone choose anything but a 9-dB antenna? Because with higher gain comes higher directionality. The "sweet spot"

for reception in a 9-dB antenna is a flat ring around the antenna. The plane of this ring stays perpendicular to the antenna as the boat pitches and rolls, alternately pointing at the water or the sky. A 9-dB antenna may do the best job in calm seas or a big, stable motoryacht, but not necessarily in a small boat in rough waters.

The 3-dB antenna, with its fat donut of reception, experiences much less of a problem with roll-related blind spots but also has a shorter effective range. Sailboats are often equipped with 3-dB antennas, but powerboats don't heel like sailboats. A 6-dB antenna is in the middle, offering decent range with fewer roll-related problems. Go for a good 6-dB antenna.

The second criterion is the construction of the antenna. You can find 6-dB antennas at prices ranging from under $50 to over $250. Low-end antennas are made with filament-wound fiberglass exterior tubes. After a couple of years on the boat, the exterior finish starts to deteriorate. If you grab one of these antennas at that stage, you'll get a handful of fiberglass splinters. And the antenna elements in low-end antennas are usually just a length of coax cable.

Mid-range antennas have a smooth polyurethane coating on the antenna tube that will hold

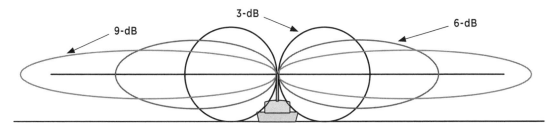

A VHF antenna with a 3-decibel (dB) gain gives good local transmit-and-receive coverage at the expense of range. A 9-dB antenna trades coverage at large roll and heel angles for longer range. A 6-dB antenna represents a good compromise for a powerboat.

up for years and will not shed fiberglass splinters. The element inside the antenna is usually some sort of brass wire.

High-end antennas have a polyurethane coating as well as more complicated and efficient brass and copper radiating elements inside the antennas. The very best antennas have silver- or gold-plated elements inside the antenna tube.

Lower-end antennas generally have mounting ferrules made of nylon. Mid- and high-end antennas have stronger chrome-plated brass or stainless steel ferrules.

Most antennas are a standard 8 feet long. Exceptions are 3-foot stainless steel whip antennas designed for mounting on sailboat masts and small powerboats. These have a cylinder at the base used to house the loading coil, required to match the short antenna to the VHF frequencies.

Most antennas come with 15 feet of coax cable and the coax fitting needed to connect the antenna to the radio. If a longer cable is needed, you can buy coax cable and splice fittings at most marine stores.

All but a few special antennas have 1"-14 (1-inch diameter by 14 threads per inch) threaded bases. These fit a wide variety of antenna mounts, many of which have a ratcheting adjustment arrangement that allows the antenna to be folded down easily, as when going under a low bridge. You can find mounts designed to be installed on flat surfaces, on vertical surfaces, or on pulpit or stanchion tubes.

An 8-foot antenna whipping in the breeze can exert a lot of force on the antenna mount. Be sure to use sufficiently strong mounting bolts and a backing plate if necessary.

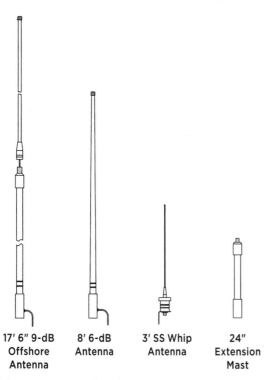

17' 6" 9-dB
Offshore
Antenna

8' 6-dB
Antenna

3' SS Whip
Antenna

24"
Extension
Mast

An assortment of marine VHF antennas.

A stainless steel ratchet mount for a VHF antenna. (Courtesy Shakespeare Electronics Products Group)

INSTALLING TRANSDUCERS FOR FISHFINDERS AND DEPTH SOUNDERS

Installing a transducer for a depth sounder or fishfinder is a common DIY project, but one that generates more questions than most. There are three basic types of transducer installations: transom-mount, through-hull, and in-hull.

Transom-mounted transducers are usually made of plastic and come with a mounting bracket that is screwed to the transom. Transom-mounted transducers can sometimes be mounted as in-hull transducers, but only at some loss of sensitivity and with a complete sacrifice of the optional speed- or temperature-sensing capabilities that some units offer.

A subset of the transom-mounted transducer is a trolling motor transducer, designed to mount on the lower unit of an electric trolling motor. Some trolling motors even come with a mount already in place.

Through-hull transducers require drilling a hole through the bottom of the hull and bolting the transducer in place with a big nut on the threaded transducer stem. The bodies of through-hull transducers are generally plastic or bronze. Some come with a fairing block attached or as an option to orient the transducer beam straight downward when the unit is mounted in a deep-V hull.

In-hull or puck-style transducers are designed to be mounted inside the hull, against the bottom of the boat. A well-designed in-hull transducer loses very little sensitivity.

Transom-Mounted Transducer

Transom-mounted transducers are the simplest to install. A plastic bracket is fastened to the transom, and that bracket holds the transducer at the proper level in the water. Some transducers also carry a paddle wheel to measure speed as well as a sensor to detect water temperature.

Proper location of the transducer is critical for accurate readings. It must be installed parallel to the waterline and at a height that remains slightly underwater when the boat is at speed. The transducer should also be at least 15 inches from the prop and in an area free of turbulence and bub-

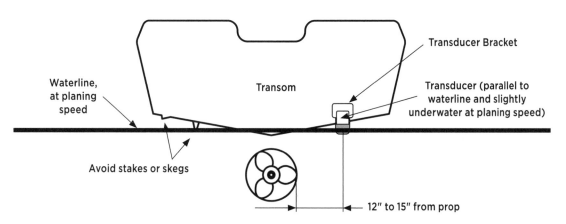

Siting a transom-mounted transducer.

bles, which may be caused by rivets, strakes, or other appendages or protrusions on the boat's bottom. Look over the transom when the boat is at speed to identify an area where water comes off the transom smoothly and without bubbles.

Be sure to properly seal the fastener holes used to hold the bracket to the transom. Drill the holes oversize and fill them with epoxy/filler before redrilling them to the proper size. If not sealed, even a small screw hole can allow enough water to leak into the transom to cause rot.

Being exposed on the transom also means that the transducer is subject to damage from hitting debris or during launching from or retrieving to a trailer. Luckily, these transducers are also among the cheapest, so replacement won't bankrupt you.

Transom-mounted transducers can also be removed from the bracket and installed as a through-hull mount. Again, follow the manufac-

turer's instructions for proper mounting and orientation.

Closely allied to the transom mount is the trolling motor mount. If you decide to install your transducer on your trolling motor, make sure you have the appropriate style of transducer. Most manufacturers will exchange an unopened, unused transducer for the proper style at little or no cost.

Through-Hull Transducer

Most through-hull transducers have a mushroom-shaped head on a threaded shank. The transducer is installed from the outside, and a nut is threaded onto the shank inside the boat to hold it in place.

As in most jobs, the details are important. If the hull is fiberglass, it is important to seal the edges of the fiberglass with epoxy. If the hull is

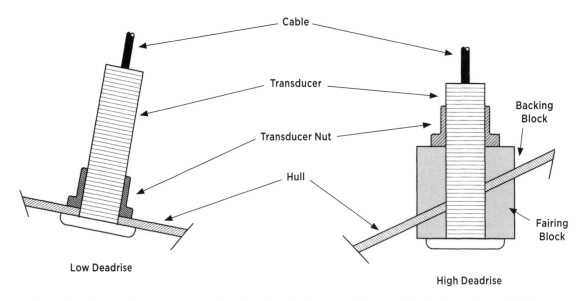

A through-hull transducer mount on a low-deadrise hull is straightforward (left), but a deep-V hull requires an exterior fairing block and quite possibly a matching block inside the hull.

cored, remove the core around the hole and replace it with epoxy/filler to prevent water intrusion and keep the transducer nut from crushing the core.

Some plastic-bodied transducers are incompatible with certain sealants, so follow the manufacturer's recommendations for the proper sealant to use. Plastic transducer bodies generally hold up well as long as the unit isn't overtightened and the right sealant is used. Bronze transducers are more expensive but stronger.

Transducers must be oriented close to vertical for accurate, reliable readings. If the angle of the boat's bottom, known as deadrise, is less than 10 degrees or so, it may not pose a problem when mounting a transducer. On a deep-V bottom, however, a normal through-hull mounting may aim the transducer 20 degrees or more from vertical. In such cases a fairing block may be required.

A fairing block has its top surface angled to match the boat's deadrise, while the bottom surface is horizontal. A matching block may be installed inside the hull to permit the mounting nut to be tightened evenly. A properly designed fairing block can reduce turbulence around the transducer, actually improving its performance. The block may be made of wood (not recommended), plastic, or bronze. Some transducers are available with a fairing block attached.

In-Hull Transducer

Given all the potential problems incurred by drilling big holes in the bottom of a boat, it is not surprising that in-hull transducer mountings are popular. They work well in solid fiberglass hulls that are not cored. Any core or even bubbles in the glass will produce erroneous readings. Some hulls already have a pocket molded in the bilge

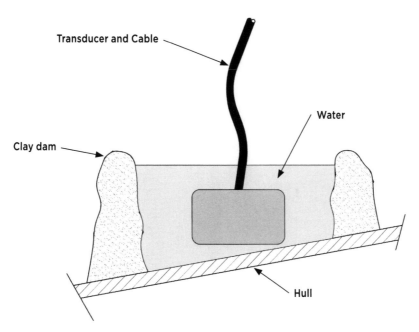

A clay dam allows you to test a transducer's location before permanently installing it.

for such a mounting. If you can't find it, ask the manufacturer if there is one.

Some people simply mount the transducer and hope for the best, but a more successful approach is to systematically test the transducer's accuracy in a given location. To do this, you need to have the depth sounder or fishfinder display installed and powered up and the transducer connected.

With the boat motionless over a level bottom, hold the transducer in the water and note the depth. Then hold the transducer against the bottom inside the bilge at the trial location. If the area can be dammed off, fill it with water and place the transducer in the pool. Take a reading. If it closely matches the reading taken with the transducer held over the side, you're good to go. Mark the location and proceed with the installation.

If you can't provide a pool of water in the bilge, cut one end of a short length of PVC tubing

at an angle to match the deadrise of the hull so that the tubing can be mounted on the vertical. Temporarily seal the tubing to the hull with strip caulk or silicone sealant. Fill the tube with water and place the transducer in the tube, weighting it down if necessary to sink it to the bottom of the tube before taking the reading.

It sounds like a lot of work, but once you've done it you'll know that the location is correct. Remove the tubing or pool of water and dry out the mounting area.

Here is where practical experience differs from manufacturers' instructions. The manufacturers suggest epoxying the transducer in place using a thick, slow-setting epoxy. They recommend coating both the hull and the transducer and pushing the transducer in place with a twisting motion to ensure that there are no air bubbles underneath.

A more common mounting method that works just as well is to place a large blob of sealant

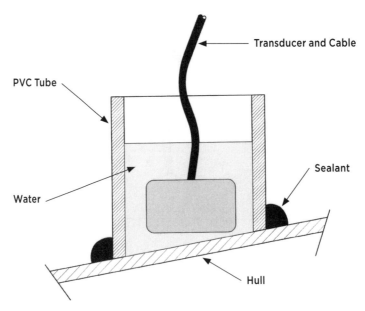

A PVC tube is an excellent way of testing a mounting location for an in-the-hull transducer.

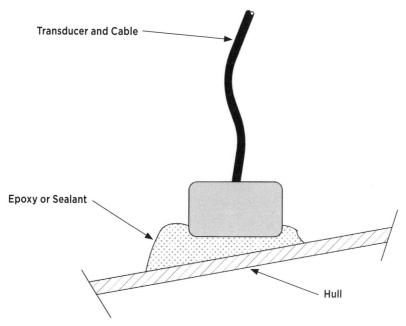

Transducer and Cable

Epoxy or Sealant

Hull

Epoxy or sealant blobs are often used to mount in-hull transducers. Make sure there are no air bubbles in the sealant.

in the mounting area and push the transducer into the sealant, ensuring that no air bubbles are underneath. Make sure you use the appropriate sealant suggested by the manufacturer, as some sealants will attack the plastics used in the transducer. If you ever want to remove the transducer, using the right sealant will make the job a lot easier.

Special considerations apply for mounting transducers in metal or wood hulls. Most manufacturers provide good, detailed installation directions. Spend some time on their websites reviewing selection and installation procedures.

CHAPTER 8

Engine and Drivetrain

The engine and drivetrain are the heart and muscles of your boat. While few of us will be doing heart transplants (engine repowering), there is ample opportunity for do-it-yourselfers to maintain and upgrade these vital systems. Many of us have changed the oil and filters in our cars, and those same procedures transfer easily to our boats. (In fact, many inboard and stern-drive engines are based on automotive engines.) Developing a familiarity with your engine and drivetrain is also good for safety's sake. When you're in a pinch, you can't fix what you don't know.

CHANGING ENGINE OIL

There should be a law forcing boat designers to service the boats they create. That might make common maintenance tasks, such as changing the engine oil, a little easier. Most owners of inboard or inboard-outboard (I/O, also called stern drive) engine installations anticipate changing the engine oil with the same enthusiasm they feel when going to the dentist.

Most marine engine manufacturers recommend changing the engine oil after every one hundred to two hundred hours of operation, or at least annually. Frankly, most marine engines aren't used often enough to cause any appreciable breakdown in the oil. The marine environment being what it is, however, moisture may well accumulate in an idle engine. Changing the engine oil (as well as the filter) on a regular basis will help prolong the life of your engine.

Consider yourself lucky if you can get a catch pan under the engine and let the oil drain from the crankcase by gravity. The rest of us must resort to various workaround methods of draining the oil, ranging from simple to complex.

Make a few simple preparations for this task, regardless of how simple or complex your method is. Have enough containers to hold all the old oil. (Many people use old plastic milk jugs to capture the used oil.) Tight-fitting tops lessen the likelihood of a messy spill. Have a good supply of oil-absorbing pads ready to deploy around and under the engine. Have enough of the right grade of new oil and the proper replacement oil filter at hand. Don't forget a filter wrench.

Warm up your engine. Warm oil drains more quickly and completely out of the engine, and by running the engine, you put many of the contaminants in the oil into suspension so that they can be drained out before they settle to the bottom of the oil pan, or crankcase.

Apart from direct draining through a plug in the oil pan, the simplest oil-change method uses a manual pump. You snake the small, flexible pickup hose down the dipstick tube to the bottom of the oil pan, then pump the oil out.

Three varieties of manual pumps are readily available at your marine store. The first is a metal container with a pump attached. The pickup tube is equipped with a clamp that seals the hose in the dipstick opening and allows the pump to build up a vacuum in the metal container. When the clamp is loosened, the vacuum sucks out the oil.

These pumps are simple and well built and last for years. The downside is that the capacity of the container is limited, and it may need to be emptied during the course of an oil change. The pickup hose is easy to insert through the dipstick tube, but because of its small diameter, the flow of oil is rather slow.

The second type of manual pump has a direct action, meaning that you simply operate the handle up and down to suck the oil out of the dipstick tube and into a built-in plastic container. You don't have to build up a vacuum as in the previously mentioned pump, but the container has a limited capacity and may need to be emptied during an oil change.

The third choice is a handheld piston pump that looks like a small handheld bilge pump. The pickup hose either screws onto a threaded dipstick tube or is snaked down through the tube, and there is an output hose instead of a built-in container. The output hose directs the waste oil into any convenient container (such as a milk jug) while you pump. The volume expelled by each stroke is small, making the oil change a long and tiring effort, and the loose output tube stuffed into a jug is a mess just waiting to happen. You did put oil pads under the jugs, didn't you?

Three manual oil-change pumps. The one at left works by pulling a vacuum in the metal container, which may require fifty or so strokes on the handle. Releasing a pinch clamp on the suction hose (not rigged in this photo) then sucks the oil out of the engine crankcase via the dipstick tube. Operating the direct-action pump at right applies a vacuum directly to the dipstick tube, thus requiring fewer strokes to build a vacuum, but the receiving container is smaller and more likely to require emptying during the oil change. The handheld piston pump at center includes a small-bore pickup hose for dipstick insertion; you must supply a waste container to receive the old oil.

If the manual pumps sound like a lot of work, let's see what electricity can do for us. The simplest electric pump uses a rubber impeller in a plastic housing to pump the oil, while the motive power to spin the impeller comes from an electric drill. Tighten the pump shaft in the drill chuck, insert the pickup hose down the dipstick tube, stick the discharge hose into a jug, and turn on the drill, holding the pump body in one hand and the drill motor in the other. See any potentially messy problems here? One other caveat: Make sure the impeller in the pump is rated for petroleum products; some drill pumps are rated only for water.

This Jabsco electric pump mounts on a 5-gallon bucket. The power leads with alligator clips will clamp to your ship's battery for power.

Pumps mounted in buckets represent a step up from handheld drill pumps. These usually comprise a 12-volt impeller pump mounted on the lid of a 3- to 5-gallon metal or plastic bucket. A power cord with alligator clips on the end allows the pump to be connected to a 12-volt battery for power. Most have on/off switches and some also have reversing switches so the contents of the bucket can be pumped out.

The pickup hose can be the type that screws onto a threaded dipstick or simply a tube to snake down through the dipstick opening. There are a few nagging problems with this style of pump, however. Empty, the buckets with the pump mounted in them are top-heavy and hard to store. Some users solve this problem by storing the unit in a plastic milk crate for stability. Put an oil pad in the bottom of the crate to soak up any dribbles. It is sometimes hard to find a flat, stable location for the unit in the bilge of the boat, and ready access to 12-volt power may be problematic. When filled, the bucket becomes a heavy object to move around and off the boat.

One refinement of this system is to replace the oil pan drain plug with an elbow and a length of hose, the other end of which comes out from

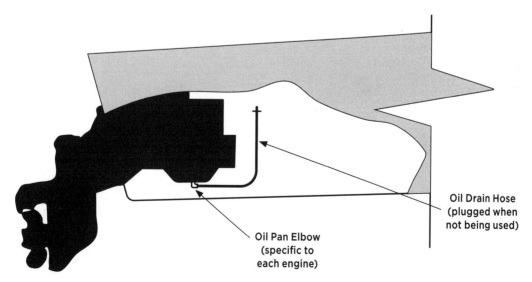

Permanently connecting a drain hose to the oil pan will provide a convenient method for draining the oil. The elbow specifications will vary with the engine make and model.

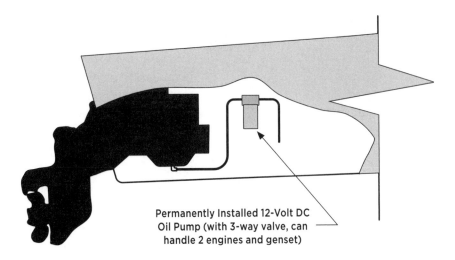

Permanently Installed 12-Volt DC
Oil Pump (with 3-way valve, can
handle 2 engines and genset)

Adding an electric pump to a permanently attached oil-drain hose will make oil changes a breeze.

under the engine and can be connected to the pump. Make sure the hose is rated for petroleum products, can be sealed at the open end when not in use, and isn't subject to chafe or wear.

Many larger boats, especially trawler yachts, have permanently installed oil-changing systems. These usually consist of a hose from the bottom of the oil pan (or from each oil pan in a twin-engine boat) connected to a manifold and pump assembly that is permanently bolted to a bulkhead. Unfortunately, these systems are too large for most of the small boats that this book is concerned with.

No oil change is complete until the old oil is properly disposed of. Many if not most marinas provide for the proper disposal of old oil. If your marina does not, many auto parts stores will accept used oil free or for a nominal price. Be careful when moving the containers around, since you are liable for any spillage, whether of fuel or oil.

If you have a diesel engine, another way of disposing of old engine oil is to mix it with the diesel fuel. It is claimed that you can mix up to 10 percent old oil in the fuel, though the oil should be filtered and well mixed with diesel before being put into the tank. Check your engine manual to see if the manufacturer approves of this practice. It is controversial among diesel engine manufacturers and owners, and it is probably unnecessary if you have access to proper disposal sites. If you were on a long cruise or at sea without proper facilities, however, it would be better to burn the old oil than to dump it over the side.

Find out what oil-change option works best for you, and change your oil often. Don't make a mess, and dispose of waste oil properly.

FUEL SYSTEM MAINTENANCE

The advent of E10 gasoline (gas with 10 percent ethanol) has caused major problems for boaters. The fuel dissolves some fiberglass fuel tanks and can attack hoses and seals on older boats. The stuff that it dissolves may end up clogging your carburetor or injectors. The fuel itself deteriorates much faster, too, because it can attract fifty times more water vapor from the atmosphere than conventional gasoline. When too much water is absorbed, a phenomenon called phase separation occurs, in which the water and ethanol drop to the bottom of the tank and the gas floats to the top, losing about three points of octane in the process. Needless to say, you can't burn the water-rich stuff on the bottom, and the reduced-octane gas on top isn't much good either. The bottom line is that boaters should inspect their fuel systems annually and be prepared to spend more time on fuel system maintenance than ever before.

Gasoline is dangerous to work around, so before we get started, let's review a few safety tips: Have a Class B fire extinguisher rated for flammable liquids close at hand. Turn off the boat's electrical system at the batteries. It should go without saying that while working on your fuel system or while pumping fuel you should not smoke or use any tools that create sparks, including most electrical power tools. When gawkers come by to visit, make sure they observe the rules.

At the same time, take appropriate steps to avoid polluting the water either directly or through groundwater runoff. If you put so much as a light sheen of oil on the water, you may be liable for stiff Coast Guard pollution fines. When draining a fuel system, have plenty of absorbent pads to catch drips. Check with your marina or municipal authorities about the proper disposal of used oil and bad gas.

Here's what you can do to maintain the health of your fuel system:

- **Inspect.** All hoses should be regularly checked for brittleness, cracks, or softening. If you detect changes in your fuel lines, change them earlier rather than later. A soft hose indicates that the interior structure is deteriorating and could delaminate and completely plug the fuel line.
- **Replace.** Replacement fuel line should be purchased at a marine store, not an auto parts store. There are three types of fuel line in common use, and all three need to have the appropriate USCG (U.S. Coast Guard) and SAE (Society of Automotive Engineers) certification notices printed on the hose itself. Type A1 hose is black and is used for fuel and vent lines. Type A2 hose is also black and is used for fuel fill lines. Type B1 fuel lines are gray and are used with outboard fuel systems. Measure all the lines you need to replace before you go to the marine store, and allow extra in case you have mismeasured. All fuel hoses must be double clamped at each end, so buy hose clamps at the same time, and pick up a few spares. I don't like reusing old hose clamps, especially on something as critical as a fuel system. Again, buy them at a marine store, and ensure that they're stainless steel. When you install them, make sure the second hose clamp lands entirely on the barb and not half on the barb and half off. That could pinch or cut the inside of the hose and lead to a fuel leak.
- **Prep for Storage.** Experts disagree on the best way to prep your fuel tank for winter storage. Some recommend draining the fuel system as much as possible and then adding a fuel stabilizer to what remains in the lines. While this prevents phase separation from occurring to a full tank of gas, its downside is that a great deal of condensation can occur in an empty tank, so you're still stuck with water in the tank. Other experts, including some oil company experts, recommend filling the tank to about 95 percent capacity, leaving some room for expansion while minimizing the amount of air available for condensation.

Both sides in this debate agree that the worst solution is to leave the tank half full.

• **Stick It.** An engine that knocks, hesitates, or fails to reach its accustomed top speed at wide-open throttle (WOT) may be suffering from phase separation in its fuel. You can test the gas in your tank for separation by applying a special "water-finding" chemical paste to a dipstick and sticking it through the fuel filler or tank access port down to the bottom of the tank. The paste will change color if water is present. Be sure to use a paste specifically formulated for E10 fuel.

• **Separate It.** Install a fuel/water separator as described in the next section.

Installing a fuel/water separator is an easy do-it-yourself project and well worth the time in these days of ethanol-laced gasoline. (Courtesy Moeller Products Company, Inc.)

ADDING A FUEL/WATER SEPARATOR

E10 gasoline is hygroscopic, which means that it absorbs water from the air. It will do this readily enough in your gas tank, but it is even more susceptible to water contamination in the distributor's or dealer's storage tank. As a result, your chances of buying a tank of bad gas are higher than ever, and that's why you should consider adding a fuel/water separator to your fuel system. It is easy to install.

Several firms manufacture add-on separator kits, including Racor and Sierra. These consist of a cast aluminum or stainless steel bracket that accepts a spin-on separator cartridge. This separator cartridge also acts as a fuel filter and is commonly referred to as a filter or filter cartridge. The kits also include one or two spin-on filters and several brass plugs. The brackets have two inlet ports and two outlet ports to handle either single engines or a twin-outboard instal-

lation. For single-engine use, the brass plugs come into play to block off one set of inlet and outlet ports.

Most kits do not include the hose barb fittings to connect the fuel lines, so these must be purchased separately to match the size of your existing fuel lines. The port diameters are either ¼ inch or ⅜ inch, with an NPT standard thread. Generally speaking, the ¼-inch ports are used for engines rated below 200 horsepower (hp), and the ⅜-inch ports for engines of 200 hp and up.

Fuel/water separators with clear plastic bowls make it easy to spot water in the fuel, but they are legal only for gas outboards. If you have anything else—inboard, stern-drive, or even a diesel engine—you need a metal bowl or a plastic bowl with a metal fire shield.

American Boat & Yacht Council standards require that fuel lines slope uphill from the tank to the engine. Identify a strong mounting location that meets this requirement and provides access to the fuel lines. Leave enough vertical clearance under the filter cartridge so that it can be unscrewed and removed. Even better, leave enough space so that a container can be placed under the filter to catch any drips during removal.

The filter bracket must be mounted firmly to withstand the weight of the filter when full as well as the stresses placed on it when removing the spin-on filter cartridge. Most brackets use ¼- to ⅜-inch fasteners. One common installation option is to lag-bolt the unit to the transom. The transom is more than strong enough to support the unit, but be sure to seal the transom core (see Chapter 6) to prevent water damage.

With the bracket mounted, cut the fuel line from the tank and connect it to the separator inlet, then run a line from the outlet to the engine. Often you can just disconnect the fuel intake line from the engine and hook it to the inlet hose barb on the separator bracket. Remember to double-clamp the hoses, and use only marine fuel hose certified and marked as such. Take all the usual precautions when working with gasoline. Drain the lines, clean up spills, and have a fire extinguisher handy.

Once you have your fuel/water separator installed, be sure to include a couple of extra filter cartridges in your spare parts supply. If you are out on the water and your engine starts sputtering from a bad case of water contamination, it may take a couple of filters to get you home. Be sure to have a proper container aboard so you can hold the dirty filters for proper disposal ashore.

Place the container under the filter and unscrew the filter. The container will catch the drips.

20 Ways to Beat the High Price of Gas

As I write this in summer 2008, gas prices—including prices at gas docks—are at their highest levels ever. But before you rail at that "price-gouging marina owner," consider things from his perspective.

Most gas dock operations are seasonal, so the annual cost of maintaining the fueling facilities—tanks, pumps, license fees, and perhaps the dock itself—has to be paid for with income generated during just a few months. In addition, many gas docks don't sell enough gas to qualify for volume discounts. In many cases, the marina may pay just about as much for their gas as you do.

Many boaters are already curtailing their boating due to high fuel costs. To keep your boat from becoming little more than a floating picnic table tied to the dock, here are twenty ways to get as much mileage as possible out of every gallon. Not everyone will be able to make use of all these suggestions, but surely some of these ideas will help you save fuel and keep boating.

1. Keep a clean bottom. Even a mild growth of slime will increase the resistance of a boat through the water. If you are in a slip, have a diver clean the bottom or pull the boat to get the bottom scrubbed. Trailer boaters should clean the bottom after every use.

2. Apply fresh bottom paint. Antifouling paint loses its effectiveness over time. When the intervals between required bottom cleanings get shorter and shorter, it's time to pull the boat and apply new bottom paint. In less salty waters, use bottom paint with high levels of slime-killer additive. (See Chapter 6.)

3. Remove unnecessary appendages. If you have a depth-sounder transducer that's no longer being used, or anything else sticking out below the waterline that you don't need, get rid of it to reduce water drag. Remove large canvas enclosures when they're not needed to cut resistance through the air.

4. Keep the engine in tune. Not only will you burn less fuel, the engine will run smoother and last longer. Although you should carefully observe your owner's manual for maintenance schedules, you should also keep an eye on your boat exhaust. It should be invisible. If it's black, blue, or white, you need at least a tune-up, if not more serious engine repairs.

5. Make sure you have the right prop. Most of us expect the right prop to be on the boat when we get it, but that's not always true. Do some research; check the prop to determine its diameter and pitch, and check with the boat manufacturer to get their recommendations. Installing the correct prop could be a quick and inexpensive way to increase both performance and fuel economy.

Your owner's manual will give you the engine speed range for wide-open throttle (WOT). This is usually between 5,000 and 5,500 rpm. Select a prop that just barely allows your engine to reach that range at WOT. Increasing the prop's pitch reduces rpm and vice versa. Too much pitch is better than too little, because exceeding your WOT will burn fuel without adding appreciable performance, and may damage your engine.

6. Keep an eye on your prop. If your boat speed starts dropping at accustomed throttle settings, it may be a sign that your prop is dinged or its pitch has changed.

7. Get the best deal on fuel. Shop around for lower prices as well as discounts. Discounts are sometimes given to members of BoatU.S. Other marinas may offer discounts for cash or for purchases over 50 gallons, and possibly bigger discounts for larger purchases. Trailer boaters should consider filling up at a landside gas station instead of a marina fuel dock.

8. Find the most economical cruising speed. Note the amount of fuel added at each refueling and keep a log of times, distances, and speeds run. This requires some record keeping, but it's not difficult to find the speed range that uses the least fuel per mile. Almost invariably it will mean slowing down, but that's the price you pay for efficiency.

9. Add a fuel-flow meter to your instrumentation. A fuel-flow meter is a better way to determine your most economical operating speeds. It can also be used to monitor your engine's health; increased fuel consumption can indicate problems with the engine or reflect the need for a tune-up. A fuel-flow meter will set you back about $300, but it might pay for itself within just a few tanks of gas.

10. Avoid phase separation and fuel degradation. There is no way to recombine phase-separated gas, so avoidance is the only solution. Under ideal conditions of moderate temperatures and low humidity, E10 gas will resist phase separation for three months or so. Don't leave a tank full of gas sitting longer than that, and make sure you use it up sooner in hot, humid weather.

If you have a 100-gallon tank and use only 20 gallons, consider installing a secondary, smaller tank and use it instead of the bigger tank. It's bad enough when *any* gas phase-separates, but even worse when you lose 100 gallons that way.

11. Unload the boat. Remove any unused equipment from the boat. There is no sense in hauling around weight you don't use. Clean out lockers and storage areas. Reducing the weight of the boat, even a little bit, will reduce your fuel consumption.

12. Empty the water tanks. Fresh water weighs 8.33 pounds per gallon, and most of us hardly use the onboard water supply unless we are cruising. Why drag it around if you don't use it?

13. Trim the boat correctly. Boat hulls are designed to run level on plane. Distribute weight on board (including passengers) and use trim tabs and engine trim to keep the boat in proper trim. Not only is it more fuel-efficient; the boat will handle better too.

14. Get up on plane quickly. The longer you spend struggling to get over the hump and onto plane, the more fuel you burn. Those trim tabs and engine trim controls can help you get up on plane quicker, where most planing hulls operate more efficiently.

15. Steer small. Check your wake and see how straight you're steering. The less correcting you do, the shorter your trip and the less fuel you'll consume. Use an autopilot whenever practical, and adjust cable steering systems to eliminate excessive play.

16. Plan your trip and navigate properly. You can use less fuel if you spend less time wandering around trying to figure out where you are. Before setting out, establish an efficient course to follow with proper waypoints and course directions.

17. Check the tide tables. Plan your trip around the tides to avoid running against contrary currents. Starting a few minutes earlier or later can have a big effect on fuel consumption.

18. If you fish, use a trolling motor. Lugging a big 150 hp outboard at trolling speed is not good for either fuel economy or the health of the engine.

19. Find less-horsepower-intensive ways to use your boat. Find destinations closer to home; ski less and picnic more; discover the pleasures of becoming a superb boat handler rather than just going fast. Party at the dock and enjoy the marina ambiance and amenities.

20. Go out on a friend's boat. This is the ultimate fuel saver—at least while you still have friends. To make this sustainable, form a "boat-pool" with fellow boatowners.

INSTALLING A FUEL-FLOW METER

Given the price of fuel, it only makes sense to understand your boat's "sweet spot" of fuel consumption. While it is possible to estimate fuel consumption by tracking distances traveled and the amount of fuel needed to replenish your tank, such calculations are inexact at best.

A much better way of monitoring fuel consumption is with a fuel-flow meter. A sensor installed in your fuel line tracks the amount of fuel flowing to the engine, and a dashboard-mounted gauge gives the fuel consumption in gallons per hour (gph) while the engine is running. The gauge also has a fuel totalizer counter that tracks the gallons of fuel consumed, helping you to keep from running out of fuel.

One of the largest manufacturers of this equipment, FloScan Instrument Co., makes flow meters for almost every type of engine installed in a boat, including I/Os, outboards, gas and die-

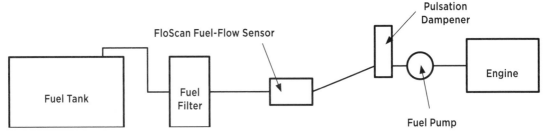

The heart of the fuel-flow meter is the flow sensor. (Courtesy FloScan Instrument Company)

This fuel-flow gauge indicates rate of consumption on the dial and total consumption since last reset in the digital readout. (Courtesy FloScan Instrument Company)

sel inboards, and single- and twin-engine inboards. With so many meters available, the first task is to select an appropriate unit for your boat. This section covers the installation of a flow meter on a single-engine gasoline-powered boat.

There are three main components to install: the fuel flow sensor, the gauge, and the required switches. The sensor needs to be installed in the fuel line after any fuel filter and before the fuel pump inlet. An additional requirement is that the sensor be installed at least 12 inches from the fuel pump inlet and at least 1 to 2 inches below it. This is to minimize pressure fluctuations for the operation of the fuel pump. The sensor should be bolted solidly in place but not to the engine. FloScan offers a metal bracket as a mounting option for the sensor.

The sensors for gas engines have ¼-inch NPT ports. These can accept standard barbed hose fittings if that is what your engine uses and what you prefer to use, but some engines use JIC (Joint Industrial Council) or SAE fuel hose connections. These fittings require a special copper sealing washer unique to each style of fitting; make sure you use the right washer. You will have to have these fuel hoses made up by a hose supplier or hydraulic shop. Measure for the hoses before ordering, and allow for engine movement between the fuel pump and the sensor.

Use a fuel-proof pipe thread sealant when installing the hose fittings. Do not use Teflon tape! Fuel lines must be double clamped. Make sure the hoses have an ample radius to avoid kinking. Hose should also be supported every 2 to 4 feet to minimize chafing. Padded stainless steel cable clamps can be used to secure the hose.

The next component to install is the gauge itself. It will need to be at least 12 inches from the compass to avoid interference, and it should be out of direct sunlight, which might overheat the LCD screen and temporarily turn it black.

Once you've selected a location, it's time to cut the hole. I start by taping off the area around the hole with blue masking tape, then marking the center of the hole on the tape. In most cases, the instrument panel is fiberglass. The blue tape protects the surrounding fiberglass from scratches and inadvertent drill contact.

My first choice is to cut the hole with an appropriate size holesaw. Saws as big as the gauges are seldom available in home improvement stores, however, so I buy most of mine online. I drill a small (about ⅛ inch) pilot hole on the center mark, because a small pilot drill is much easier to locate and control than the center drill in a holesaw. This small hole will keep the pilot drill in the holesaw from wandering. Drill slowly through the instrument panel.

You can also use a jigsaw or saber saw to cut the hole. I use a medium-toothed metal-cutting blade when cutting fiberglass. You will need to mark the hole circumference on the tape and then drill a big enough access hole for the jigsaw blade. Cut slowly, and hold the line. You did check to see that nothing was behind your cut before starting, didn't you?

Once the hole is complete, remove the tape, smooth any rough edges, and trial-fit the gauge. It is better to cut the initial hole slightly undersize and enlarge it as needed by sanding than to cut the hole oversize.

The last component to be installed is a totalizer reset switch. This switch returns the "total fuel used" display to zero. It might be a single-pole, single-throw (SPST) toggle switch or a momentary on/off switch, depending on the model of meter you've choosen. Do not use illuminated or back-lit switches.

If you are installing a FloScan flow meter on an older, carbureted engine, you will also need to install a fourth component, a pulsation dampener. This device smoothes out the pulses from the diaphragm fuel pump used on carbureted engines. Pulsation dampeners are available as accessories from FloScan but are no longer standard, as carbureted inboard and I/O engines are no longer made. A pulsation damper is installed after the fuel flow sensor, with the arrow pointing up.

The system can now be wired according to the wiring diagram provided with the instrument. Use 18 AWG (American Wire Gauge) wire for runs under 50 feet long, and 16 AWG for runs over 50 feet. Use either tinned crimp connectors or ring connectors, properly sealed with adhesive-lined heat-shrink tubing (see Chapter 7).

Once the system is installed, it should be calibrated. The back side of the gauge holds a series of small dip switches for this purpose. First top off your fuel tanks and then run the boat in your normal manner. Once you've run about 20 gallons through the engine, refill the tank to the same level, noting the quantity of fuel used. Compare this amount to the amount shown in the totalizer window in the gauge. The instructions provided with the instrument include a chart to show how to set the dip switches to correct any error you see.

With a fuel flow monitor in place, you can now determine how much fuel your engine consumes at any given operating speed and boat weight. Please note that extended periods of operation outside your normal engine-speed range may throw off the totalizer calibration.

EXHAUST MANIFOLD CARE AND REPLACEMENT

Not long ago a friend stopped by my boat with a tale of woe. In spite of having his boat's Outboard Marine Corporation (OMC) stern-drive engine serviced by his dealer for many years, he ended up with water in his engine, which had to be replaced for a goodly sum. The cause of his problem was that the exhaust manifolds looked like new from the outside but had rusted on the inside, finally allowing water into the combustion chambers. The next time he turned over the engine, the pistons tried to compress water instead of air, and things bent inside—lots of things.

Exhaust systems on boats differ fundamentally from those installed in automobiles. The engine block may be the same old GM 350, but the exhaust system certainly isn't.

Boats are equipped with water-cooled manifolds and water injection into the exhaust gases. This cools the exhaust and allows the gases to be conveyed to the outside world through flexible rubber exhaust hoses. The water is pulled off the raw-water cooling circuit and circulated around the exhaust manifold, spacer (if used), and riser.

From there, it is injected into the exhaust gas flow. The resulting mixture of exhaust and cooling water is ejected overboard. This can be done above water through transom ports or below water through an outdrive propeller.

On V-6 and V-8 engines, the exhaust manifolds are separate from the intake manifolds. On in-line fours and sixes, the intake and exhaust manifolds are contained in a single casting. Most

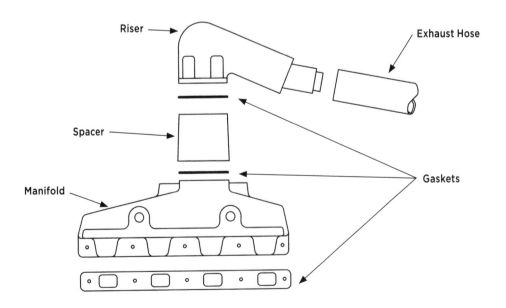

A typical manifold design for a V-8 inboard or I/O engine.

manifolds are cast iron—cheap and easy to cast, but susceptible to rust and attack by salt water. Some manifolds are aluminum, and a few very expensive units are cast of stainless steel and coated with ceramics.

Almost every exhaust system also includes some sort of riser. This item bolts on the exhaust manifold and allows an engine package to be custom fitted to a particular boat by providing for different exhaust hose sizes and attachment angles. In some installations, a spacer is bolted between the manifold and the riser to elevate the riser's exhaust outlet.

Finally, there are gaskets, mounting kits, drain taps, drain plugs, and hose barbs and hoses with which to further adapt an exhaust system to a boat and engine combination. Warm manifolds, cold manifolds, and freshwater-cooled manifolds use basically the same manifold-riser-spacer configuration. The differences are in the details of each.

It is a good idea to remove your manifolds every three years or so to check them for excessive corrosion or blocking of coolant passages with salt and rust buildup. Regularly flushing a cast-iron manifold with fresh water will significantly extend its life. If your engine manifold is equipped with zincs for corrosion protection, now is a good time to check them. The rule of thumb is that when a zinc is more than 50 percent gone, it should be replaced.

Excessively blocked or corroded manifolds should also be replaced. After you've gone through the trouble of getting a manifold off the engine, trying to milk a few more months or years out of questionable hardware isn't worth it. A $750 to $1,000 do-it-yourself manifold job beats a $15,000 engine replacement anytime.

New manifolds are available from several suppliers. OSCO, Sierra, Indmar, and Barr are among the more popular sources. Typical manifold prices range from $140 to over $350 each, depending on the popularity of the engine. Risers run from $120 to over $200.

Unbolting and replacing the exhaust system isn't rocket science. It can be dirty and messy but is certainly within the ability of the average boater. Make sure your supplier has all the parts you need in stock and on hand. Don't expect to walk into a boat store unannounced on a Friday night and pick up a complete exhaust system for an obscure engine you want to work on the following day. Call ahead and make sure the parts are there.

Drain the cooling system before removing the manifolds. Most manifolds have petcocks at their lowest points through which they can be drained for winter storage if antifreeze isn't used.

The most common problem when removing an old manifold is dealing with rusted and corroded nuts, bolts, and studs. Breaking off a stud or bolt in the engine block will ruin your whole day. Spray fasteners with a penetrating oil such as PB-Blaster or Kroil to help loosen them. WD-40 is less effective, as it is a water displacer, not a penetrating oil. Start treating the fasteners well in advance of when you are actually going to replace the manifolds to give the penetrating oil a chance to work. Tapping the fastener head lightly sometimes encourages the oil to penetrate, but don't damage the threads on the end of the fastener.

Some manifolds have hose barbs for the water outlet or inlet. If these have to be replaced, make sure you know their sizes. You may also need several pipe plugs to fit threaded holes in the sides, top, or bottom of a new manifold. These holes are often required as part of the casting process and are sealed with the pipe plugs. Make sure these are in the manifold box when you buy the manifold. These plugs also make nice inspection ports if you can get them out after they've been rusting in place for years. The threads on these plugs are tapered and seal by being wedged in place. Do not use thread-sealing compounds that contain Teflon, as they will allow you to overtighten the plug and possibly crack the manifold. The plug doesn't have to be flush with the manifold to seal properly.

If you are installing new studs, use a thread lock compound, like those from Loctite, to keep the studs from backing out of the block. Tighten the nuts and bolts to the recommended torque specifications in your engine's shop manual. If you don't have a shop manual, get one! While you're at it, get a torque wrench. Don't overtighten hose barbs or pipe plugs. They just need to be snug enough not to leak.

The need for gaskets between components is obvious; they keep water inside the manifold, where it belongs. What isn't obvious is that these gaskets come in several different configurations. This is especially true of the gaskets between the manifolds, spacers, and risers. Depending on the coolant flow, these may completely block the water flow or have several open passages. Take special note as to the type and orientation of these gaskets when you remove the old parts. Make sure that you have the right gaskets when purchasing your replacement system.

Often you have the choice of buying a gasket or a mounting kit. The mounting kit will contain the gasket and whatever studs, nuts, or bolts are needed to mount the unit. Different combinations of riser and spacer sizes require different mounting kits. Murphy's Law states that you won't need the kit if you have it, because you will be able to get the nuts or bolts off okay, but if you bought only the gasket, you'll break a stud or strip a nut and will need the kit you don't have.

Use only rubber hoses rated as wet exhaust system hoses—anything else will melt or burn. There are both wire-reinforced and no-wire hoses available. Replace yours with whatever was originally used. This may take some effort, because

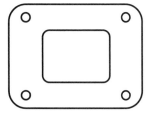 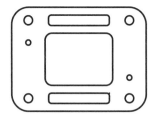 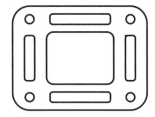

Used on the same risers and spacers to configure them differently;
make sure which you have and which way they go!

Gaskets for manifold risers and spacers are designed to configure water flow through the manifold. Freshwater-cooled engines require different gaskets than raw-water-cooled engines. The gasket designs shown here are representative, but there are others.

4-inch wire-reinforced exhaust hose is sometimes like an immovable object.

Some stern-drive exhaust systems use an exhaust bellows to connect the inboard exhaust components to the outdrive. On some OMC and Volvo stern-drive installations, don't be surprised if one side of the exhaust bellows has been trimmed away. This was done on purpose to relieve excess back pressure. Some installations may also use a short length of hose, called a hump hose, to connect components together. These are commonly used where there is a great deal of movement between the riser and the rest of the exhaust system.

INSTALLING AN ENGINE FLUSH SYSTEM

Most of us running inboard/outboards (I/Os, or stern drives) and inboards in salt or brackish water understand the potential harm that water can inflict on our expensive machinery. Corroded and leaking manifolds and risers, blocked cooling passages, and overheating engines comprise just a few of the hazards.

One partial solution is a freshwater cooling system, in which outside water (called *raw water*) is used to cool the engine antifreeze in a heat exchanger. This will help eliminate the ill effects of salt in the engine block, but the raw-water side of the cooling system is still vulnerable to salt and corrosion.

Another, better option is to install a freshwater flushing system in your boat. Such a system allows the engine to be flushed with fresh water after you have returned to your slip. Most of these

units have to be added after purchase of the boat and vary widely in concept and execution.

A new system that I like is the Quick Flush Valve kit from Marine Technology Group, LLC. This engine flush system consists of three ball valves mounted on a bronze T-shaped body. One leg of the T is for the inlet water from the seawater pickup on the outdrive or from the engine-cooling inlet through-hull. A second leg of the T is the outlet for the cooling water going to the engine. The third leg is the inlet for the flushing water. This connection is equipped with a quick-release hose coupling, making the job of connecting the freshwater hose to the Quick Flush unit easy. Three different Quick Flush versions are available: the inboard-I/O model shown in the accompanying illustrations, another one designed for air conditioners and generators, and a third designed specifically for diesel engines. The second two options have slightly different valve configurations to suit their specific applications.

As with all marine ball valves, the handle position on the Quick Flush indicates whether the valves are open or closed. When the handle is parallel with the hose, the valve is open. When the handle is at right angles to the hose, the valve is closed. No ambiguity here.

When the engine is in normal operation, the two main valves are open, allowing cooling water to flow from the seawater pickup to the engine, while the flush water inlet valve is closed. To flush the engine at the dock, the inlet valve from the seawater pickup is closed. A standard garden hose is connected to the flush water inlet, and the flush water inlet valve is opened. This allows flushing water to flow into the engine.

Up to this point the Quick Flush system is no different from other engine flushing systems. But

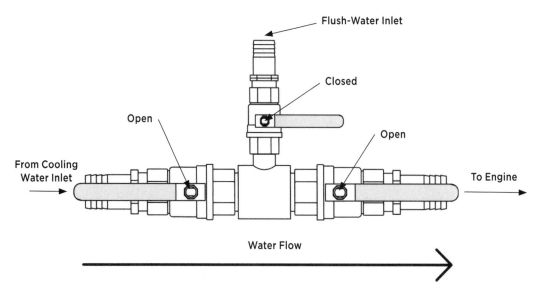

With the quick-flush valve closed in normal operation, water flows from the raw-water intake to the engine.

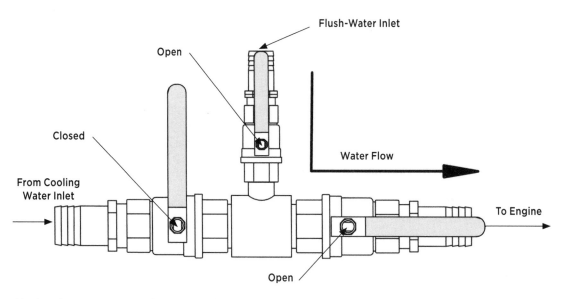

Closing the raw-water intake valve and opening the flush-water inlet allows the engine to be flushed with fresh water.

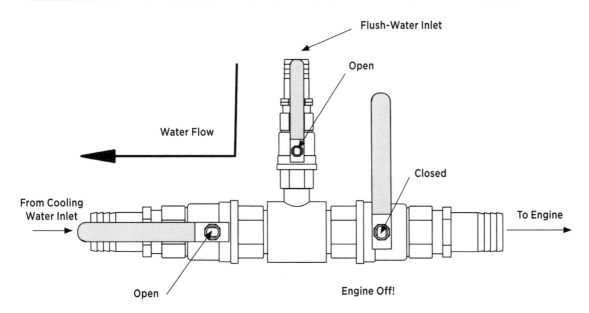

Closing the engine cooling valve and opening the intake and flush-water valves directs the flush water or antifreeze back through the outdrive of an I/O engine.

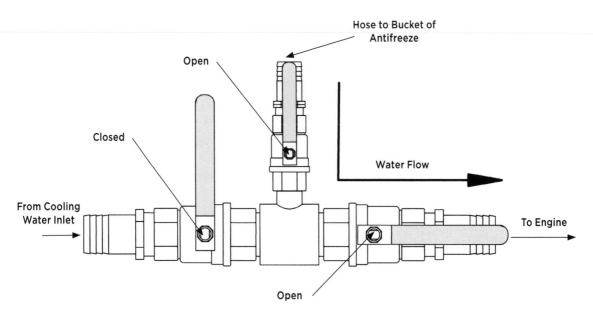

Feeding the flush-water valve from a bucket of antifreeze makes quick work of winterizing an engine.

by closing the cooling water inlet to the engine while leaving the flush water inlet open, you can backflush an outdrive. Of course, the engine must be shut down at this point, as there will be no cooling water flowing to the engine.

With an optional inlet hose and strainer, you can also use the Quick Flush system to make winterizing your boat engine a snap. The strainer and hose assembly is connected to the flush water inlet port and then dropped into a bucket of antifreeze. When the engine is started, the antifreeze is sucked through the engine. Run the engine until antifreeze is spitting out with the exhaust. Do not use automotive antifreeze, since it contains ethylene glycol, which is toxic to animals and an environmental problem. Use only marine antifreeze, which contains nontoxic propylene glycol and can safely be spilled on the ground.

The optional strainer and hose can also be used as an emergency bilge pump. This is accomplished by dropping the hose assembly into the bilge and closing the valve from the seawater inlet. The water from the bilge is pumped through the engine as cooling water while draining the bilge.

The Quick Flush unit is simple to install. If you have an engine with a cooling water inlet through-hull, cut the hose from the through-hull and insert the Quick Flush valve, using hose clamps on the raw-water inlet and outlet.

If you have an I/O engine, locate the cooling water line from the outdrive to the engine and insert the Quick Flush in that line. Tighten the hose clamps and you are done. You can double-clamp the hoses if and only if the hose barb is long enough that both clamps land fully on the barb. Straddling the end of a short barb with a second hose clamp risks pinching, constricting, and possibly tearing the hose and runs a bigger risk than

a single hose clamp. Only fuel hoses are required by the Coast Guard to be double clamped.

PROPELLER MAINTENANCE, REPAIRS, AND REPLACEMENT

Propellers require relatively little servicing. Many people remove their propellers at the end of the season and store them inside. This protects the expensive propeller from theft and ensures that it won't become frozen in place due to corrosion. Trying to remove a prop from a corroded spline can end up damaging either the prop, the spline, or both.

Removal is straightforward. Straighten out and remove the cotter pin, then unscrew the keeper nut. Beneath that is the prop nut, the unscrewing of which will require a special wrench or a big socket on a ratchet. To prevent the prop from turning when you unscrew the prop nut, use a block of wood to hold it steady, bracing the wood against the lower unit. When the nut is off, you should be able to pull the prop off the shaft, revealing the thrust washer beneath.

If the prop won't come off easily, you can use a hub puller. These have two claws to hook under the lower edge of the hub, and a large screw that you tighten against the prop shaft. Be gentle with aluminum props, as some parts of the hub are thin and can easily be damaged.

Remove and grease the thrust washer, and clean and regrease the hub splines and the shaft. Use a marine grease made specifically for this purpose.

Small nicks in the edges of the prop blades can be carefully smoothed out with a fine-toothed file and blended into the surrounding blade area. Inspect the aft surfaces of the blades for small pits, which are a sign of cavitation and a sure indication that your prop isn't pitched right for your boat and motor combination.

If blades are badly nicked or bent, or if you want to change the pitch of the blades, take your propeller to a competent prop shop. Sometimes they can even weld broken blades back onto the hub—although how likely is it that you'll find the broken blade? If the rubber insert has come free of the metal hub of your outboard or I/O prop (this is called a "spun hub"), a pro can replace the insert. Be sure to get a quote before repairing a prop. In many cases the cost of repairing an aluminum prop is close to the cost of a new prop, especially if your marine store is having a sale.

You will need several pieces of information to purchase a new propeller. The first is the propeller diameter—that is, the diameter of the circle described by the tips of the blades. The second is the *pitch*, which in effect describes the angle of the blades but is measured in inches, not degrees. Imagine a wood screw with a spiral thread. Turning the screw once will advance the screw into the wood by a certain amount; in similar fashion, one rotation of a propeller advances it through the water. Because water isn't solid, the propeller will *slip* to some extent, but slip is ignored when determining pitch.

You also need to know the make, model, and year of the engine, because the configurations of the prop shaft and splines differ from engine to engine. In many cases, the replacement prop will come without a hub, and you must purchase a separate hub kit to match the prop to the engine. This is an ideal setup for the retailer, as he has to carry only one model of prop for each pitch and diameter and match the props to the engines with

a hub kit. It is also ideal for the consumer, as these hubs also act as a fail-safe mechanism. If the propeller hits a rock or debris, the hub breaks before the prop does—most of the time.

REPLACING WATER PUMP IMPELLERS

Have you ever stopped to think how much your boat depends on a little rubber impeller, or how many of them you have aboard? Depending on the size of your boat, there could be from one to as many as seven or even more impellers on board.

Flexible-impeller pumps are commonly used to pump cooling water through outboard, sterndrive, and inboard engines of all sizes. More mundane applications include things like macerator pumps—which, for obvious reasons, usually incorporate chopper blades. Engine oil change systems, especially portable ones, often use impeller pumps, as we saw earlier in this chapter. Impeller pumps are also common in washdown pumps and live well aerators.

Flexible-impeller pumps are mechanically simple, having only one moving part, and are therefore reliable. They are also versatile, being able to pump anything from water or oil to the "stuff" in your holding tank. They handle small debris well. They are self-priming and use the pumped fluid to lubricate the rubber impeller. A well-sealed pump can push fluids 15 to 25 feet. Impeller pumps are also scalable, meaning they can be built large or small, depending on the application.

Impeller pumps are quite simple in operation as well. The impeller runs in a cavity that, at first

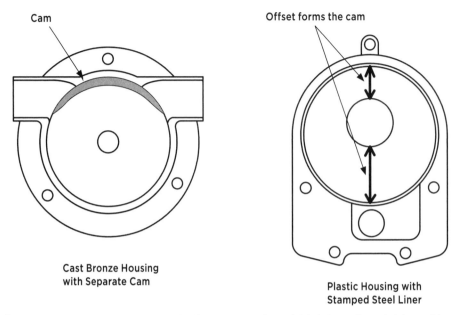

Cam

Offset forms the cam

Cast Bronze Housing
with Separate Cam

Plastic Housing with
Stamped Steel Liner

Impeller pumps require an asymmetry in the pump cavity, which is introduced either with a cam along one side of the housing (left) or an off-center pump shaft (right).

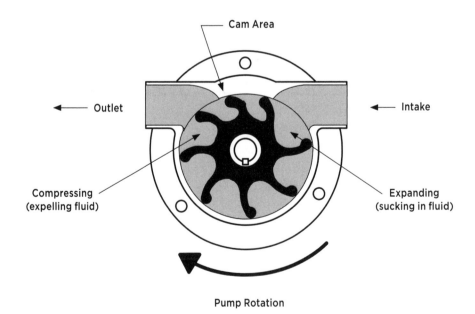

Cam Area

Outlet

Intake

Compressing
(expelling fluid)

Expanding
(sucking in fluid)

Pump Rotation

The flexible impeller blades are forced together by the cam or shaft offset as they approach the outlet, and the resultant volume reduction expels water picked up at the intake.

glance, looks cylindrical. A closer inspection, however, reveals that the cavity or housing is either offset from the centerline of the pump shaft or indented to form a cam on one side of the cylinder.

This cam provides the pumping action. As the blades of the impeller depart the cam, the volume between blades expands, sucking or drawing in fluid through the intake. As the blades approach the cam on the other side of their rotation, the volume between blades contracts again, expelling the pumped fluid through the outlet. The continuous rotation of the impeller provides a smooth, even flow.

The heart of the impeller pump is obviously the impeller itself. These come in several different materials, the most common of which is neoprene rubber, which is ideal for pumping water-based fluids. Nitrile rubber is used when pumping petroleum-based fluids.

A variety of materials is used for pump housings. Most outboard water pumps use a plastic housing with a stamped steel liner in the cavity. A wear plate and gasket seal the open end of the pump. The pump shaft is also the prop driveshaft and passes completely through the pump.

Water pumps on inboard and large I/O engines are often made of cast bronze. These units have a separate, arc-shaped cam that bolts into the pump cavity. A bronze cover plate seals the open end of the pump and allows access to the impeller.

Macerator pumps usually have plastic housings. They can be built into the base of the toilet or operate as a stand-alone pump.

Pump shafts are usually steel and come equipped with one or more seals to prevent leakage. Belt- or engine-driven cooling pumps also have bearings and bearing supports as part of the

design. Keys, gaskets, and cover screws complete the pump bill of materials.

Impeller pumps generally fail in one of two ways. The first is a gradual degradation in pump performance and flow. This is usually due to impeller or housing wear or impeller age.

The second failure mode is sudden and catastrophic failure, with the impeller usually losing some or all of its blades. This is usually caused by running the impeller pump dry. Remember, the fluid being pumped provides the cooling and lubrication for the pump. If you forget to open the cooling-water inlet seacock, or if a plastic bag covers the water inlet strainer, no cooling water will reach the impeller and it will soon destroy itself.

The impeller often sheds its blades in such a failure, and the errant blade fragments must be tracked down and removed from the system, especially in an engine cooling application. Failure to do so will usually lead to further problems and blockages later on.

Some manufacturers recommend replacing the impeller every year. Some recommend removing the impeller from its housing during winter layup. Most of us don't do either, but carrying a spare impeller on board is a highly recommended, commonsense precaution.

Impeller pump maintenance is well within most boatowners' capabilities. Before you decide to perform maintenance on your impeller pump, however, take a few preliminary steps. Don't be afraid to review the service manual or rebuild kit directions. Make sure you have identified your exact make of pump and have the appropriate rebuild kit or replacement impeller on hand. There are several pump and impeller manufacturers, and many impellers are interchangeable. Have all the part numbers available when you shop for spare parts. Your store may carry only one brand or the other. (You *did* document those numbers in your onboard maintenance manual, didn't you?)

Make sure you have the right tools available. Do a dry run to make sure the tools fit the jib. Special wrenches or short screwdrivers might be required. Trying to replace an impeller at night on a rolling sea isn't the time to develop your repair strategy.

Outboard engine pumps are probably the most difficult to maintain. Changing the impeller requires separating the lower gear case from the engine. This also may require disconnecting the shift linkage. Consult your engine manual for the specific steps required to get to the pump.

When the lower unit is free, you will usually find the pump on top of the gear case. The housing can then be unbolted and the impeller replaced. Carefully inspect the housing and the stamped steel liner for signs of wear or overheating. A lower-end rebuild kit includes just the impeller and gasket, but other kits also include the upper and lower housing as well as the wear plate. If in doubt about a component, replace it. You don't want to have to drop the gear case any more frequently than necessary.

Most engine cooling pumps have a cover plate held on with several screws. Removing the screws and cover plate exposes the impeller. If the impeller has been changed regularly, it should slide easily off the shaft. In many case, however, it will need to be pried out with a couple of screwdrivers. Take great care not to damage the housing, since these can be expensive to replace.

Many manufacturers make impeller pullers, much like a gear puller, for extreme cases. These are pricey, however. Some manufacturers have threaded the inside of the exposed end of the impeller. Removing this type of impeller is a simple matter of threading a bolt of the right size into the open end. As the bolt is tightened, it bears on the pump shaft and backs the impeller out. More manufacturers should consider this design feature.

Provided they are accessible, freestanding impeller pumps are usually easy to disassemble and service. When servicing a macerator pump, place plenty of adult diapers around and under the pump to soak up any "stuff" that may dribble out.

REPLACING STEERING AND THROTTLE CABLES

Years of little maintenance and no lubrication can result in a seized or broken steering or throttle cable. That's the bad news. The good news is that it is well within the capabilities of the average boater to replace these cables.

Finding the right cable can be difficult. Take a look at any major marine supplier's catalog and you will see dozens of variations in end styles and lengths. Look for identification numbers on the old cable housing, as this makes finding a replacement much easier. Failing that, drag the old cable to the marine store and let them measure the length and inspect the end fittings. Some cables are measured by overall length and others by the length of the outer sheath.

For years, Morse Cables was the main supplier of throttle and steering cables, but then Morse was purchased by Teleflex. The good news is that many of the old Morse cables can still be supplied by Teleflex, but most are built to order. Plan on a lead time for these cables, as they won't be available off the shelf. Some cables may just be too old

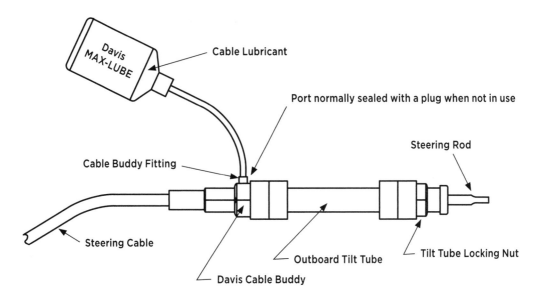

Davis Instruments Company's Cable Buddy provides a quick and easy way to lubricate steering cables.

to find a replacement, in which case you may have to convert to modern end fittings.

Removing a cable can be a great deal of fun. Often it will be snaked around components and under gunwales and decks. If it passes through spaces where access is restricted, tie a strong line to the end of the cable as you remove it. This messenger line will make pulling the new one much easier.

Be careful not to kink or bend the cable as you work it back through the boat. Support the new cable in the same locations as the old one. Stock cables have no provisions for lubricating the cable inside the sheath, but aftermarket kits are available to fit many popular sizes of cables. Davis Instruments, for example, makes the Cable Buddy, which provides a zerk (grease) fitting through which you can apply grease or 90 weight (90W) gear oil to the inside of a steering cable.

Keep the steering tube that connects the cable end to the motor well lubricated during the year.

This is usually the first place you will notice stiffness in your steering system. Some tubes have grease fittings; be sure you apply grease once or twice a season.

ADDING A KICKER AND OUTBOARD MOUNT

There are two reasons to add an auxiliary outboard motor, or kicker, to your boat. It gives you a secondary means of propulsion if the main engine quits, and it is a better option for slow-speed trolling. Running a large outboard at trolling speeds for long periods wastes fuel and is bad for the engine.

Most kickers I've seen are around 8 to 9.9 hp and are of the four-stroke persuasion. Occasionally you see a 15 hp kicker. Your selection will depend, among other things, on the options you

This articulated lift-up mount is designed for outboard engines up to 9.9 hp.

desire (tilt, tiller versus remote steering, et cetera) plus the weight and cost of the motor and the size and type of your boat.

Brackets for small outboards include solid mounts that hold the engine at a fixed height, and lift-up mounts that allow you to raise the engine out of the water. Either type needs to be rated for the weight of your outboard. Don't try to get by with a marginal rating. If you're on the cusp, go up to the next sturdier size. Most new outboards sold today are four-stroke models that weigh more than their two-stroke equivalents, so take that into consideration.

The kicker will be mounted to the side of the main engine. Tiller-steered engines have the throttle mounted on the tiller handle. The shift lever is usually mounted on the side of the engine, but there is a trend toward mounting the shift, too, on the tiller handle. Operating the outboard will require you to reach and operate the controls easily and comfortably while maintaining clear vision forward. The configurations of many boats simply don't permit this, in which case an engine with remote steering will be required.

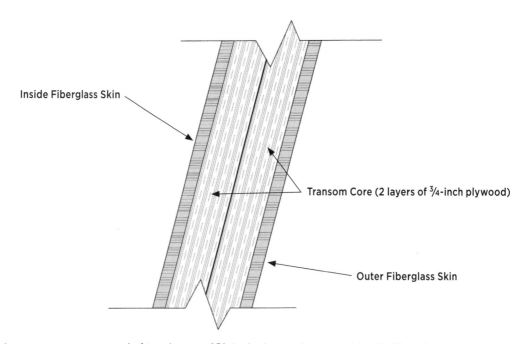

Inside Fiberglass Skin

Transom Core (2 layers of ¾-inch plywood)

Outer Fiberglass Skin

Many transoms are composed of two layers of ¾-inch plywood encapsulated in fiberglass.

Although remote steering is more expensive and its installation more complex, it is often well worth it. The shift and throttle can be mounted where they are accessible, convenient, and comfortable to use while permitting good forward vision.

Once you have made all these decisions, but before you buy anything, it is time to look at the transom where the mount will be installed. On many boats the entire transom is reinforced, usually with two or three layers of plywood achieving a combined thickness of about 1½ inches. If the transom is solid and in good condition, it will be strong enough to support the mount.

In rare cases the mounting area will not be strong enough to support the weight of the kicker and may be only a single thickness of fiberglass. In cases like this, the area will have to be stiffened and strengthened with a backing plate.

If the area in question is flat, a single piece of good-quality marine or MDO plywood about ¾ inch thick is usually sufficient. The plate should extend beyond the bolt pattern of the mount both top and bottom and side to side. The edges of the plywood should be tapered at 45 degrees, and the entire piece should be given three coats of epoxy to seal it from water damage.

If the mounting surface is curved, a different approach works better. The backing plate should be made from three layers of ¼-inch plywood, each layer slightly smaller than the last. Coat each layer with epoxy adhesive and then temporarily

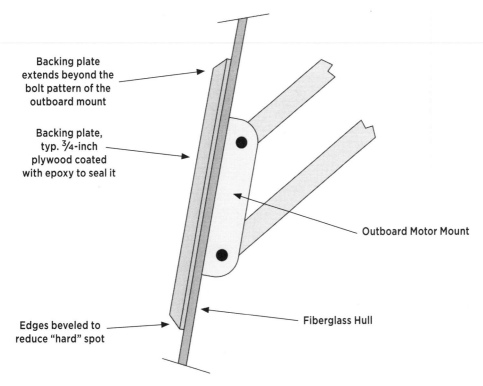

Backing plate extends beyond the bolt pattern of the outboard mount

Backing plate, typ. ¾-inch plywood coated with epoxy to seal it

Outboard Motor Mount

Edges beveled to reduce "hard" spot

Fiberglass Hull

When a flat transom needs reinforcing to mount a kicker, a flat backing plate is easy to install.

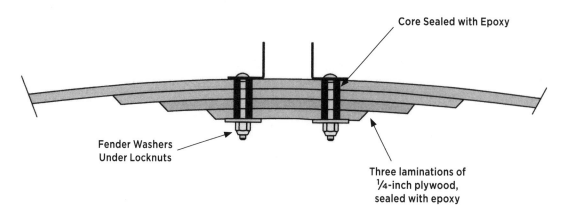

Core Sealed with Epoxy

Fender Washers
Under Locknuts

Three laminations of
¼-inch plywood,
sealed with epoxy

Curved transoms require a curved backing plate. This one is made from three layers of ¼-inch plywood epoxied together.

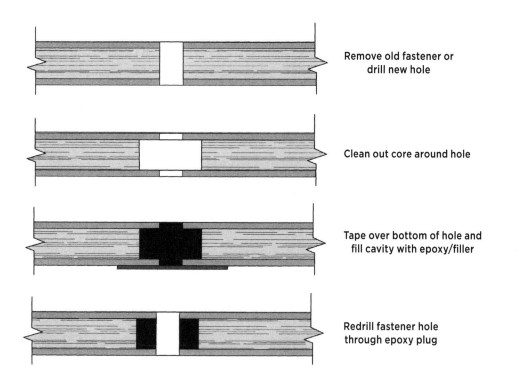

Remove old fastener or
drill new hole

Clean out core around hole

Tape over bottom of hole and
fill cavity with epoxy/filler

Redrill fastener hole
through epoxy plug

As covered in Chapter 6 and elsewhere throughout this book, filling fastener holes in the transom is critical to keep water from saturating a plywood transom core.

bolt it in place using the mounting holes. Place plastic between the first layer of plywood and the transom and coat the bolts with wax or Vaseline to keep the epoxy from gluing them in place.

The backing plate will conform to the curvature of the hull when the epoxy cures. Remove it from the boat and sand any rough spots or epoxy drips, and then apply the three coats of epoxy.

Place blue masking tape over the area where the mount will be installed. The masking tape will prevent the transom from being scratched and make it easy to draw locating marks. Carefully locate the exact position of the mount and the required fastener holes. As you drill the holes, inspect the drill cuttings (swarf) coming out of the hole. If you find wood chips in the swarf, you will have some additional work to do.

Once the fastener holes are drilled, place the backing plate in place and drill the holes through it, using the holes in the transom as a guide.

One of the problems with drilling through a plywood backing plate or a wood-cored transom is the possibility of water leaks and core damage. To prevent this, the mounting holes now need to be drilled oversize and then filled with epoxy/filler, as discussed in Chapter 6. Once the epoxy has cured, the mounting holes are redrilled through the epoxy plug.

Now it is time for the final assembly. Temporarily bolt the mount in place and tape around it. This is to keep any sealant from squeezing out on the fiberglass. Place the mounting bolts through the holes on the mount and place a neoprene washer on the back side of the fasteners.

Apply a good bead of sealant like 3M 4200 around the fasteners and place the mount in position. On the inside, apply more sealant around the bolts and the area where the backing plate will be. Push the backing plate in place and install large washers (fender washers) and locknuts on the fasteners. Tighten snugly but not overly tight. The neoprene washers will keep you from squeezing out all the sealant.

Allow the sealant to cure properly, which will require up to seven days for regular-cure 3M 4200. You can then further tighten the nuts as long as someone holds the bolt heads to keep them from turning. If you let a bolt turn at this stage, you will have broken the sealant bond around it and provide a ready path for leaks.

INSTALLING REMOTE ENGINE CONTROLS FOR A KICKER

Once the engine mount for your kicker is in place, it is time to install the controls for it. The assumption is that you purchased an outboard setup for remote operation. If you have an outboard with a tiller, you can control it either by seating yourself in the stern or by having your dealer convert it for remote operation.

There are three controls to consider: throttle, shift, and steering. Throttle and shift are controlled by cables attached to the outboard at one end and a control head on the other. That control head usually has a shift lever and a throttle lever, each controlled by its own cable.

The control head can be mounted on an external surface or recessed into the structure of the boat. External controls are easier to work on, and their cables are somewhat easier to rout. Recessed controls look neater but are harder to work on, and routing the cables can be difficult.

In either case, work through your marine supplier to make sure you get the right cables for your motor, the right controls for your cables, and the

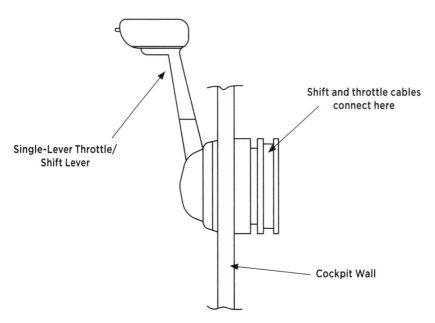

Shift and throttle cables
connect here

Single-Lever Throttle/
Shift Lever

Cockpit Wall

This Teleflex SL-3 engine control unit is designed to mount on the side of the cockpit, with the cables concealed behind the cockpit wall. A single lever controls both shift and throttle.

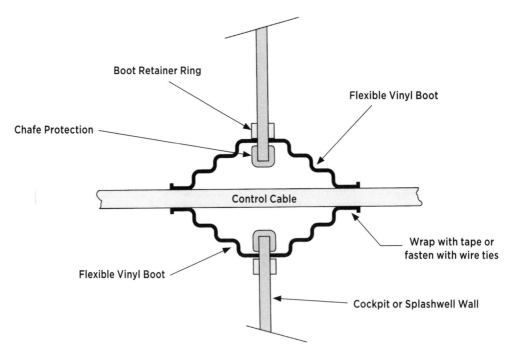

Boot Retainer Ring

Flexible Vinyl Boot

Chafe Protection

Control Cable

Wrap with tape or
fasten with wire ties

Flexible Vinyl Boot

Cockpit or Splashwell Wall

Place molded vinyl boots around control-cable openings to prevent water from leaking into the boat.

correct connectors with which to attach cable ends to the outboard and the controls. Test-fit the components on the bench to ensure that you have all the parts you need to finish the job as well as a good understanding of how all the parts fit together and what kinds of clearance you'll need to install them.

The external controls are usually simply bolted to a vertical surface on the side of the cockpit. Use stainless steel bolts and nylock nuts to make sure the bolts don't work loose. The cables will then need to be routed back to the kicker. This will usually mean running them through some part of the boat's fiberglass structure. Install a large grommet or edge protector around any clearance hole through fiberglass to avoid chafe, and put a cable boot on the cable on each side of the hole to keep water out. Do not try to cut cables to shorten them. If they are too long, coil them and hide the coils out of sight.

Internal or flush-mounted controls have the cable connectors and much of the associated mechanism hidden below a horizontal surface near the helm station. The instructions for the controls will contain a template for the cutout required for the flush-mounted controller.

Tape off the area with blue masking tape and then transfer the shape of the opening from the template to the tape. Cut out the opening with a jigsaw, using a medium-toothed metal cutting blade at slow speed. Take your time and cut as accurately as possible to minimize any sanding or filing required to get the controls to fit. The cables will have to be routed to the stern of the boat and then out to the kicker. Again, make sure there are no possible chafe points, and use a cable boot to seal the opening through the transom.

The third control required is some method of steering the kicker. If you have an outboard or a manually steered inboard/outboard, you can con-

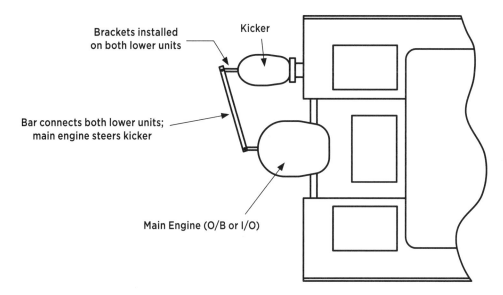

Brackets installed on both lower units

Kicker

Bar connects both lower units; main engine steers kicker

Main Engine (O/B or I/O)

If you have a mechanically steered I/O or outboard engine, you can connect it to your kicker, allowing the boat's steering wheel to steer both engines.

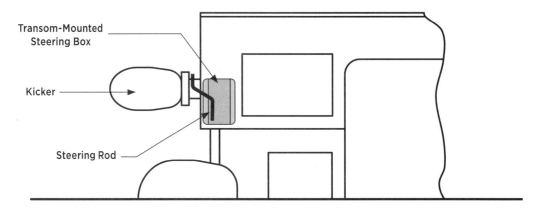

You can bolt a remote steering unit to the transom and steer the kicker via the short rod. These units are available wired or remote control.

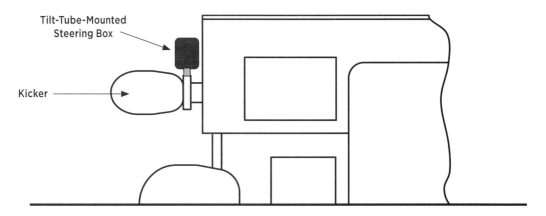

Remote steering units can also be attached to the kicker's tilt tube. These, too, are available wired or with remote control.

nect the kicker to the outdrive using a connector bar kit and one of several styles of available brackets. These kits are available from Cabela's in a wide range of prices.

If you have an I/O with hydraulic steering, you will need another option, as you may well troll with the main engine shut off and hydraulic steering unavailable. There are several options to choose from. One is to install a full steering system, with a cable and a steering wheel, somewhere on the boat. However, places to mount gear on a small boat are sometimes hard to come by. A remote steering unit might be a better bet.

These come in two styles. The first mounts on the transom and is connected to the kicker with an actuator rod. The rod may need to be bent to suit your installation, but that is probably the hardest part. A second type attaches to the stock steering tube mount on the outboard. Both types are available with an optional wireless remote control unit so you can steer from anyplace on the boat.

These items are available at many marine stores or at Cabela's. Prices range from under $60 for a simple connector bar from your main engine up to almost $500 for a full-blown wireless remotely controlled steering system.

TRIM TABS

Trim tabs help correct trim problems and help a boat get up on plane faster. Once on plane, tabs allow the operator to dial in the exact trim needed for best operation.

There are two major manufacturers of trim tab systems: Lenco manufactures electrically operated trim tabs, while Bennett produces hydraulic tabs. Both product lines are excellent. I prefer hydraulic trim tabs, so that's the installation we'll pursue here.

The first step is to size the tabs for your boat. The manufacturers' websites give plenty of information on appropriate tab sizes, including *span* (the length from side to side) and *chord* (the fore-and-aft width). A good rule of thumb for proper sizing is 1 inch of span per foot of boat length per trim tab. A 24-foot boat could use two 24-inch tabs with a standard chord of 9 inches. If the transom won't accommodate a proper span, you can substitute shorter tabs with a 12-inch chord. A

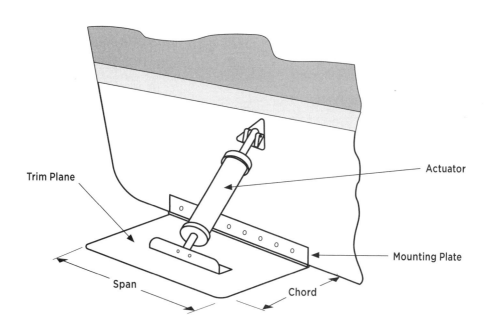

Trim tabs are easier to understand if you know the nomenclature.

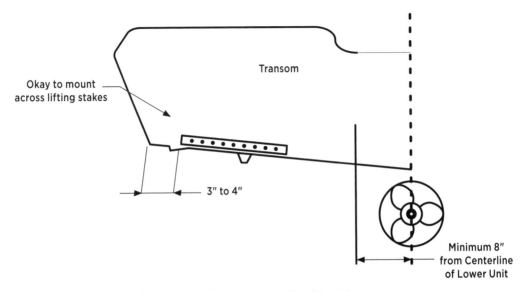

These are the important offsets for locating and mounting trim tabs.

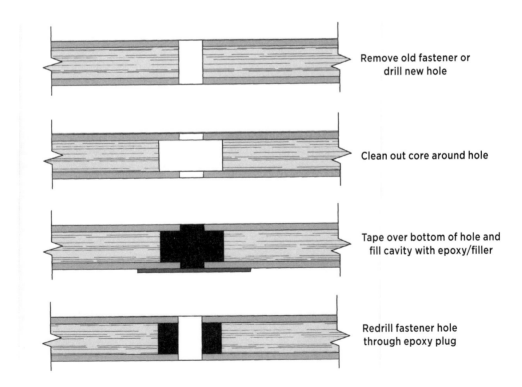

Remove old fastener or drill new hole

Clean out core around hole

Tape over bottom of hole and fill cavity with epoxy/filler

Redrill fastener hole through epoxy plug

It bears repeating (yet again!) that filling fastener holes is a critical precaution to keep water from saturating a transom core.

12-inch chord is also suitable for slower boats, semidisplacement hulls, and large boats.

The tabs should be mounted 3 to 4 inches inboard of their respective chines and should angle down toward the boat's centerline along the transom's bottom edge.

Begin the installation by positioning one of the trim tabs along the bottom edge of the transom. With the tab temporarily in place, hold its hydraulic cylinder (that is, its actuator) in place to check its upper mounting location. The area inside the boat where the cylinder will be fastened needs to be clear and accessible. If this isn't practical and you can't find an alternate trim-tab position, contact Bennett for additional options. If the location is accessible, you can proceed with the installation. The tabs are held in place with #10 x 1¼″ stainless steel screws. The instruc-

tions that come with the tabs give the exact drill sizes needed for these screws. If the drill hits wood in the transom core, drill out the holes oversize and fill them with epoxy/filler as described in Chapter 6. Once the epoxy cures, redrill the holes. This will keep water from invading the transom core.

If the transom is crowned rather than flat, you will need to make a shim to provide a flat mounting surface. StarBoard is excellent for this as it won't rot, delaminate, or soak up water.

The next step is to attach the top ends of the actuators to the transom. First, however, the tabs need to be trimmed to their neutral angles. Hold a straightedge or wood batten up against the bottom of the hull such that its aft end extends underneath and past the tab. Place a spacer on the batten, under the aft edge of the tab, to properly

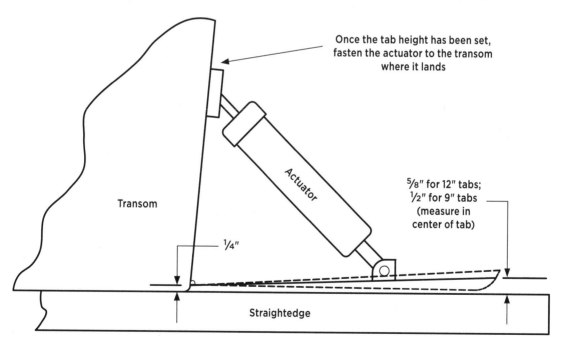

Once the tab height has been set, fasten the actuator to the transom where it lands

Actuator

Transom

⅝″ for 12″ tabs; ½″ for 9″ tabs (measure in center of tab)

¼″

Straightedge

Once the trim tab is mounted, you will need to set the tab height before mounting the actuator.

position it. The spacer should be ½ inch high for a 9-inch chord and ⅝ inch high for a 12-inch chord.

With the tab properly located and trimmed, the top end of the actuator will fall against the transom at its proper mounting location. Place a mounting template, provided in the kit, under the cylinder's top mount and tape it in place. This template will provide the proper location for the three mounting holes and the center clearance hole for the hydraulic connection.

Find a location inside the boat for mounting the hydraulic power unit (HPU). The ideal location will be near the stern of the boat in a place that is convenient to both cylinders, keeps the HPU high and dry, and allows sufficient access to run the hydraulic hoses. The HPU slips into a bracket from above, so you'll need at least 3 inches of clearance above the mounting bracket in order to slide the unit into place. Fasten it in place with #10 screws. The hydraulic lines can now be connected from the cylinders to the HPU. The ports on the HPU are marked port and starboard.

Bennett offers several choices for tab control. A single-lever joystick is one option, and another is a pair of rocker switches. In either case, the control unit is mounted in the dashboard in a location that is easy to see and reach from the helm and provides access to the back side of the installed unit. Apply blue masking tape to the area to protect the surrounding gelcoat from chipping, and mark the center of the hole. Drill a ¼-inch hole to serve as a pilot hole for the holesaw. (The product instructions specify the exact size required.) Drill the mounting hole slowly and evenly.

Plug the wiring harness into the hydraulic power unit and run the wires up to and through the mounting hole. Use wire ties to support the wiring under the deck edge and keep it secure and free from snagging. The HPU draws about 18 amps in use, so provide a 20-amp fuse or circuit breaker in the power line. A connection to the boat's 12-volt DC ground is also required. Cut the wires to length, install the crimp connectors, and connect to the control unit. See Chapter 7 for more information on wiring procedures.

With everything connected and ready to go, fill the hydraulic reservoir with automatic transmission fluid. Place the control in "bow-down," then "bow-up" position for three cycles of fifteen seconds each. This will purge any air from the system. Then place the system in full-down position and check for leaks. Do the same in full-up position. Refill the reservoir as necessary.

Bennett suggests installing zinc anodes on the tabs if they are used in salt water.

REPLACING A SPEEDOMETER PITOT PICKUP

This is a pretty simple repair. Most hull-mounted marine speedometer sensors have a nylon arm called a pitot tube, or simply a pitot, that extends into the water. This arm is hollow and carries a hose barb at its upper end. Small-diameter plastic tubing runs forward from the barb to the back of the dash-mounted speedometer display unit. As the water pressure on the end of the pitot tube increases, the air pressure in the connecting tube increases, driving the pointer in the speedometer dial.

The most common causes of failure include damage to the pitot tube from striking something and breakage of the connecting tube due to impact or age. Teleflex sells a universal replace-

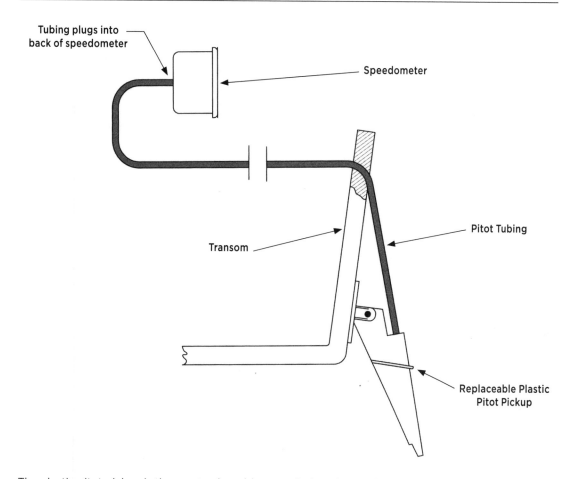

Tubing plugs into back of speedometer

Speedometer

Pitot Tubing

Transom

Replaceable Plastic Pitot Pickup

The plastic pitot pickup is the most vulnerable part of a boat's speedometer system.

ment pitot tube for around $15, while the replacement tubing goes for about 50 cents a foot.

Replacing the pitot tube is as simple as unscrewing the broken one and replacing it with the new one. Replacing the tubing is a little more difficult, because it snakes through the boat to the back of the speedometer. Always tie a messenger line to the end of the old tube before you pull it out, and use that line to pull the replacement tube back through the boat.

If your speedometer still doesn't work, it's usually time to replace it.

REPLACING ZINCS

It's an unpleasant fact that water and metals do not always cooperate. Nowhere is this more obvious and important than on a boat. The combination of two dissimilar metals in the presence of water results in *galvanic corrosion*, and salt water makes the reaction worse.

Metals can be ranked in a galvanic table from least to most reactive. Gold is at the top of the list as least subject to galvanic corrosion, while beryllium is ranked at the bottom. All other metals are ranked somewhere between. Two dissimilar metals placed together will produce an electrical voltage. The strength of the voltage and its corrosive effects will depend on how dissimilar the metals are in terms of reactivity, or *nobility*—that is, how far removed they are from each other in the galvanic table. Beryllium in contact with gold will produce 1.85 volts, the worst-case scenario. In all cases, the more reactive of the two metals will be the one that suffers corrosion—that is, the *anode*. The other metal will be the *cathode*.

Zinc is more reactive than aluminum or steel, so connecting zinc electrically to one of those metals will result in the zinc being attacked rather than the metal it's protecting. As a result, *sacrificial anodes* made of zinc are used on boats to protect expensive metal parts from corrosion. Commonly called *zincs*, these anodes are installed externally on outboard and stern-drive lower units, trim tabs, metal rudders, and propeller shafts from inboard engines. Zincs can also be found inside engine cooling circuits and water heaters.

"Zincs" has become something of a generic term for sacrificial anodes, some of which are actually made from aluminum or magnesium. Their use will be specified by the engine manufacturers using them. Be sure to check your engine manual for the proper metal type.

It is standard practice to inspect your zincs at the start of the boating season. The general rule of thumb is that when a zinc is more than 50 percent gone, it should be replaced.

A zinc needs a good electrical connection to the metal part it is protecting. When you install a new zinc, be sure the area under the zinc and the fasteners used to attach it are as free of corrosion as possible. *And don't paint zincs!* Doing so totally undermines their protective value.

Even if you install new zincs at the beginning of the season, you should inspect them periodically. Are they shrinking faster than they should be? Even if the zincs are okay, is the lower unit, prop shaft, or rudder corroding faster than normal?

If your zincs are wasting away faster than usual, you may have another kind of problem. Stray electrical currents can be introduced into the waters around your boat from faulty AC wiring. It may be the marina wiring, or perhaps a nearby boat has its 110-volt AC service wired incorrectly. Either way, your zincs will disappear at a faster than normal rate and, if not replaced, other metal parts on your boat may soon follow. Aluminum lower units and metal through-hulls are all vulnerable. Galvanic corrosion can destroy a through-hull with startling speed, and if your boat loses a through-hull it is likely to sink at the dock. Your best option is to ask the marina to find the source of the stray current. It's their responsibility, and it's not only a matter of protecting their customers' boats; electrical leakage could represent an electrocution risk to anyone who enters the water nearby.

Zinc "fish" are available for extreme cases. These are heavy fish-shaped zincs to which a wire is attached, and at the other end of the wire is an alligator clip. You drop the fish over the side and connect the alligator clip to the metallic part on the boat that is being corroded. A good electrical connection is critical: no connection, no protection. If necessary, sand or file the part to reveal bare, clean metal before attaching the clip.

CHAPTER 9

Trailers

For trailer boaters, the trailer is an essential but often neglected component of the boat package. A bearing failure on the highway can ruin your whole day. At any given time there are more trailered boats in use than trailers to carry them, which keeps the prices of trailers, even used ones, high, and should motivate us to take better care of our trailers.

ADDING A POWER WINCH

It's easy to appreciate the advantages of an electric trailer winch. Aside from being easier to use than a manual winch, it's also a little safer, because it's easier to keep an eye on the boat as it comes onto the trailer. In contrast, when you're cranking on a manual winch, you're sometimes facing away from the boat.

Winches are rated by pulling power. Many people assume that the winch rating should equal the weight of the boat, but that's excessive. You aren't trying to lift the boat straight up, after all; you're sliding it onto the trailer. The required rating therefore depends more on the slope of the trailer on the ramp and whether you have bunks (more friction) or rollers (less friction) on your trailer. Winch manufacturers provide guidelines to choosing a winch. If in doubt, go up one size.

Most power winches have a universal base with a variety of mounting holes to fit most common winch stand patterns. Mounting the winch requires unbolting the manual winch and bolting the power winch in its place. When the boat is on the trailer with its bow snubbed against the stop on the winch stand, there must be a distance of at least 12 inches between the towing eye (mounted on the stem of the boat) and the winch. Any less than this risks dragging the winch hook into the cable drum. The winch should be at the same height as the towing eye. If necessary, reposition the bow stop or the winch stand.

Electric winches are powered from the tow vehicle's 12-volt starting battery. The winch comes with a wiring harness for the vehicle and a special plug that fits the winch. A circuit breaker is mounted on the battery's positive post, and the positive wire runs back along the vehicle frame to the vicinity of the trailer hitch and is held in place with nylon wire ties. Be sure to avoid sharp edges, areas of potential chafe, and hot spots near the exhaust system. The negative wire bolts to the tow vehicle's frame to provide the ground. Be sure to clean any paint or rust off the frame to establish a good electrical connection. Cut the

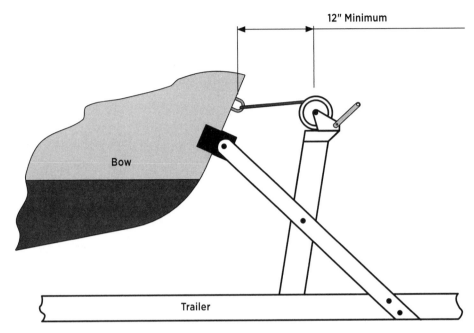

Allow at least 12 inches from the winch to the bow eye to avoid binding or jamming the cable

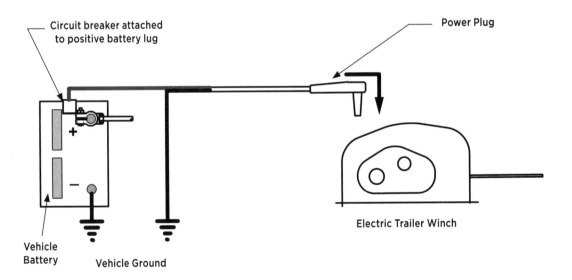

Wiring a trailer winch is straightforward.

two wires long enough to reach the winch, and then install the plug. Test the winch for proper operation.

Stand to one side when operating the winch to avoid being hit if the cable or towing eye should break. Don't use the winch to hold the bow in place while you tow the boat. Instead, disconnect the winch cable and use a dedicated bow tie-down to secure the bow.

BUILDING A TRAILER STAND

I had just backed our new 20-footer into our driveway and cranked the tongue jack down so that I could unhitch the trailer from the pickup. After I climbed on board, I opened up the cabin and poked around a bit. Then I walked aft and had a sinking feeling—literally. My weight in the aft part of the cockpit was enough to lift the trailer tongue off the ground!

Fast forward to the next spring. Taking the cover off on the first nice day, I discovered that, even with the trailer tongue jacked down all the way to raise the bow, water had collected in the cockpit and then frozen. Luckily the pool hadn't reached the level of the cockpit drains, or water would have frozen in the drains and split them.

My solution to both these problems was to build a trailer stand for our boat. After we trailer her home from the lake, we unhitch her and place the trailer tongue on the stand. It's just high enough to give the cockpit sole an aftward slant to drain it completely, and heavy enough to allow us to walk around the cockpit with impunity.

You could buy a stand at a boating store, but I find these to be narrow, unstable, and not heavy enough to counterbalance weight in the stern.

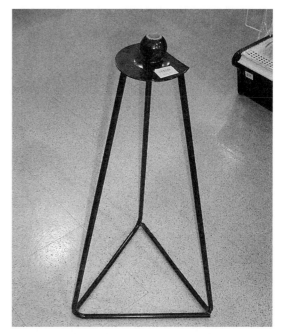

An off-the-shelf trailer stand like this one lacks the weight and base width for long-term use.

My trailer stand is made of 4 x 6 and 1 x 4 treated lumber. Galvanized deck nails and a trailer ball of the appropriate size are the only other things you'll need.

First determine the correct height for your stand. Pour a bucket of water into the cockpit and raise the trailer tongue until all the water drains out. Measure this height. If you can't lift the trailer tongue, have someone give you a hand by hanging onto the stern. If you still can't raise it, you'll need to rebalance your trailer or forget this project.

With the height of the center post known, you can lay out the rest of the stand on a piece of graph paper and scale off the dimensions. Nothing is terribly critical as long as all sides are symmetrical. I used two pieces of 4 x 6 for the base, one on edge and one lying flat. The two pieces cross each

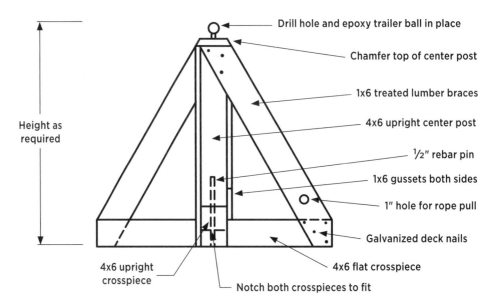

Drill hole and epoxy trailer ball in place

Chamfer top of center post

1x6 treated lumber braces

4x6 upright center post

½" rebar pin

1x6 gussets both sides

1" hole for rope pull

Galvanized deck nails

4x6 flat crosspiece

Height as required

4x6 upright crosspiece

Notch both crosspieces to fit

This simple homemade trailer stand will keep the bow elevated and allow water to drain through the transom plug(s).

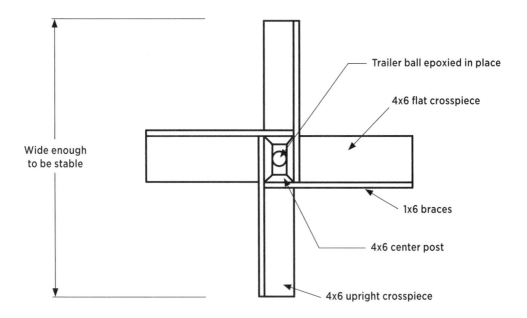

Trailer ball epoxied in place

4x6 flat crosspiece

1x6 braces

4x6 center post

Wide enough to be stable

4x6 upright crosspiece

A top view of the homemade trailer stand, which provides sufficient counterweight to allow you to walk around the cockpit.

other at right angles, and I notched both pieces to fit together securely. The length of the center post should equal your required height minus the height of the edge-set 4 x 6 base piece (most likely 5½ inches) and the height of the trailer ball.

Screw a long lag bolt up from the bottom through the two base pieces into the center post. Nail 1 x 4 braces from the base pieces to the center post. To fasten the trailer ball in place, drill a slightly oversize hole in the top of the center post deep enough to receive the ball's threaded stem. Fill the hole with epoxy and drop the ball into place.

Chamfer the top of the center post to allow water to drain off quickly. If you use pressure-treated lumber, you can leave it unfinished, or you can seal it with a deck sealer/waterproofer.

You could make the trailer stand from lighter stock if you don't need the weight to counterbalance someone standing in the stern. Of course, if you want to hold a square dance in the cockpit, you might have to add a few concrete blocks to the stand for additional ballast.

REPACKING AND REPLACING TRAILER BEARINGS

I have friends who replace their trailer bearings every year. That is probably overkill, but I bet there are more trailers out there that need new bearing than ones that don't. By repacking the bearings annually, you'll avoid the need to replace them for several years.

The first order of business is to check the bearings. Jack the trailer up and support it so it can't fall. Spin each wheel and listen. If you hear a growling sound or notice a lot of friction, you may have to replace the bearings. In extreme cases, the axle shaft may be scored and may also need replacing.

You can now proceed with removing the wheel and tire. Removing the lug nuts can be hard or easy, depending on how long ago you last changed tires. Lower the tires back to the ground and loosen—but don't remove—the nuts; then raise the trailer again so the tires are off the ground and the trailer is supported securely on jack stands. Finish removing the lug nuts and take off the wheel.

You can now remove the sheet metal cover in the center of the hub. This will expose the castellated nut holding the hub on the axle. Remove the cotter pin that runs through the axle and castellated nut, then unscrew the nut and remove the washer behind it. With any luck you can now pull the hub off the axle. Catch the bearings and place them on a clean rag. The inner race will remain on the axle, while the outer race will remain in the hub.

If you are reusing the bearings, clean them in kerosene and set them aside to dry. Clean the axle shaft with kerosene or brake cleaner. If the shaft is scored, you should replace it. This may mean replacing the entire trailer axle if it is a one-piece unit.

If you are replacing the bearings, the next step is to find replacement parts. Bearings are available in complete kits as well as individually. You will need the inner bearing, the outer bearing, and a grease seal.

Trailer axles come in two versions, stepped and straight. Stepped axles have a larger inner bearing and a smaller outer bearing. Straight shafts use the same size bearings in both races. Don't count on identifying marks on the bearings, as manufacturers use many different bear-

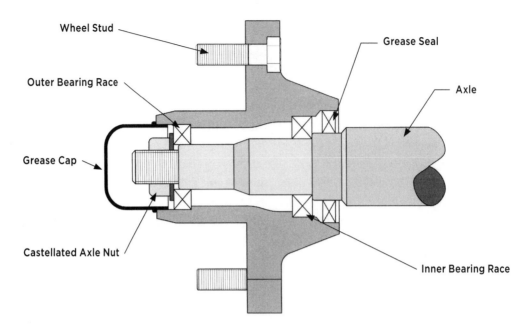

Wheel Stud

Outer Bearing Race

Grease Cap

Castellated Axle Nut

Grease Seal

Axle

Inner Bearing Race

This cross section of a trailer hub shows the inner and outer bearings as well as the grease seal.

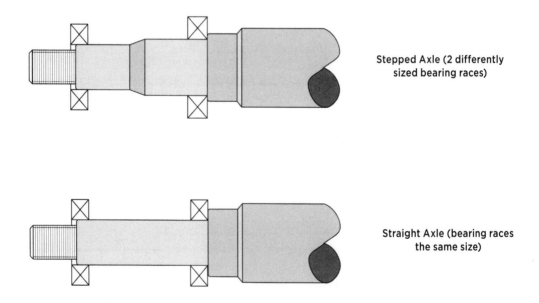

Stepped Axle (2 differently sized bearing races)

Straight Axle (bearing races the same size)

Stepped axles require two differently sized bearing races, while straight axles use two races of the same size.

ing suppliers and, as far as I know, there is no single reference showing what bearings go with what trailer. Unless you buy the parts from a dealer specializing in your brand of trailer, be prepared either to measure your bearings with a set of calipers to determine their size, or to take the old ones to the dealer. Once you open a package and get grease on the bearings, dealers won't take them back.

Remove the grease seal and outer race from the hub by tapping them with a light hammer and a block of hardwood or a brass drift pin. Tap lightly and evenly around the periphery to work out the race without damaging the bearing surfaces in the hub.

To remove the inner race from the axle shaft, you may need to use a bearing puller. Again, take care not to mark or damage the bearing surfaces on the shaft.

The outer race can now be installed in the hub. Seat the race squarely in the bore, making sure it is facing the right way, and gently tap it in place with a block of wood and a hammer.

At this point the bearings should be either new or clean. Pack the bearings with wheel bearing grease, forcing the grease in and around the bearings and the bearing cage until they are completely filled. Place the inner bearing race in the hub and tap the grease seal into place with a block of wood and a hammer. Carefully place the hub on the shaft.

Place the washer on the shaft and then tighten the nut. Spin the wheel as you tighten the nut to make sure the bearings are seating properly. Once the nut is firmly tightened, back it off about an eighth of a turn, until the cotter pin hole in the shaft lines up with a gap in the castellated nut. Install a new cotter pin and bend the ends around to keep it from backing out. The wheel should

now spin freely and without noise. Tap the dust cover back on and proceed to the next wheel.

INSTALLING BEARING PROTECTORS

Picture this: you drive many miles to the launch ramp. When you get there, the bearings and hubs are nice and warm. You then proceed to dunk them in cold water. The suddenly cooled hubs shrink and contract, sucking in water.

One of the most common causes of trailer wheel bearing failures is getting water in the hubs and bearings. One way to minimize this problem is to install bearing protectors, often known by the popular brand name Bearing Buddies. Bearing protectors replace the dust caps on your trailer hubs.

Bearing protectors are spring loaded and exert a slight pressure on the grease in the hub. This pressure overcomes the force of the outside water trying to get in. Most bearing protectors have a centrally located grease fitting for refilling and a pressure relief valve to prevent overfilling. Overfilling one of these protectors results in blowing out the grease seal in the hub and allowing all the grease to escape while allowing water in.

The hardest thing about installing these units is determining the right size to buy. The bore in the hub that accepts the dust cover comes in three different diameters: 1.781 inches, 1.980 inches, and 2.328 inches. If you don't have the means to measure your dust cover, take one to the parts store and match it up.

Installation is as simple as filling the hub with wheel bearing grease and tapping the protector into place with a block of wood and a hammer.

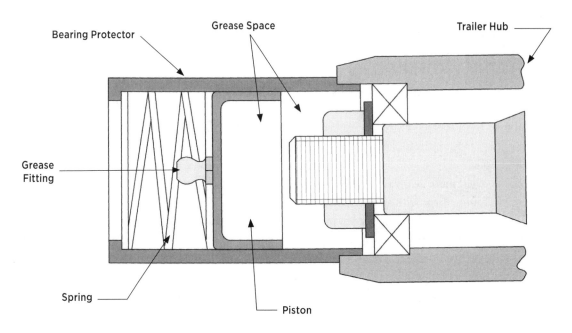

A bearing protector keeps a slight pressure on the grease inside a trailer hub, which in turn helps keep water out.

The grease level can be checked by pressing the edge of the piston. If the piston rocks slightly, the protector is properly filled. If it doesn't rock, add grease until it does. The piston should move outward about an eighth of an inch.

You should use a manual grease gun. Using an automatic grease gun might blow the hub's rear seal.

CORROSION PROTECTION AND REMEDIATION

More trailers have died from neglect than for any other reason. One of their chief enemies is corrosion. This is especially true if the trailer is regularly used in salt water. The best thing you can do for your trailer is to give it a regular freshwater bath.

Steel boat trailers are either painted or galvanized. Part of your annual spring commissioning should be inspecting your trailer for corrosion. Wire-brush any rust spots on a painted trailer. Although you can prime spots before painting them (zinc chromate primers are the best choice), a better approach is to treat the areas with a phosphoric acid compound that reacts with the metal to convert rust into iron phosphate. These treatments go by many brand names, including Ospho and RustBlock. The iron phosphate surface makes an ideal substrate for paint.

On rusted galvanized steel frames, wire-brush off the surface rust, then spray the areas with a zinc-rich primer. These are available at marine and trailer stores and are described with terms such as "cold galvanizing" or "instant galvanizing." The original galvanizing was applied to the steel by dipping it in molten zinc. Any primer or coating applied after that original galvanizing has started to fail and will not be as strong as the original, so keep a regular check on those areas and respray as often as necessary.

Aluminum trailer frames are impervious to rust, but problems arise due to the steel fasteners or components attached to them. This can create galvanic corrosion, especially if the trailer is left dirty or used in salt water. Be diligent in washing the trailer with fresh water to keep corrosion at a minimum. Another solution is to use tough nylon washers or spacers between the aluminum and all steel fasteners and fittings.

A COMPLETE TRAILER OVERHAUL

I inspected the trailer for my 20-footer when I had the yard put the boat on jack stands for bottom painting. What I saw was worse than I thought. I hadn't done any maintenance on the trailer, except for new tires and packing the wheel bearings, for over ten years. It showed.

The springs were rusty and sagging; insulation on the wiring was cracked; the bunks needed help; and the coupler and chains were rusty and suspect. The list went on. The aluminum frame was in good shape and needed no welding repairs—that was the good news. But with the boat off the trailer, I knew I'd been given an ideal opportunity to overhaul the trailer.

The biggest job was to replace the springs, which I don't think had ever had a high enough load rating even when new. Luckily, my neighborhood boating store stocks an impressive inventory of trailer parts and accessories. I was to make frequent visits there during the overhaul.

My springs had an eye at each end; other trailers have different spring configurations. With the eye-to-eye spring measurement, I was able to find an exact size replacement with a higher load rating than the originals. I also purchased new spring pads, axle U-bolts, shackles, shackle bolts, and shackle bushings.

After I jacked up the trailer and supported the frame, the fun commenced. All the nuts and bolts were corroded solid and had to be cut off with a fiberglass-reinforced cutoff disc in my Dremel. (Don't use unreinforced discs, as they will shatter!)

The next problem was bolting the shackles and springs together. The shackles are heavy steel plates that connect the spring eyes to the frame. A large bolt goes through the shackles and the bushing in the spring eye. The problem was that the head portion of the shackle bolt had ridges that were meant to force their way into the shackle hole, keeping the bolt from rotating.

I'm sure a trailer manufacturer could have put these bolts in place quickly with an impact wrench, but I didn't have one. I ended up buying a heavy-duty socket and an 18-inch breaker bar. That, in combination with a length of pipe over the breaker bar handle, finally gave me enough leverage to seat the bolts.

The rest of the spring installation went quickly. The new spring pads went under the spring and over the axles, and the new U-bolts held everything in place.

Next I attacked the electrics. As long as I was removing the old wiring, I decided to replace the lights as well. My boating supply store had a wiring kit for my trailer size containing all the neces-

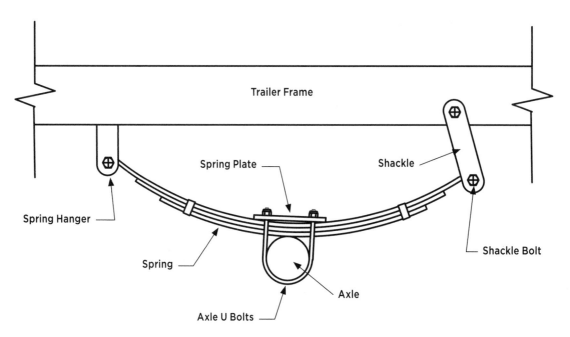

Any good trailer store will be able to provide replacement spring components like these.

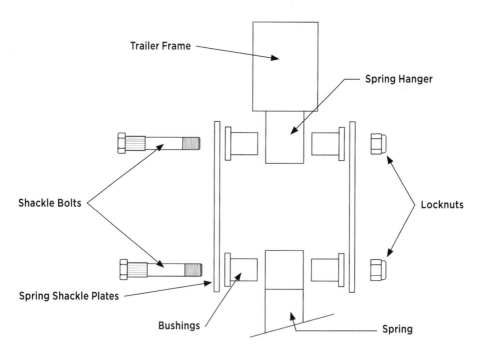

Shackle plates, bushings, and bolts can be replaced easily.

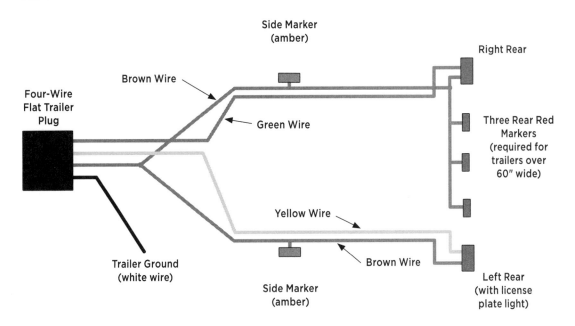

Side Marker
(amber)

Right Rear

Brown Wire

Four-Wire
Flat Trailer
Plug

Green Wire

Three Rear Red
Markers
(required for
trailers over
60" wide)

Yellow Wire

Trailer Ground
(white wire)

Brown Wire

Side Marker
(amber)

Left Rear
(with license
plate light)

When addressing bad trailer wiring, it is often easiest to replace all the wiring with a standard wiring harness. This diagram shows a split harness with a flat four-pin trailer connector.

sary wiring, the trailer plug, and very good directions.

There are two types of trailer wiring harnesses. One is a central harness with leads branching off to the side-mounted lights. The other is a split harness with one leg going down each trailer side rail. That was the style I needed.

The old wiring had been exposed to the weather, which had contributed to its deterioration. It was also vulnerable to physical damage. To avoid these problems and make a neater installation, I placed all the wiring in split black plastic wire conduits. These are available in various sizes from your marine store. I held the conduit in place with nylon wire clips screwed into the trailer frame.

I used adhesive heat-shrink butt connectors to make the connections waterproof. I followed the directions religiously and, to my complete

I elected to enclose my trailer wiring in corrugated plastic conduits to protect it from damage.

amazement, the lights worked correctly the first time I tried them.

On to the coupler. The old one was rusted and hard to work, and the safety chains, although probably as strong as new, were rusty. Since I had to unbolt the chains to get the coupler off, I decided to replace the whole mess. Couplers are standardized based on weight ratings, so finding a replacement was easy, right down to the bolt pattern.

It's possible to crush an aluminum trailer frame by overtightening the coupler bolts. To prevent this, I installed a tight-fitting block of oak inside the trailer tongue, and redrilled the coupler mounting holes.

The front end of the trailer was supported by an ancient-looking tongue jack that worked, but only under protest. My parts store carried the exact same model, and replacing it was a simple bolt-off/bolt-on affair.

I had replaced the winch cable once, but the winch itself was getting rusty to the point of being dangerous, so it was time to replace that too. Luckily, the sizes and mounting dimensions of trailer winches have changed very little over the years, and I was able to find a bolt-on replacement that fit perfectly. Instead of the usual galvanized

My new coupler, shown here, was a direct bolt-on replacement for the old one. I also installed new safety chains at the same time.

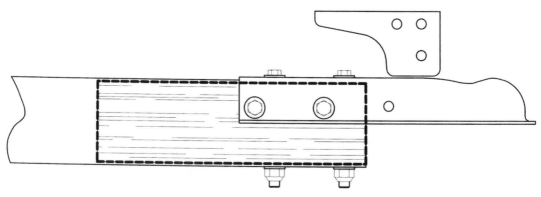

Oak block prevents coupler bolts from crushing tongue

A tight-fitting hardwood block in the trailer tongue will keep the coupler bolts from crushing the tongue.

Because the original jack model for my trailer was still being made, replacing the jack was a simple matter of unbolting the old one and bolting in the new—no redrilling required.

Replacing my trailer's manual winch was a simple matter of buying a new one and bolting it in place. Most winches have enough mounting hole options to meet just about all possibilities.

steel cable, I decided to use low-stretch line instead. I made sure the breaking strength of the line was greater than the rated capacity of the winch.

The original fenders had removed themselves when the steel fender brackets rusted away, more evidence of saltwater immersion. Not wanting to repeat that mistake, I made new brackets from heavy aluminum bar stock I purchased at the local home improvement store. To these I bolted new plastic fenders that, while not strong enough to stand on, do protect the hull from errant rocks, spray, and mud.

The last task was to fix the trailer bunks. These were aluminum extrusions—two inboard and two outboard—curved to conform to the boat's hull. They had originally been covered with a rub-

ber extrusion that had long since deteriorated into nothingness.

A call to the trailer manufacturer revealed that those rubber pieces were no longer available, so I decided to use standard trailer bunk padding. I draped the material over the bunk extrusions and temporarily held the edges together underneath with spring clamps. I then used an awl to make a hole through both edges and bolted them together with stainless steel bolts and big fender washers.

Tightening the nuts and bolts nicely tensioned the padding and kept any fasteners away from the hull. Standard trailer bunk padding was just the right size to go around the aluminum bunks, but if I had needed wider strips, I could have used outdoor carpeting.

I bent the fender brackets on my trailer from stock aluminum extrusions I found in a local home improvement store.

I purchased the plastic fenders from a local marine supply store.

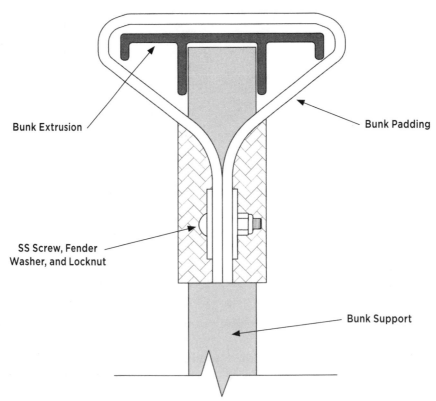

I elected to cover my curved aluminum trailer bunks with outdoor carpeting.

I wrapped the outdoor carpet around the old bunk supports and simply bolted it in place with stainless steel bolts and large fender washers.

CONSIDERATIONS WHEN STORING A BOAT ON A TRAILER FOR THE WINTER

If you keep your boat on a trailer, jack the wheels off the ground to minimize sidewall cracking. Grease the wheel bearings now; it's one less thing to do in the spring. Give the ball socket on the trailer coupling a light coat of grease to prevent rusting. Make sure the boat sits bow up, so any water that gets aboard will drain through the transom plugs. And, of course, remove the plugs and store them in a place you'll remember.

A trailered boat is best protected with a properly sized cover. The cover should fit well and be firmly tied underneath the boat. Use support poles or bows to eliminate any sagging areas of

A good-fitting cover minimizes the chances of it flogging in the wind and damaging the gelcoat.

Trailered boats often have their cover securely tied to the trailer.

the cover that could collect water or snow. Such pools can become heavy enough to tear the cover or even damage the boat if not emptied out.

Finally, consider adding a tarp over the fitted cover. Tarps are cheap, covers aren't, and a tarp will keep a lot of the bird droppings, snow, and rain off the more expensive cover. See Chapter 10 for more winterizing suggestions.

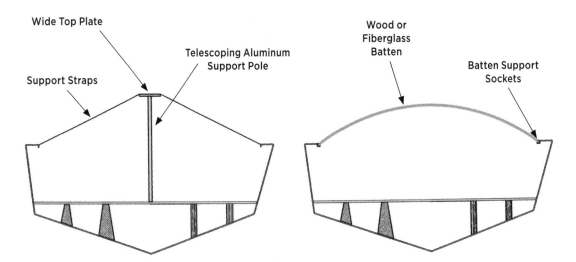

Use some sort of support system for your boat cover to prevent water from pooling in low spots and damaging the cover.

CHAPTER 10

Winterizing

Once Labor Day has passed, while there is still good boating weather to be had, many of us need to start thinking about winterizing.

Most people think of winterizing only in terms of the engine and water systems, but there are really six main areas of concern, not all of which apply to all boats and all storage scenarios:

1. Cleaning the boat
2. Winterizing the engine and outdrive or lower unit
3. Winterizing the fresh- and wastewater systems
4. Preparing the cabin
5. Inspecting the trailer
6. Installing the winter cover

CLEANING THE BOAT

Let's face it, the more you do in the fall, the less you have to do in the spring. This means you should take time in the fall to thoroughly clean the boat. That way the summer's accumulation of dirt and debris won't be fossilizing itself onto your boat during the winter.

Take the time to scrub the nonskid and get all the dirt out. Wash and wax the hull. Get a good bottom cleaner and clean the growth off the bottom now. You will thank yourself in the spring when it comes time to apply another coat of bottom paint.

Don't forget the canvas. Clean off any mold or mildew and clean and polish the clear vinyl. Remove the canvas and take it home if possible.

Arrange to have your boat power washed as soon as it's pulled from the water. The longer you delay the washing, the harder it becomes to remove the marine growth.

WINTERIZING ENGINES AND OUTDRIVES

This is the area that most people think about when you mention winterizing. It can be done quickly if you have all the needed supplies ready:

- Oil for engine and outdrive or lower unit
- Oil filters
- Fuel filters
- Fogging oil
- Antifreeze
- Winterizing kit for antifreeze
- Spark plug wrench
- Fuel stabilizer

Start the process by warming up the engine or engines, making sure you supply cooling water through a garden hose if your boat is out of the water. This does two things: it warms up the oil and opens up the thermostat. Once the oil has warmed up, change both the oil and the oil filter. This will leave nice fresh oil sitting in your engine, without the summer's buildup of acid, water, and gunk. It will also be one less thing to do in the spring. If you don't change the oil, at least add some crankcase conditioner to the oil.

While you are at it, change the fuel/water separator cartridge and either top up the fuel tank or drain it. (See Fuel System Maintenance in Chapter 8 for a further discussion.) Add fuel stabilizer to the tank.

The next task is to run antifreeze through the system. Buy 3 to 5 gallons of nontoxic (propylene glycol) marine antifreeze. Don't use automotive (ethylene glycol) antifreeze, as it is toxic. It also tastes sweet to animals, which will die if they lick up any spills. Marine antifreeze comes in three temperature ratings: $-50°$ F, $-60°$ F, and $-100°$ F.

These are the temperatures at which the antifreeze will turn to slush. The $-50°$ F rating is fine for water systems, but use a $-60°$ F or $-100°$ F rating for the engine. Any residual water in the cooling loop will dilute the antifreeze and impact its ability to protect the engine. The $-60°$ F and $-100°$ F varieties also have more corrosion inhibitors for use in engines.

Most marine stores carry a winterizing kit that includes a plastic container for the antifreeze and a plastic hose to connect to the flushing muff on the outdrive. Some I/Os and inboards have separate cooling water intakes in the bottom of the boat. In these cases, remove the intake hose from the seacock and place it in a bucket of antifreeze.

With the engine warmed up, begin running the antifreeze through the engine and/or outdrive. As you near the end of the antifreeze in the container, start spraying fogging oil in the carburetor. Smaller engines and outboards will probably die, while larger engines will just bog down. As the last of the antifreeze runs through, shut down the engine if it doesn't stall of its own accord. The fogging oil will give the cylinder walls a healthy coating of oil and corrosion blockers for the winter.

Don't attempt to fog a diesel or a fuel-injected gasoline engine in this manner. In the case of a fuel-injected gas engine, you need to mix a fogging solution and then run it through the fuel system. This typically is an amount of two-cycle oil added to the fuel/water separator cartridge and allowed to run through the injection system and engine. Your engine manual will spell out the specifics. Do not do this to a diesel!

Drain and change the lower unit or outdrive oil. Check the oil for water (it will look like coffee) and metal chips. Water in the oil indicates a leak-

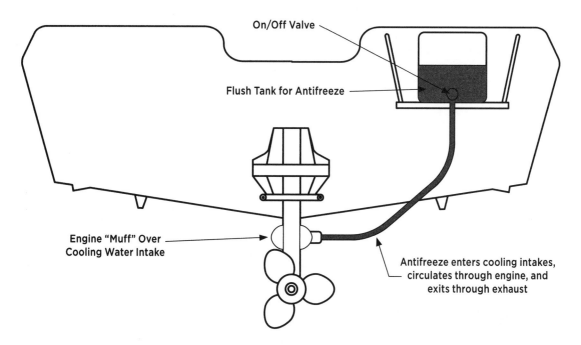

On/Off Valve

Flush Tank for Antifreeze

Engine "Muff" Over
Cooling Water Intake

Antifreeze enters cooling intakes,
circulates through engine, and
exits through exhaust

Most marine retailers sell an engine-flush kit like this one. The hose is designed to connect to standard garden hose fittings on engine muffs. Use propylene glycol antifreeze, which is nontoxic. Do not use ethylene glycol for this application.

Engine muffs fit over the cooling water intakes on an outboard motor or outdrive. Attaching a garden hose allows you to run the engine at idle for tuning or winterizing. (Courtesy Moeller Products Company, Inc.)

ing seal, and chips indicate mechanical problems. Four-stroke engines, both outboard and stern drive, need to have the crankcase oil changed as well.

Clean the carburetor flame arrestor with carburetor cleaner, and lubricate any grease points spelled out in the owner's manual. Check for loose or missing fasteners on the engine and outdrive. Replace the zincs if they are more than 50 percent gone.

If you haven't checked or changed the water pump impeller recently, do it now.

This is also a good time to check the prop for damage, and it wouldn't hurt to pull the prop and grease the splines while you're at it. If the prop is damaged, the winter season is the ideal time to have it refinished. No sense in waiting until the busy spring season to get it done.

Store outboard engines upright, on a rack or on the boat.

It doesn't sound like fun at all, but the more time you spend properly winterizing now, the better off your boat will be, and you'll speed up the commissioning process in the spring.

WINTERIZING WATER SYSTEMS

Simple water systems require little maintenance. If you have a portable tank, take it out when you winterize, clean it with a bleach solution, and put it away for the winter. If your sink is plumbed to a through-hull and you are storing the boat on land, make sure the seacock is open and the drain line is empty so that freezing does not rupture the hose or crack the seacock. If you store your boat in the water, add water system antifreeze to the drain line and cycle the seacock to allow some antifreeze to drain through to ensure that the line is completely filled with antifreeze.

The antifreeze must be propylene glycol based and intended for use with water systems. Standard ethylene glycol-based automotive antifreeze is poisonous and should never be used in any water system. Marine/RV antifreeze should not be diluted: use it straight from the jug.

More complex water systems require more work. The usual practice is to drain the water tank, then add several gallons of antifreeze so that it replaces all the water that remains in the system. The amount of antifreeze required is determined by the size of your tanks and the complexity of your water system.

Pump out as much of the water as you can from the freshwater tank, then add several gallons of antifreeze to the tank. Turn the pump on to pressurize the system, or pump the antifreeze through your water system until it comes out of every outlet, starting with the one farthest from the tank and working your way back. Remember to flush the water heater, if you have one, with antifreeze. Make a note and fasten it to the switch that controls power to the water heater to remind yourself to flush the water heater with fresh water before you turn it on in the spring, or you will have terrible tasting water from cooked antifreeze.

Have the holding tank pumped. Leaving that stuff sitting in the boat all winter isn't good, even if there is antifreeze in it. After it's pumped, add antifreeze to the head and pump it through to the holding tank. Don't skimp on antifreeze; make sure it gets through all the head hoses to the holding tank.

Don't forget to put antifreeze in the AC cooling loop, hot water heater, shower sumps, and any sea strainers you have. If there is usually a little water in the bilge, add a little antifreeze there too.

PREPARING THE CABIN

Go through the cabin and remove anything you can to a cool, dry place in your house. Any food or drinks should be removed. Cushions, curtains, life preservers, towels, and spare clothing should all be taken home. If possible, remove the electronics and take them home too. Wipe down the refrigerator or icebox with a mildew cleaner or bleach solution and leave the door propped open.

Open all doors, drawers, and compartments to minimize enclosed spaces. Place dehumidifier tubs throughout the boat to absorb excess humidity. Don't forget to check them once or twice during the winter, if possible.

Remove the batteries and take them home. They should be fully charged and stored in a cool, dry place, not on a concrete floor in the garage. Don't forget to check the electrolyte levels and add distilled water if necessary. A trickle charge now and then won't hurt, but leaving the battery charger hooked up all winter can cook the batteries.

PREPARING THE BOAT FOR SHRINK-WRAPPING

Many of us complete our winter preparations with shrink-wrapping. While few of us do the job ourselves, we can save some money by making sure the boat is properly prepared for shrink-wrapping, and end up with less cleanup work in the spring.

Fold down any antennas and secure them. Some shrink-wrappers ask that any canvas be taken down before their arrival. At least one company I talked to will do it for you, but at a cost.

In some cases, a frame may be necessary to support part or all of the shrink-wrap, to keep it from sagging and allowing puddles of snowmelt to collect, freeze, and provide a base for additional snow to collect in such quantities that it could split the film. A frame may also serve to break up unsupported spans of film into smaller sections, and so prevent it from flapping itself to pieces. In some cases, netting or tape straps can be substituted for a rigid frame. Apply padding to any posts or projections that might puncture the film. Most installers will handle all this for you, but again, you may be able to save yourself some money by doing it yourself.

Removing the cover in the spring is simple. Cut it away, being careful not to scratch the gelcoat. Remove any tape, strapping, or temporary frames. Don't just dump the film in a dumpster. Most marinas have special bins for the material, to make sure it is recycled properly.

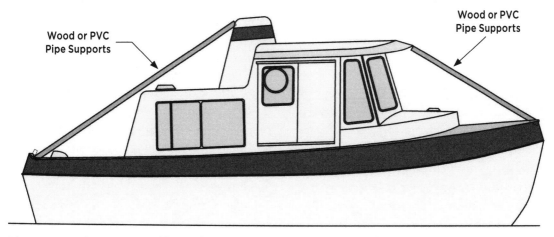

Wood or PVC Pipe Supports

Wood or PVC Pipe Supports

Place support in open areas, like cockpits, to prevent the shrink-wrap from sagging and collecting water or ice.

This go-fast boat is ready for winter with an excellent shrink-wrap job.

WINTER COVERS AND TARPS

There are several good reasons to use a cover or tarp and frame instead of shrink-wrapping. If you plan to keep the boat indoors, for example, an inexpensive cover will suffice to keep the boat clean. If you plan to keep the boat for several years, the cost of a custom cover and frame can be amortized and will cost less than annual shrink-wrapping. A properly designed frame can provide sufficient headroom and access to various parts of the deck to make winter repairs feasible. Finally, you may have an oddly configured boat that may make shrink-wrapping difficult and a precisely fitted cover more practical.

For every boat with a neatly fitted cover, I see a dozen using the old standby, a poly tarp. These tarps come in a wide range of sizes, colors, weights, and prices. You used to be able to tell the quality of the tarp by the color, with blue being the lowest quality and silver or green being the best, but this has changed, and the color no longer signifies the quality. Probably the best indicator of quality now is the weight; the heavier the tarp, the better the material. Even the highest-quality tarps are less expensive than any sewn canvas cover.

The tarp must be longer than the boat to provide enough material to wrap around the bow and stern and tuck it into place. Tarps have regularly spaced grommets for tying down, but if you need to tie off at locations where there are no grommets, you can add grommets or use special tarp tie-down fittings, both of which will probably be available where you bought the tarp.

Tarps are much harder to tie down and are more subject to flapping in the wind than other types of covers. Spend the extra time and the extra line to get your tarp tied down securely, and

The ubiquitous polypropylene tarp is frequently used to cover boats. Don't expect much more than a season's use from one, and check the boat often to make sure the tarp is secure.

don't expect the tie-downs to remain tight all winter. Check them regularly; if you don't, you risk the cover shredding prematurely or the loose lines scuffing your gelcoat.

Never tie the tarp or cover to boat stands! The constant motion of the tarp and lines from the wind can work the stands loose, allowing the boat to topple and ruining your whole boating experience, not to mention your neighbor's. Be sure that opposite boat stands are chained together beneath the hull to keep them from "walking" out from under the boat.

Almost every tarp cover requires at least a simple frame to prevent low spots that could collect water or snow. See the following three projects (Wooden Tarp Frames, PVC Tarp Frames, and Electrical Conduit Tarp Frames) for different approaches.

Lacking a convenient tie-off point for a tarp grommet, hang something heavy from it—like this jug filled with water—to keep wind from getting under the edge and causing havoc. Do not tie a tarp to a boat stand. If you do, the action of wind in the tarp could loosen the stand.

Wooden Tarp Frames

At one time almost all frames were made of wood. Some of these frames were works of woodworking art, intricately shaped and assembled with precision. These frames were knocked down and stored each spring for use in the next fall haulout. Other wood frames were cobbled together from furring strips and common lumber and were often discarded at the end of a season.

The more time you spend designing and laying out your wood frame, the less material you will use and the quicker it will go together. Most wood frames use a series of A-frames spaced the length of the deck, and these support a ridgepole. The widths of the A-frame bases will decrease toward the ends of the boat, and especially toward the bow. Despite this, you can keep the height of the A-frames fairly constant if you're willing to let the A-frame vertexes become more acute over the foredeck. This allows the ridgepole to remain level. Alternatively, you can keep the A-frame vertex angle constant, meaning that the frames will become progressively shorter as you move forward. The ridgepole height in this option will obviously decrease with frame height.

A level ridgepole makes the fitting of a square or rectangular tarp a little easier and allows more headroom near the bow, but tall A-frames with narrower bases are less stable. A-frames that shorten as their bases narrow are more stable, but the ridgepole height will decrease toward the bow. Either way, the frames will need to be securely braced fore and aft to keep the structure from collapsing. A commonsense approach is to incorporate sufficient headroom amidships and aft but let the ridgepole height decrease forward. This reduces windage on the cover during winter storms.

The frame pieces should be securely bolted together with locknuts so that vibration from the wind will not work the fasteners loose. It is also best to secure the frame to the deck instead of the stanchions. Winter winds can introduce a great deal of vibration in the tarp and frame that might loosen or bend stanchions.

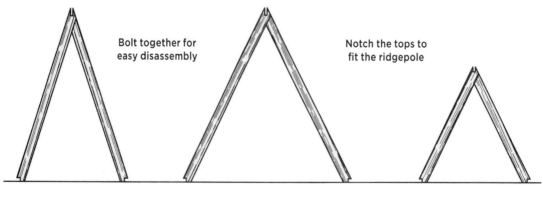

Keep the height the same and the ridgepole will be level

Bolt together for easy disassembly

Notch the bottoms to fit the toe rail

Notch the tops to fit the ridgepole

Keep the angle the same and the ridgepole height will change

Many winter storage frames are made using wood A-frames.

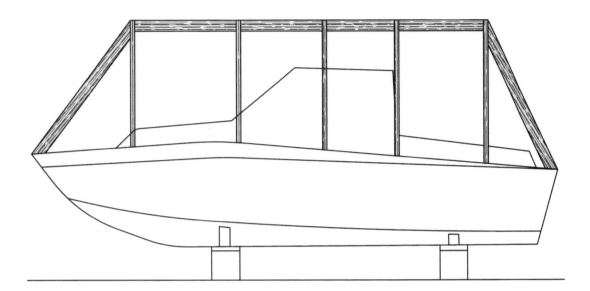

If you keep the A-frames a consistent height, the ridgepole will be level and you will have more head-room, but those A-frames with narrower bases will be less stable. If stability might be a problem, keep the vertex angle the same for all A-frames (see the next illustration).

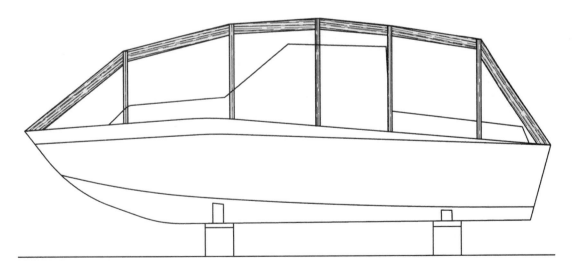

If you keep the A-frame vertex angle consistent for stability, the A-frames with narrower bases will be shorter but no less stable. This means less headroom in the ends of the boat.

One of the most important factors in a successful winter frame is the elimination of sharp corners or rough spots on the frame or the boat. Any of these will ruin a cover or tarp in no time. Pad sharp corners with carpet scraps well fastened in place.

If you plan to reuse your frame next year, mark each piece clearly and make a sketch or diagram of the frame so you know where each piece goes. Depend on your memory and you'll be standing among a bunch of parts wondering where they go.

PVC Tarp Frames

The availability of various sizes of PVC plumbing pipe and fittings has provided another alternative for constructing winter cover frames. Two methods of constructing these frames are in common use.

The first uses small-diameter lengths of PVC pipe. These are bent into arches and fastened to the sides of the boat, often the stanchions, with wire ties, hose clamps, or even duct tape. When a single length of pipe is too short to complete a full arch, two pieces are joined together with a length of metal rod or pipe. Additional lengths of pipe are then added as a ridgepole and fore-and-aft bracing, again secured with wire ties or duct tape.

This type of structure works well for smaller boats but becomes flimsy as the size of the boat increases. The PVC pipe itself soon reaches a diameter that won't readily bend into arches without fracturing. Another problem with this "bent arch" style of construction is that the frames are

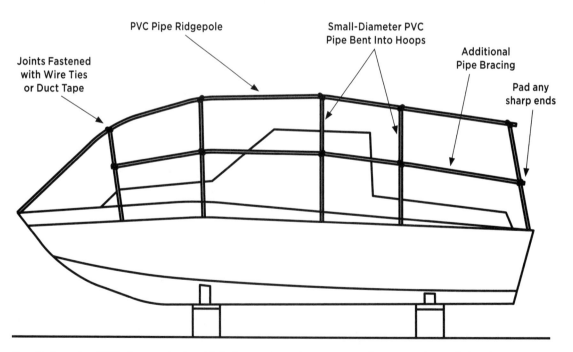

Small-diameter PVC pipe can be bent into hoops to make a storage frame. Horizontal pipe bracing can be fastened in place with wire ties or duct tape.

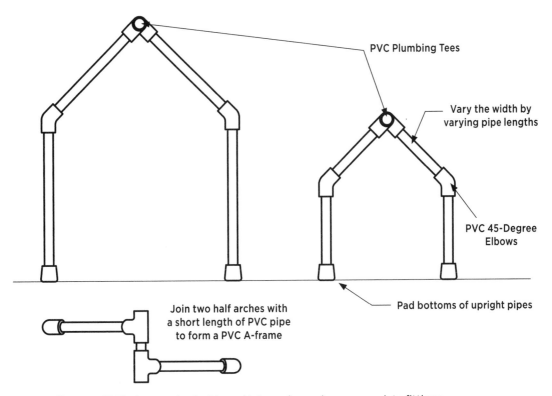

PVC Plumbing Tees

Vary the width by
varying pipe lengths

PVC 45-Degree
Elbows

Join two half arches with
a short length of PVC pipe
to form a PVC A-frame

Pad bottoms of upright pipes

Larger-diameter PVC pipe can be fashioned into arches using appropriate fittings.

often fastened to stanchions, which is, as noted before, a Bad Thing.

Large frames are therefore often built out of larger-diameter pipe, say 1¼ inches and up, in conjunction with standard off-the-shelf PVC plumbing fittings. The limited number of fitting configurations does make the design of the frame more difficult.

For example, the standard construction of a support arch usually consists of two lengths of pipe for the uprights. Each upright is joined to an arch leg by means of a 45-degree elbow, and the ridgepole end of the arch leg is inserted into a tee. A short length of ridgepole pipe then connects the two arch legs to form a completed arch. The difficulty is that the lengths of the arch legs will have

to vary from arch to arch to accommodate the fixed 45-degree elbow.

Longer lengths of ridgepole pipe then connect the arches to each other to form the frame. Since the lengths of pipe are inserted in the open ends of each arch tee and the arches vary in height, the arches themselves will have to tilt slightly from the vertical to accommodate the connector pipes.

In some designs, the arch tubes are permanently joined to the tees and the 45-degree fittings but are not otherwise permanently joined. Connections are made by using stainless steel sheet metal screws driven through the fittings into the pipe beneath. The bottoms of the arches should also be padded to avoid any wear on the deck. If sufficiently large pipe is used, cross bracing may

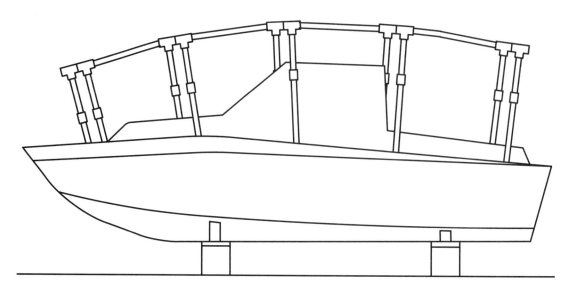

The ridgepole in a PVC pipe frame will have to be bent slightly to fit into the open ends of the arch tees, and the arches will have to cant slightly from the vertical for the same reason.

be eliminated. If in doubt, add it; it can't hurt. It is also a Good Idea to mark each joint and tube so it can be reassembled for use next year.

Electrical Conduit Tarp Frames

Another option for frame material is electrical conduit, or EMT. This tubing is available at any home improvement store in 10-foot lengths and at a dirt-cheap price. It can be cut to length with a simple tubing cutter. Bending is also simple with an electrician's conduit bender.

A specially designed clamp system called Kover Klamps makes assembling a conduit frame easy. Each clamp joins two pieces of tubing at any angle. The complete system includes protective rubber pads that snap around the clamps to protect the tarp from sharp edges, splice connectors for connecting lengths of conduit, and rubber feet to protect the deck gelcoat.

These Kover Klamp accessories are used to build a frame from electrical conduit, which is widely available and extremely cheap.

Split-foam pipe insulation works well as padding on conduit as long as it's firmly taped in place.

DO AS I SAY . . .

Don't just cover up your boat and wait for spring. Check it regularly for loose ropes, slipped frames, and holes in the cover. Fix the problem before the cover or tarp is ruined and lets the elements in. There is nothing like trying to horse a heavy cover or large tarp into place during a snowstorm with a −10°F windchill factor.

Case in point: I didn't check one of my boats for a four-week period. During that time we had several rainstorms and a snowstorm. Finally I got a call from a friend whose boat was stored next to mine, saying I had a problem. When I checked, I found that part of the PVC frame had broken and allowed the tarp to sag down into the cockpit. Water and ice were collecting in the depression. Luckily, it was a new tarp and it held, keeping the water out of the boat. I should follow my own advice.

This is what happens when you don't check your boat often enough. A PVC support broke and allowed several hundred gallons of water to accumulate in the cockpit. Luckily the tarp held and prevented water from invading the boat's interior.

Sources of Information

The Big Book of Boat Canvas
Karen S. Lipe
International Marine
ISBN 0-915160-35-8

Blue Sea Systems
bluesea.com/resources
Application Briefs
Reference Material
Technical Briefs

Boater's Guide to Cabin Ventilation
Marinco/Nicro
Online PDF
www.marinco.com/files/support/product/
    manuals/minivent%20manual.pdf

Boatowner's Illustrated Handbook of Wiring
Charlie Wing
International Marine
ISBN 0-07-071092-9

Capt'n Pauley's Virtual Boatyard
www.thevirtualboatyard.com
Boat advice for the nautically addicted
Author's blog on projects, upgrades, and
    maintenance information

David Pascoe
http://www.yachtsurvey.com
Online articles covering survey-related problems
    and solutions

The Don Casey Archive at BoatU.S.
http://www.boatus.com/howto/howto_lib.htm
Boat maintenance and repair articles

Ed Sherman's *Powerboater's Guide to*
    Electrical Systems
Ed Sherman
International Marine
ISBN 07-134326-1

Gougeon Brothers on Boat Construction
WEST System, Inc.
www.westsystem.com

Nigel Calder's *Boatowner's Mechanical and*
    Electrical Manual
Nigel Calder
International Marine
ISBN 0-07-009618-X

WEST Epoxy
Using WEST System epoxy
www.westsystem.com

West Marine Advisors
www.westmarine.com
The West Advisor
Advice on West Marine products

Sources of Gear and Supplies

3M Marine Products
www.3m.com/product/

American Boat & Yacht Council (ABYC)
613 Third Street, Suite 10
Annapolis, MD 21403
Phone: 410 990-4460
Fax: 410 990-4466
www.abycinc.org/index.cfm

Ancor Wire (Division of Marinco)
707 226-9600
www.marinco.com/brand/ancor

Attwood Corporation
1016 N. Monroe Street
Lowell, MI 49331
Phone: 616 897-2290
www.attwoodmarine.com

Barr Marine by EDM (manifolds)
100 Douglas Way
Natural Bridge Station, VA 24579
Phone: 866 255-9265
Fax: 540 291-4185
www.barrmarine.net/wordpress

Bearing Buddy, Inc.
Check website for dealers
Phone: 787 839-2688
Fax: 787 839-2735
www.bearingbuddy.com/index.shtml

Beckson Marine, Inc.
65 Holland Avenue
Bridgeport, CT 06605
Phone: 203 333-1412
Fax: 203 384-6954
www.beckson.com

Bennett Marine
550 Jim Moran Boulevard
Deerfield Beach, FL 33442
Phone: 954 427-1400
Fax: 954 480-2897
www.bennetttrimtabs.com

Blue Sea Systems
425 Sequoia Drive
Bellingham, WA 98226
Phone: 800 222-7617
Fax: 360 734-4195
bluesea.com

Boater's World Marine Centers
Check website for locations
Fax: 877 552-2284
www.boatersworld.com

BoatExec
Sales: Sales@BoatExec.com
Support: Support@BoatExec.com
www.boatexec.com

BoatLIFE (Life Industries Corporation)
4060 Bridge View Drive
N. Charleston, SC 29405
Phone: 800 382-9706
Fax: 843 566-1275
https://boatlife.ipower.com/overview.asp

BoatNotes
www.xchangingminds.com/latsatts/boatnotes/
    index.htm

Bomar
P.O. Box 1200
South West Street
Charlestown, NH 03603
Phone: 603 826-5791
fax: 603 826-4125
www.pompanette.com/bomar

Boston Whaler
100 Whaler Way
Edgewater, FL 32141
Phone: 877 294-5645
Fax: 386 423-8589

Bosun's Buddy Electronic Log Books
SelfTailing Software
325 North Washington Street
PMB 302
Olympia, WA 98501
Phone: 360 704-0384
www.bosunbuddy.com

Bristol Finish
C Tech Marine
2280 Avocado Avenue, Unit 4
Melbourne, FL 32935
Phone: 800 582-7508
Fax: 321 752-5899
www.bristolfinish.com

C. E. Smith Co.
Tech Support
Phone: 336 273-0166
Fax: 336 273-0570
www.cesmithco.com

C. Sherman Johnson Co., Inc.
1 Matthews Drive
East Haddam Industrial Park
East Haddam, CT 06423
Phone: 860 873-8697
Fax: 860 873-8589
www.csjohnson.com

Cabela's
See website for locations
Phone: 800 237-4444
www.cabelas.com

Capt. Tolley's Creeping Crack Cure
See website for where to purchase
www.captaintolley.co.uk

Cetol (Interlux Paints)
www.yachtpaint.com/usa/sikkens/default.asp

Collinite Corporation
520 Lincoln Avenue
Utica, NY 13502
Phone: 315 732-2282
www.collinitemarine.com

Davis Instrument Corp.
3465 Diablo Avenue
Hayward, CA 94545
Phone: 510 670-9229
Fax: 510 670-0589
www.davisnet.com

E-Paint Company
25 Research Road
East Falmouth, MA 02536
Phone: 800 258-5998
Fax: 508 495-3210
www.epaint.com

East Penn Manufacturing Company, Inc.
   (batteries)
Deka Road
Lyon Station, PA 19536
Phone: 610 682-4231
Fax: 610 682-4781
www.eastpenn-deka.com

E-Z Steer Systems
3923 88th Street NE, Suite J
Marysville, WA 98270
Phone: 800-634-7838
Fax: 360 651-6743
www.ezsteer.com

FloScan Instrument Co., Inc.
3016 NE Blakeley Street
Seattle, WA 98105
Phone: 206 524-6625
Fax: 206 523-4961
www.floscan.com

Fulton Trailer Parts
Cequent Trailer Products
1050 Indianhead Drive
Mosinee, WI 54455

Phone: 715 693-1700
Fax: 715 693-1799
www.fultonperformance.com/home.html

Garelick Manufacturing Co.
644 Second Street
P.O. Box 8
St. Paul Park, MN 55071-0008
Phone: 651 459-9795
Fax: 651 459-8269
www.garelick.com

Gibco Flex-Mold
6657 E Peden Road
Fort Worth, TX 76179
Phone: 817 236-5021
Fax: 817 236-5020
www.gibcoflexmold.com

Gougeon Brothers (WEST System Epoxy)
West System Inc.
102 Patterson Avenue
P.O. Box 665
Bay City, MI 48707-0665
Phone: 866 937-8797
Fax: 989 684-1374
www.westsystem.com

Grady-White Boats, Inc.
P.O. Box 1527
Greenville, NC 27835
Phone: 252 752-2111
www.gradywhite.com

Groco
7240 Standard Drive
Hanover, MD 21076
Phone: 410 712-4242
Fax: 410 712-0160
www.groco.net

HobbyCast division of Freeman Manufacturing & Supply Co. (RTV mold materials)
Phone: 440 934-1902, ext. 102
Fax: 440-934-7200
E-mail: contactus@hobbycast.net
www.hobbycast.net/contactus.htm

Indmar Products Co., Inc. (manifolds)
5400 Old Millington Road
Millington, TN 38053
Phone: 901 353-9930
Fax: 901 358-4292
www.indmar.com/index.html

Interlux Paints
International Paint LLC
2270 Morris Avenue
Union, NJ 07083
Phone: 800-468-7589
www.yachtpaint.com/usa

Jabsco
www.jabsco.com/index.htm

Jamestown Distributors
17 Peckham Drive
Bristol, RI 02809
Phone: 800 497-0010
Fax: 800 423-0542
401 254-5829
www.jamestowndistributors.com

Kover Klamps
P.O. Box 94
City Island, NY 10464
Phone: 718 885-2400
Fax: 718 885-2202
www.koverklampframes.com/boat_cover_framing.html

Magma Products, Inc.
3940 Pixie Avenue
Lakewood, CA 90712
Phone: 562 627-0500
Fax: 562 627-0550
www.magmaproducts.com/index.html

Marinco/Nicro
www.marinco.com/brand/nicro

Marine Technologies Group, LLC
812 Bayside Drive
Cape Canaveral, FL 32920-3556
Phone: 877 415-9188
Fax: 321 392-3035
www.marinetechgroup.com

Maxwell America, LLC (windlasses)
2907 South Croddy Way
Santa Ana, CA 92704-6302
Phone: 714 689-2900
Fax: 714 689-2910
www.maxwellmarine.com

Meguiar's Inc.
17991 Mitchell South
Irvine, CA 92614
Phone: 800 347-5700
www.meguiars.com

Merton's Fiberglass & Marine Supply
P.O. Box 399
East Longmeadow, MA 01028
Phone: 800 333-0314
Fax: 413 736-3182
www.mertons.com/index.html

Moeller Marine Products
801 North Spring Street
Sparta, TN 38583
Phone: 800 432-8344
Fax: 931 738-9835
www.moellermarine.com

MyShipLog
myshiplog.com/welcome

OSCO Motors
245 E. Union Street
Hatfield, PA 19440
Phone: 800 762-6726
Fax: 215 822-5394
www.oscomotors.com/index.asp

Panther Marine Products
MarineTech Products
1760 Buerkle Circle
St. Paul, MN 55110
Phone: 651 486-2010
Fax: 651 486-6989
www.marinetech.info/pmarine/index.php

Perko, Inc.
16490 NW 13th Avenue
Miami, FL 33169
Phone: 305 621-7525
Fax: 305 620-9978
www.perko.com

Pettit Paints
Kop-Coat Marine Group
36 Pine Street
Rockaway, NJ 07866
Phone: 800 221-4466
www.pettitpaint.com

Quick USA LLC (windlasses)
509 McCormick Drive
Glen Burnie, MD 21061
Phone: 877 768-5991
Fax: 410 768-5995

Racor
3400 Finch Road
Modesto, CA 95353
Phone: 209 521-7860
Fax: 209 529-3278
Sold through distributors

Ranger Boats
Wood Manufacturing Company, Inc.
P.O. Box 179
Flippin, AR 72634
Phone: 870 453-2222
www.rangerboats.com

Rule-ITT
1 Kondelin Road
Cape Ann Industrial Park
Gloucester, MA 01930
Phone: 978 281-0440
Fax: 978 283-2619
www.rule-industries.com/index.htm

**Sailrite Enterprises, Inc. (awning, cushion,
   sewing products)**
4506 S. State Road 9
Churubusco, IN 46723
Phone: 800 348-2769
www.sailrite.com

SeaDek, Inc.
485 Gus Hipp Boulevard
Rockledge, FL 32955
Phone: 321 632-4466
Fax: 321 632-7019
www.seadek.com

SeaLand Technology
Dometic Sanitation Corporation
13128 State Route 226, P.O. Box 38
Big Prairie, OH 44611-0038
Phone: 800 321-9886
Fax: 330 496-3097

Shakespeare Electronic Products Group
6111 Shakespeare Road
Columbia, SC 29223
Phone: 803 227-1590, ext. 1320
Fax: 803 419-3099
www.shakespeare-marine.com/home.asp

Sierra Marine
Teleflex Marine Distribution Center
1 Sierra Place
Litchfield, IL 62056
Phone: 877 663-8396
Fax: 217 324-4396
www.sierramarine.com

SIS, Inc. (Scientific Instrument Services, Inc.)
Clear Seas Vinyl Restoral Kit
1027 Old York Road
Ringoes, NJ 08551
Phone: 908 788-5550
Fax: 908 806-6631
www.sisweb.com

SSI, Inc.
Sailing Specialties Inc.
43985 Commerce Avenue
Hollywood, MD 20636
Phone: 301 373-2372
Fax: 301 373-2734
www.ssicustomplastics.com

StarBoard
King Plastic Corporation
1100 N. Toledo Blade Boulevard
North Port, FL 34288-8694
Phone: 941 493-5502
Fax: 941 497-3274
www.kingplastic.com

Star brite
4041 SW 47th Avenue
Fort Lauderdale, FL 33314
Phone: 800 327-8583
Fax: 954 587-2813

Sunbrella
Glen Raven Custom Fabrics, LLC
1831 North Park Avenue
Glen Raven, NC 27217-1100
Phone: 336 221-2211
www.sunbrella.com

Suncor Stainless, Inc.
70 Armstrong Road
Plymouth, MA 02360
Phone: 508 732-9191
Fax: 508 732-9798
www.suncorstainless.com

T-H Marine
Sold through marine retailers
www.thmarine.com

TACO Metals, Inc.
50 N.E. 179th Street
North Miami Beach, FL 33162
Phone: 305 652-8566
Fax: 305 770-2387
www.tacomarine.com

Taylor Made Products
Phone: 800 628-5188
www.taylormadeproducts.com

Teleflex
Teleflex Marine Distribution Center
1 Sierra Place
Litchfield, IL 62056
Phone: 877 663-8396
Fax: 217 324-4396
www.teleflexmarine.com

Tempress Products
5052 Sharp Street
Dallas, TX 75247
Phone: 877 234-7466
www.tempress.com/index.php

Todd Marine Products
361 Neptune Avenue
West Babylon, NY 11704
Phone: 800 275-2436
Fax: 631 661-5953
www.toddusa.com/index.aspx

Treadmaster
Navimo USA, Inc.
7455 16th Street East, Suite 107
Sarasota, FL 34243
Phone: 866 383-1888
Fax: 866 214-1400
www.plastimousa.com/treadmaster.htm

West Marine
See website for locations
www.westmarine.com

Whitecap
Sold through marine retailers
Phone: 888-WHITECAP
Fax: 732-819-3559

Index